Market relations and the competitive process

MANCHESTER
UNIVERSITY PRESS

New Dynamics of Innovation and Competition

The series New Dynamics of Innovation and Competition, published in association with the ESRC Centre for Research in Innovation and Competition at the University of Manchester and UMIST emanates from an engagement of the Centre's research agenda with a wide range of internationally renowned scholars in the field. The series casts new light on the significance of demand and consumption, markets and competition, and the complex inter-organisational basis for innovation processes. The volumes are multi-disciplinary and comparative in perspective.

Series editor:
Mark Harvey is Senior Research Fellow at CRIC

Already published:
Innovation by demand: an interdisciplinary approach to the study of demand and its role in innovation   Andrew McMeekin, Ken Green, Mark Tomlinson and Vivien Walsh (eds)

Market relations and the competitive process

edited by
Stan Metcalfe
Alan Warde

Manchester University Press
Manchester and New York

distributed exclusively in the USA by Palgrave

Published by Manchester University Press
Oxford Road, Manchester M13 9NR, UK
and Room 400, 175 Fifth Avenue, New York, NY 10010, USA
www.manchesteruniversitypress.co.uk

Distributed exclusively in the USA by
Palgrave, 175 Fifth Avenue, New York,
NY 10010, USA

Distributed exclusively in Canada by
UBC Press, University of British Columbia, 2029 West Mall,
Vancouver BC, Canada V6T 1Z2

British Library Cataloguing-in-publication data
A catalogue record for this book is available from the British Library

Library of Congress Cataloging-in-publication data applied for

ISBN 0 7190 6468 6 *hardback*

First published 2002

10 09 08 07 06 05 04 03 02   10 9 8 7 6 5 4 3 2 1

Typeset in Sabon with Helvetica Neue Condensed (HNC)
by Northern Phototypesetting Co. Ltd, Bolton
Printed in Great Britain
by Biddles Ltd, Guildford and King's Lynn

Contents

List of figures and tables

Figures

Tables

List of contributors

Suma S. Athreye   Economic Discipline, The Open University

Michael H. Best   University of Massachusetts at Lowell and Judge Institute of Management Studies, Cambridge University

Mark Harvey   ESRC Centre for Research on Innovation and Competition, University of Manchester

Brian J. Loasby   Department of Economics, University of Stirling

Jonathan Michie   Department of Management, Birkbeck College, University of London

Richard R. Nelson   School of International and Public Affairs, Columbia University

Christine Oughton   Department of Management, Birkbeck College, University of London

Andrew Sayer   Sociology Department, University of Lancaster

Don Slater   Sociology Department, London School of Economics

Fran Tonkiss   Sociology Department, Goldsmiths College, University of London

Our thanks go to Deborah Woodman and Sharon Dalton for their inestimable contributions to the organisation of the seminar and the preparation of the typescript for this book.

Series foreword

The CRIC–MUP Series New Dynamics of Innovation and Competition is designed to make an important contribution to this continually expanding field of research and scholarship. As a series of edited volumes, it combines approaches and perspectives developed by CRIC's own research agenda with those of a wide range of internationally renowned scholars. A distinctive emphasis on processes of economic and social transformation frames the CRIC research programme. Research on the significance of demand and consumption, on the empirical and theoretical understanding of competition and markets, and on the complex inter-organisational basis of innovation processes, provides the thematic linkage between the successive volumes of the series. At the interface between the different disciplines of economics, sociology, management studies and geography, the development of economic sociology lends a unifying methodological approach. A strong comparative and historical dimension to the variety of innovation processes in different capitalist economies and societies is supported by the international character of the contributions.

The series is based on international workshops hosted by CRIC which have encouraged debate and diversity at the leading edge of innovation studies.

CRIC is an ESRC funded research centre based in the University of Manchester and UMIST.

Introduction

Stan Metcalfe and Alan Warde

There has been increasing interest and debate in recent years on the instituted nature of economic processes in general and the related ideas of the market and the competitive process in particular. This debate lies at the interface between two largely independent disciplines, economics and sociology, and reflects an attempt to bring the two fields of discourse more closely together. In many ways this is to return to a previous age when the study of institutional arrangements was at the centre of the study of capitalism. The contributions to this volume explore this interface in a number of ways. The purpose of this Introduction is to place these contributions in the wider context and briefly to outline the content of the various chapters.

We consider the best place to start to be with the analysis of the nature of markets by drawing a distinction between the general market system and particular markets. This inevitably leads us to a discussion of the relation between markets and competition. The central presence of markets in the operation of capitalism should require no comment, although the 'end of history debate' has focused our attention on the multiple meanings and ways in which the market system can be organised. While the market may be pervasive it is not monolithic, and while it may be spreading as the dominant mode of organisation in modern society, it remains the case that substantial areas of activity lie beyond the market. The boundary between the market and the non-market cannot be taken for granted. It is to a degree fluid and reflects the circumstances of time and place. Thus, for example, there is a whole range of economic activity that lies outside the market, as in household production, and there is also serious debate about extending market principles to other spheres including trade in genetic material.

The approach we take reflects our view that markets are indissolubly and simultaneously economic and social. As frameworks of norms that provide regularity to behaviour but permit changes in behaviour, they operate at multiple levels thereby constraining the conduct of individuals, groups and organisations. As frameworks, they are continually evolving. They emerge, grow, stabilise and decline, and it is the dynamics of these processes that are central to our conception of the operation of modern capitalism. Consider the market arrangements for the food industry in the UK. In the last half century they have been transformed irrevocably as the supermarket form has displaced almost entirely a system based on centralised wholesale markets and small retail stores (Harvey *et al.*, 2001). In the process the social, temporal and spatial nature of the activity of procuring food has also been transformed with major implications for the conduct of urban life and the social and economic behaviour of households. Similarly, in regard to mass entertainment the development of radio and television has led to the emergence of a market-based system for the provision of mass entertainment services that co-exists in many countries with a state-funded service. This reflects not only developments in technology but an extension of the space where the market operates, a development that is very obvious in relation to the broadcasting of sporting activities. In the process the very notions of the market for sports' entertainment, its social and cultural meanings, the mode in which it is consumed, the way it is financed, and the distribution of its returns to the players and organisers have changed fundamentally.

In this Introduction we raise a number of issues relevant to the appraisal of 'the market'. Markets, of course, are not natural phenomena; they are created institutions, frameworks assembled and adhered to by the market's participants. Their number varies over time as innovations of technique and organisation open up new ways of using economic resources. At one level therefore the market system is the framework for creating specific new markets and destroying existing ones, and is a basis of the dynamism of the system. Thus it is important to distinguish the *modus operandi* of the market system in general from the very specific instituted conditions that define any particular market.

The traditional economic perspective on the market has been to judge it in terms of the efficiency with which resources are allocated across rival activities and over time. Here the discussion of the market becomes indistinguishable from a discussion of the degree of competition that prevails in any particular market. This emphasis upon the efficiency properties of the market–competition complex is of course important, but it is by no means the whole story or the story that most adequately captures the operation of capitalism. Markets are devices for adapting to new possibilities and creating new resources; markets, that is, facilitate and stimulate economic and social change as well as allocating given resources. It is this creative aspect of the market system which is lost in the concern to rationalise static concepts of efficiency in the allocation of given resources to given ends using given means. What is unique about capitalism is its combination of market exchange and competitive rivalry in the promotion of internally generated change. Not only is capitalism distinguished from socialism, but different forms of capitalism are also distinguished by that fact.

Open markets facilitate and create incentives to innovation and simultaneously transform their own internal structure. However, not every innovation possible is permissible within prevailing ethical codes, social mores and political regulation, for 'markets' constrain as well as enable. The social and political dimensions of market processes – inequality, fairness, power, uncertainty, status – all influence the range and nature of what takes place in the market context. More deeply still, the acceptance of market processes and the rhetoric with which they are described and assessed tell us a great deal about different kinds of market society.

The rhetoric, discourses and doctrine of the market

In the middle of the twentieth century, a substantial proportion of the population of the globe considered market principles unjust and the operation of markets a major basis of inefficiency. The slump, the poverty and the inequality of the 1930s, the lessons of co-operation in wartime, and optimism about the prospects of democratic socialism and welfare states, contributed to an atmosphere critical of markets, not only across Europe but also in the USA. The extent to which the market was re-evaluated positively in the late twentieth century is thus remarkable. The background to the rehabilitation of market principles reflects many factors. Among these we would draw attention to the long period of post-war economic growth across the globe, the effective response to the oil crisis of the 1970s, the emergence of new right politics in most Western states, the decline of communism in Europe, the critique of the bureaucratic power of states, and the seductiveness of the notion of consumer choice.

Callon (1998) and Miller (2002) are among commentators who suggest that powerful theories, especially from economics, have a tendency to create the world which they purport to describe, reality coming to mirror theory through the policy and practice of the powerful. We would not go so far as to say that the discourse of the virtuous market has created the institutional forms that it (mis)describes. Nevertheless, there are many potential ways in which the attribution of positive functions to market relations would affect understandings of reality and thus economic, political and social action.

What we find most striking is the extent to which the market is considered to be without stain in the current period. Unparalleled, if not entirely unprecedented, confidence is being expressed about markets. What happened at the end of the twentieth century was that the market mechanism was pressed into service into new areas, as a matter of policy. In the de-regulation of what were publicly owned agencies, in the extension of quasi-market principles within public administration, for example in health services, and in the extended commercialisation of broadcasting, we find clear examples of the spread of the market. Markets were overtly promoted, and this process required strong legitimisation from a discourse of 'market virtue'.

The notion of the virtuous market is based on a number of propositions that go weakly contested. Among the most important of these are the following:

- The market enshrines the principle of consumer sovereignty.
- The market permits, sustains and delivers individual freedom of choice and action across the economic and social spheres.
- The market is an ideal mechanism for exchange because its incentive structures are consistent with basic features of human nature.
- The market is applicable to a great many, if not all, forms of human activity, its principal mode of rational calculation being suitable to all spheres of life.
- The market is the epitome of efficiency in the allocation of resources and is unfailingly superior to any other system of economic governance.
- The market is the best guarantor of reliable quality in products and services.
- The market guarantees sustained growth in standards of living in all countries, whatever their level of development.

The power of the discourse operates in several modes: as political rhetoric, in business practice and through the ghostly role of markets in economic analysis. Despite the central role of competition and markets in capitalism, in economic analysis these concepts are subsidiary to the notions of the firm, the consumer and the transaction. The even more primitive concepts are resources, technologies and preferences. Markets have no substantive status, other than as abstract demand and supply correspondences whose origin is treated unproblematically. This is not a helpful way to understand how market economies operate and develop.

Markets in capitalism

Markets are not unique to capitalism but capitalist systems are always market systems. In answer to the question 'What do markets do?', the overwhelmingly unanimous reply from economics is that they produce an equilibrium in the allocation of resources. The traditional view is that markets are institutions to facilitate exchange. Originally, 'markets' referred to the 'places' where exchanges occurred. But what is meant by the notion of the market system is that the plans of dispersed individuals to buy and sell are rendered mutually consistent within and across all the markets in an economy – markets for labour, for free capital disposal, for commodities and services more generally. Co-ordination is fundamental to the appraisal of market processes, but equilibrium is not, for equilibrium requires a state of rest from which there is no internally generated reason to change behaviour. In equilibrium, choices are not made. Market processes always generate reasons to change behaviour, to transform the prevailing way of conducting affairs, for they are contexts within which new knowledge is always being accumulated and new knowledge always opens up new opportunities. The market system is an open system: every established economic position is open to challenge from a new commodity, a new method of production or new model of business. Because economic change is open-ended it is never uniform in its effects, and although one might make a claim for economic progress, on average it remains the case that the distribution of gains and losses, of winners and losers, remains very uneven.

It is important to distinguish the instituted framework of the market system in general from the arrangements in particular markets. While the norms of the market system change only gradually, the number of distinct markets is subject to much more rapid change. Technological and organisational innovations are a powerful source of such lower level market transformations. Markets for personal computers, mobile phones or satellite television services were unknown even twenty years ago yet each is now a major market in its own right in advanced economies. Similarly, the introduction of major innovations such as derivatives and other complicated swaps contracts has transformed the way financial markets operate and has created serious doubts about the ability of the authorities to regulate financial transactions. Equally, in regard to labour markets, innovations in contractual form have had widely different effects on conditions of employment in different countries. These different types of market appear to operate in different ways, with different instituted rules of the game. In each case the relationships among buyers, among sellers and between buyers and sellers vary considerably. This raises a number of questions including that of whether there is there a general model of the market.

The social institutedness of the market system

Besides the specifically economic instituted arrangements for the conduct of market exchange there are, it is well known, also sets of necessary social conditions for the existence of markets. The very emergence of 'the economy' as an entity recognised as a separate sphere of existence, a separate 'field' in Bourdieu's terms, is itself a historical process. Exchange is only one way of facilitating economic interaction: as Polanyi (1957) pointed out, the gift economy and the redistributive economy are alternative socially mediated systems for interlinking production and consumption. The idea that the market was its own pure and necessary logic diverts attention from the social conditions in which particular markets and the market system itself exist. Non-economic conventions of social interaction which are consistent with the operation of markets in economic life include phenomena like social capital, trust and moral codes of conduct. There are also, as Max Weber pointed out, formal institutional conditions for the operation of rational capitalist economic activity. He emphasised the importance of rational calculation as a defining characteristic of capitalism and made clear that rational capital accounting required free markets for labour and commodities, as well as private property and a stable legal and administrative framework, including the rule of law, private property rights and enforcement of contracts (commercial law). The market also presupposes sets of politically generated regulations governing market exchange, which vary from time to time and from country to country. Interventions, conditioned by ethical considerations, may limit what might be offered for sale – for example limitations on the sale of alcohol, or the sale of human tissue material – and alter the distributive effects of particular markets through taxation, controls on consumption, and so forth. Finally, the extant unequal distribution of resources is also a social pre-condition of the operation of any actual market or market system. Different original distributions always affect the operations and outcomes of market competition. That is to say, power influences the making of markets, with some agents having more 'influence' than others in setting the rules.

The general point is that markets are constructed and operated within wider institutional frameworks. They are instituted, first, by the prevailing norms in relation to property rights, contracts and the conduct of competition. They are instituted also by the broad social acceptability of particular activities reflecting ethical stances of time and place. Finally, they are instituted in relation to the specifics of particular goods and services: the limitation on who may trade, the definition of quality, the standards of measurement, the uses to which a product is put, are examples of the specific rules of the game in particular markets. These instituted frames are not given but evolve with the development of the production and consumption activities in question. If, following Hayek, it is suggested that the market process is one of discovery, then what is being discovered is also the way to arrange and regulate market activity.

The contributions

Chapters 1–3 treat the instituted relation between economy and market from a number of complementary perspectives. Richard Nelson approaches the issues through an assessment of the complexity and varied nature of market arrangements and an appraisal of the limits to markets. Although the current consensus is in favour of markets, that has not always been so and Nelson traces the swings of the pendulum from Adam Smith to the debate on 'the end to history'. The core of his argument is that it is misguided simply to presume that markets are the best solution to the problem of production and distribution. The case needs to be argued – and to be sensitive to the fine details of different market contexts. In many cases the pro-market argument is clear. Equally there are other cases where the pro-market argument fails. However, it is the middle ground which matters, because the middle ground reflects the shifting balance of the mix between market and non-market forms of economic governance. Even in the situations where the market case prevails, for example air transport and pharmaceuticals, public regulation is an important feature of the market's operation. Thus contests over boundaries help us understand the complexities of the market system and the ways in which it can be governed more effectively. Here Nelson identifies three broad classes of argument to facilitate a judgement of the proper scope of markets. The first is the familiar economists' class of market failure suitably bolstered to reflect the fact that the strength of markets is not typically to be found in their efficiency at allocating given resources but rather in their adaptivity to unforeseen change and in their openness to innovative activity. The second concerns the role of the state in taking responsibility for the rules of the market game and in providing, through the political process, the means to challenge and vary the rules in particular cases. The third reflects distributional issues in a broad sense, the possibility of a mismatch between market outcomes and social perceptions of what those outcomes should be – what Nelson calls the problem of social cohesion and human rights. Nelson concludes with an interesting taxonomy of the factors that contribute to the appraisal of the applicability of the market to specific cases. That this list is as much concerned with social as with economic matters highlights their mutually instituted nature in market capitalism.

The second chapter, by Andrew Sayer, provides a critical evaluation of the idea of the market as the definitive form of co-ordination and of the socially embedded nature of market processes. Sayer draws attention, first, to the multiple uses of the word 'market' and to the difference between the market in general and markets in particular. The inclusiveness of the market definition determines the scope of what is to be explained and how. As an exemplar, Sayer addresses the problematic question of the boundary between market and production. He points out that firms do not do what markets do and conversely, so that the Coasian idea that firms fill the residuum left when markets have reached their limit is a distorting mirror. While recognising the importance of networks and trust, Sayer develops a critique of 'embeddedness' in terms of its overly benign view of economic relations. For the disruptive and retrogressive aspects of market processes are as much embedded as are their constructive and progressive tendencies. Sayer traces this mistaken view to a belief in the superiority of co-ordination through networks and to the neglect of power relations. Similarly, he argues, there is an excessively positive assessment of the role and the origins of trust in the working of market relations. Thus he observes that contractual relations can be exploited opportunistically, that trust is malleable and contingent, and that networks allow for exit.

The third chapter, by Brian Loasby, is an exposition of the connections between market arrangements and what might be called the 'problem of knowledge'. Loasby begins by observing that the standard and pervasive use in economics of the notion of equilibrium precludes choice and decision; for in equilibrium clock time passes, yet nothing happens, so nothing new needs to be assessed. Out of equilibrium, decision is essential, and for decision to be possible sense must be made of the world. Sense depends, in turn, on the possibility of pattern formation, and Loasby links capacities for pattern formation to the structure of the sensory and mental apparatus, to the limitations that this creates on the range of patterns that an individual can hold, and thus to the division of personal knowledge in society. In turn, the division of knowledge corresponds to a division of labour in relation to decision making and thus raises the fundamental economic problem – how are the multiple decisions of multiple agents to be rendered consistent? After all, the division of labour is a pattern beyond the comprehension of any single mind. Loasby finds the answer to the question of consistency in the institution of particular rules and conventions that facilitate market processes. It is the advantages offered by particular arrangements that justify the costs of instituting markets. The primary function of market conventions is to provide information that improves the knowledge, and thus the decision-making abilities, of consumers and producers. As Loasby points out, a neglected aspect of these conventions is their aesthetic appeal. Thus knowledge of market arrangements is an important feature of the knowledge possessed by consumers: in Marshallian fashion, markets are part of their external organisation.

The second group of essays, chapters 4–6, conveniently occupies the middle ground between the entirely conceptual material of the first and the empirical papers that form the final group of three in the volume. In chapter 4, Mark Harvey explores the idea of competition as an instituted economic process and poses the important question: 'Why does competition not destroy the competitive process?' He traces the interdependence of competition and markets through the writing of Weber and Polanyi and on to the modern sociology of embeddedness and networks. However, embeddedness is not fixed, nor is it absolute; economic relations can be just as equally disembedded and, as it were, the polarity reversed with the social framing the economic. Thus Harvey suggests, in Polanyian style, that three ideas capture the concept of institutedness. First, the relation between the social and the economic is variable and contingent, so creating the possibility of varieties of capitalist system. Second, the the economic and social are mutually conditioning. Third, the relations between competition and markets are constructed at widely diverse interdependent levels in economy and society. There follows a rich discussion of the units of competition and the scales on which competition takes place. Harvey also observes that competitive processes require accumulative processes and the differential growth in capacities and capabilities underpins the dynamic nature of competition. The chapter concludes by applying these ideas to the co-evolution of competition and market arrangements in the UK retail trade. Neither the market nor competition has remained constant in form: they have mutually shaped each other, as innovations have created new units of competition, and as new scales of market have emerged together with new rules of the competitive game.

Don Slater, in chapter 5, is also concerned with how markets come to be made, framed or 'stabilised'. Locating his reflections on the nature of markets in the context of arguments about the emergence of the 'new economy', he finds many of the central and accepted propositions about change mistaken. For Slater, what we witness today is much more rapid destabilisation of categories of goods. Since a market is defined in terms of substitutable items, he reasons that the delineation of the boundaries of any market depends on agreement as to the particular definition of the items being sold therein. This focuses attention on what he calls the 'the process of materialization'. Not a new process at all, this involves a recognition of the process whereby a particular item, including an event, comes to be recognised as one thing rather than another. It requires examination of 'the social processes by which things come to be treated as things in the social world' (p. 96). This normally requires recognition in terms of both functional and symbolic attributes, as he demonstrates with reference to the notion of a 'product concept', an integral element of the marketing armoury. The product concept contains a high potential for destabilization, as producers purposively manipulate both the physical content and design of the object, and its associated cultural meanings, into a new, or rather a recognisably distinct, type of product, fully cognisant that the process is one of 'conceptualising and choosing the different things a given product could be' (p. 107). This is a process which Slater sees as indicating corporate intervention becoming more reflexive, rationalised and institutionalised. So what is distinctive about the present is the level of commercially inspired contestation over the stabilisation and destabilisation of the fundamental categories of material culture which declare what things are. Moreover, it is not only producers who are aware of the malleability of the identification of goods, but the general public, the consumers, are becoming more adept at problematising the meaning of goods and, indeed, of improvising their use for their own purposes. This position, conducted in dialogue with Callon, permits Slater to issue an incisive challenge to several of the most widely employed distinctions in understanding contemporary economic life. He argues that conventional sharp distinctions between material and non-material goods, between the physical and symbolic aspects of commodities, between goods and services, and ultimately between the economic and the cultural, are fundamentally misleading.

Fran Tonkiss, reflecting in chapter 6 on an empirical study of cultural industries in East London, addresses a related and currently topical issue, that of the distinctiveness of the operations of 'cultural industries'. She addresses the debate about whether we currently can be said to have a 'cultural economy' with newer principles of operation than those of an older industrial economy. Finding it hard to understand the producers in terms of the products being sold, she argues that attention should be paid instead to the role of specialised knowledge involved in the framing of goods to be sold in cultural markets. Distinctive firms, labour contracts and mixed forms of governance imply a definition of the boundaries of sectors in terms of knowledge and skill rather than end products. The distinctiveness of the labour processes, which in practice correspond to particular types of labour contract, have the effect of 'hollowing-out' firms in these fields. This allows some insight into alternative modes of governance of economic activities – of the related roles of firms, markets and networks – in an expanding and highly volatile field. Among the features of those sectors of the economy are the importance of cultural knowledge in developing commercial strategies, but in a context where firms are small and unstable, where expert labour in particular is likely to be freelance and imbued with an ethos of 'creativity'. Such arrangements make it less easy for firms to act as collective repositories of knowledge and know-how, such key functions tending to be met by alternative arrangements of the network type. However, networks pose problems for economic governance of cultural production, which frequently requires the involvement of the state, reminding us of how the firm is just one among several instruments of economic co-ordination. In this regard she makes use of the insights of evolutionary economics (of Hodgson and Metcalfe).

The final group of three chapters is more empirically oriented. Chapter 7, by Jonathan Michie and Christine Oughton, explores the instituted arrangements constituting the 'peculiar economics' of professional sports. The particular features of the football market in the UK include strong fan loyalty to local clubs, the importance of broadcasting revenue to the finances of the game and the managed nature of league competition. These arrangements have changed considerably over time and opened up the possibility of vertical integration between broadcast companies and football clubs, to adversely affect the future organisation of the game. The chapter concludes by arguing that a dedicated regulatory process needs to be established to ensure that football is instituted in ways that ensure its long-run survival.

In chapter 8, Suma Athreye gives an analysis of the emergence of one particular market in the UK, that for computer software. She examines some of the conditions which resulted in the UK coming to specialise in services to client companies rather than the production of software packages for an arm's length market. The explanation she finds in the scale of demand for particular services and the effect its heterogeneity had upon competences – the skills and expertise available to British companies. So, at a critical point, when demand for computer packages took off, established competences were too limited to compete effectively with US companies, skills in general management, R&D and marketing especially being lacking. Thus, Athreye elaborates a model of cumulative causation to account for the continuing weak presence of the UK in the software product segments of the global market.

In the final chapter, Michael Best provides an account of regional economic adaptation to changed market circumstances. This is the story of the dynamics of capitalism focused on the resurgence of the Route 128 region around Boston following its decline in the mid-1980s in the face of competition from Silicon Valley. The chapter addresses the question of how this resurgence was achieved. The core of the explanation is that a new model of business had to be developed to integrate and manage more effectively the well-established technological assets of the region. The old 128 model is characterised in this account as vertically integrated and inflexible. The new model, by contrast, is described as vertically disintegrated but systems integrated – it is an open system constructed around flexible networks of firms, universities and research laboratories in the region. As an open system it has strong adaptive properties that arise from the combinatorial association of the many skills and kinds of knowledge in the region. It forms an experimental system that through its innovative and entrepreneurial attributes has regenerated the region. This fits well with the notion of a restless capitalism that is creative and adapts to changing market circumstances. It fits also with Marshall's emphasis on the external organisation of a firm in developing its competitive position. This is well described here as a collective entrepreneurial capability. On what is this capability founded? Best argues that three elements are crucial: the deep technical heritage in engineering, the modular design and systems integration skills available, and the skill formation system built around MIT. Each of these has long historical roots, and it is on these foundations that the region based its adaptive and innovative response to the challenge from the West Coast. Thus entrepreneurship was crucial to recovery but was premissed upon and instituted within the wider set of arrangements that had built and maintained the available base of knowledge and skills.

The Conclusion discusses the key theoretical and conceptual advances contained in the book and identifies outstanding issues for further investigation.

References

Callon, M. (1998), *The Laws of the Market*, Sociological Review monograph series, Oxford, Blackwell.

Harvey, M., Nyberg, A. and Metcalfe, J. S. (2001), 'Deep transformation in the service economy: innovations and organisational change in food retailing in Sweden and the UK', *ESSY Working Paper*, CRIC, University of Manchester.

Miller, D. (2002), 'Some things are virtual (but not the internet)', in DuGay, P. and Pryke, M. (eds), *Cultural Economy: Cultural Analysis and Commercial Life*, London, Sage.

Polanyi, K. (1957), 'The economy as instituted process', in Polanyi, K. Arensberg, C. and Pearson H. (eds), *Trade and Market in the Early Empires*, New York, Free Press.

1

On the complexities and limits of market organisation

Richard R. Nelson

Introduction

The close of the twentieth century saw a virtual canonisation of markets as the best, indeed the only really effective, way to govern an economic system. The market organisation being canonised was simple and pure, along the lines of the standard textbook model in economics. For-profit firms are the vehicle of production and provision. Given what suppliers offer, free choice on the part of customers, who decide on the basis of their own knowledge and preferences where to spend their money, determines how much of what is bought by whom. Competition among firms assures that production is efficient and tailored to what users want.

This chapter's aim is not to gainsay the present conventional wisdom, but rather to civilise it, and make it more nuanced and subtle. Market organisation, broadly interpreted, certainly has proved an effective way to govern a wide range of economic activities, and for a number of these it is hard to think of an alternative that would do nearly as well.

However, here I want to argue, highlight, that modern societies are facing a number of challenging and contentious issues regarding how to organise and govern a variety of activities that employ a large and growing fraction of their resources, where simple market solutions do not seem a good answer. While for some of these for-profit firms free customer choice and competition can provide the core of a satisfactory governance structure, to make market governance work satisfactorily will require strong and fine-grained regulation, and perhaps a number of other supplementary non-market elements. And for a number of these activities it likely would be best to rely centrally on other basic organisational modes, with markets in an ancillary role.

This argument clearly flies in the face of conventional wisdom. Hasn't market organisation proved to be a general purpose way of governing economic activity? Haven't we learned that markets work best when there is minimal regulation or other interference from government? And hasn't negative experience with forms of economic organisation that repress markets and use other mechanisms ruled out serious consideration of non-market alternatives?

I propose that the answer to each of these questions is more complicated than that implied by the way it is posed. To assess market organisation as a governing system, it is essential to widen the analytic context. By a governing system more generally I mean a system that does two roughly separable kinds of things. First, it defines the values and interests that are to count in the determination of what and how much is to be provided and distributed; the mechanism here usually can be characterised in terms of a process. Second, it involves an assignment of responsibility for provision and a system of incentives, controls and overview mechanisms for enforcing accountability. These two aspects of governing systems show up in political science as, on the one side, political process and policy making, and, on the other side, matters of administration and implementation. In economics the former clearly relates to the organisation of demand and the latter to the organisation of supply.

Market organisation clearly provides one kind of governance system, in the sense above, and one that is widely used. However, while the conventional wisdom seems to have it that market organisation is a relatively simple structure, in fact in many sectors generally thought of as market organised, the structure of demand and supply is highly complex, involving major non-market elements. Different sectors vary greatly in their mix of market and non-market elements. And even with this variegation and complexity, and hence the ability to tailor markets to particular circumstances, market organisation is not the principal governance mode we use for many activities and sectors. Indeed in a number of areas we actually try to fence out markets. These are facts in all capitalist countries, including the USA, despite a tendency to repress them.

Part of the difficulty many seem to have in seeing the complexity and the limits of markets as governing structures stems from the tendency to think of the economy as mainly concerned with producing and distributing things like peanut butter, automobiles, haircuts, telephone messages, and computers and computer services. However, a large share of an economy's resources are employed in activities that are central to the workings of our society, our political system and our culture. Some of these are conventionally thought of as outside the economic system – and appropriately outside.

A few examples will bring out the gist of the latter argument. Thus consider the care of young children, or crime prevention and criminal justice, to identify two areas where modern societies presently are facing some difficult problems regarding organisation and governance. Neither of these activities is governed largely through the market, at least as market organisation is generally conceived. While these cases are not what most people have in mind when they think of 'economic' activities, they certainly do employ considerable resources that could be used productively in other activities. Expenditures on the police and the courts get counted in the GNP statistics. So does much of child care outside of the family, and the purchased inputs used in family child care, and feminists have not been alone in arguing that housewives' services should be counted in GNP. And it surely is important that the quantity and quality of resources dedicated to these activities be appropriate to the task, and that these resources be effectively employed to serve the values at stake.

These examples are important in their own right, because they surely do present major problems of organisation and governance of activities employing substantial resources. But they are important also because they highlight the often neglected fact that the lines between 'economic' activities, and activities that generally might be thought of as social or political or cultural are blurred rather than sharp. An economy is not a sphere of activity that is separate from child raising, or from dealing with crime, or from supporting art or religion, or from political campaigning, for that matter. Rather, economics should be viewed as an aspect of any activity. From that point of view, it should be clear that the problem of economic organisation and governance is not simply about the production and distribution of commodities like peanut butter.

In any case, under standard circumstances, child care is presumed to be the province of the child's parents or extended family. At the same time, parents or those in a parental role are presumed to have an obligation to care adequately for their children: they are not seen as having a right to choose whether or not to provide that care, as they have the right to buy whichever kind of car they like or none at all. Preventing crime, and operating the criminal justice system more generally, traditionally are viewed as basic activities of government. In general, it is expected that individuals are to be treated as equals by the system, and that justice is 'not for sale'. In both of these areas there is considerable resistance to the idea of letting market values and mechanisms play a central role in governance.

But, of course, the market does play a role in these areas. Babysitters and nannies serve for pay. The demand for extra-family child care is large and growing and there are many for-profit as well as not-for-profit providers. Persons of wealth and social status are well known for getting a better break from the criminal justice system than those towards the bottom of the social order; they can, among other things, hire good lawyers. Also, there recently has been considerable use of for-profit contractors to run prisons, and many businesses and local communities hire their own private guards. While presently the role played by the market in these areas is relatively small, there is considerable debate about whether that role should be bigger or smaller.

Thus there is major dispute about how day-care providers should be regulated, for example about the qualifications of carers, and about acceptable ratios of carers to children. Day-care subsidy is another issue. The ability of the rich to buy favorable verdicts, and the frequent inability of the poor to obtain decent legal defense for serious crimes, has raised concerns about the quality of justice dispensed by the criminal justice system. In both child care and criminal justice markets are used, but no one is arguing that they should be unfettered. On the other hand, it is not clear just where or how to draw the lines.

The governance of basic scientific research is another important area where, presently, the market plays a relatively modest role, but there is considerable debate about just what that role should be. The scientific community long has argued that it is a mistake to have conjectures regarding likely future practical application play a central role in the allocation of resources to basic research. Rather, the dominant criterion ought to be scientific promise, which the scientists themselves are in the best position to judge, and research findings ought to be published and open to anyone to test and use. For-profit companies are not much given to support research under those terms and groundrules. It long has been broadly accepted that funding basic research is an appropriate mission of government. By and large governments have provided funding for basic research under a regime of self-governance by scientists, with universities the principal locus of the activity.

However, while open publication and open access traditionally have been the norm in basic science, in recent years universities as well as business firms have begun to patent the results where they can, and to require that users take out licences and pay fees. And corporations now are important sources of support for basic research in certain fields, with their profiting from this activity tied to their ability to restrict access to results. There is a growing debate about whether or not public funds should go into fields of research that companies seem willing to support out of their own money, and regarding whether it is a plus or a minus that university research results increasingly are being patented. The debate can well be regarded as about the scope and nature of the role markets ought to play in governing the basic science enterprise.

Of course these three activities are not generally regarded as basically market governed. But consider some sectors that most people do think of as governed and organised through the market, for example pharmaceuticals or airline services. The products of both industries are highly regulated, as are some of the details of the operation of the firms in those industries. The R&D of pharmaceutical companies draws heavily on publicly supported biomedical research, and a significant portion of the sales of pharmaceuticals is funded by various government programmes that support the provision of medical care. The airlines depend on investments in airports, which in many cases are publicly financed, and on a government-funded and -operated traffic control system. Or think of automobiles that run on public roads, under a specialised system of traffic law. Or agriculture.

As one reflects on these sectors and these activities, it becomes evident that the provision of supportive and regulatory bodies of law, and the necessary infrastructure, which are widely recognised as requisite tasks for government in order to make markets work decently well, are to a considerable degree sectorally specific. While often repressed in the current discussion, markets need non market structures in order to operate.

I propose that almost all activities in modern economies are governed through a mix of market and non-market mechanisms, with the relative importance of markets, the constraints put on their workings, and the strength and nature of non-market mechanisms varying from activity to activity, and from sector to sector. My focus in this chapter is on the debates about the mix.

Thus consider hospital services, another arena where the debate is intense. The hospital sector contains numbers of both public and non-profit units, as well as for-profit hospitals. Part of hospital revenues comes from private patients and private insurance. Part comes from public programmes that support the care of persons in certain categories. Hospitals are subject to a number of different forms of regulation. Physicians, as a profession, play a major role in determining what is done. In recent years, managed-care organisations and insurance companies also have played major roles in the hospital governance structure. There is often bitter debate about the relative power that these different parties and interests should play in the governing structure, as well as about the role of public finance in supporting the system.

Or, consider some of the issues surrounding the governance of the Internet. Should the content of the Internet be regulated, and if so in what ways and by whom? Should the Government require that the Internet be made available on favorable terms to schools, and if so who should pay for it?

Other areas of dispute involve markets for things some people believe should not be bought and sold, or in some cases should not be available at all. Reflect on the controversy about the emerging market for kidneys and ova, or about the decriminalisation of prostitution and drugs.

This already is a lengthy and diverse list of areas where the appropriate role of market and non-market modes of governance is under dispute. But let me stress their common properties. They all involve a particular class of goods or services that do or arguably should show up in the GNP accounts, because they employ scant resources to meet particular kinds of human needs. And they all involve disputes about the appropriate structure of governance, that is about the values and interests that are to count in the determination of what and how much should be provided and distributed, and about who is to do the work under what regime of incentives and controls.

While there is overlap, I want to differentiate these kinds of economic governance disputes from those that are central to macroeconomic policy; the issues I am considering here are microeconomic. In some cases the issues I am focusing on here are intertwined with policies concerned with income distribution. However my focus is on disputes about the governance of particular activities or sectors, with the question of who pays sometimes figuring as part of the dispute, but the central issue is not income transfers *per se*.

Despite these commonalities, the issues I touched on above still would appear to be very heterogeneous, and appearances here are not deceiving. An important point I want to get in view is that the particular key issues of governance, and the arguments about what markets can and cannot do well, differ from activity to activity, and hence from sector to sector. However, a principal purpose of this essay is to try to make some order of this apparent jumble of issues. Later in this chapter I develop a relatively small collection of analytic categories which, I propose, encompasses a large share of the issues at stake. But first I need to set the stage.

I begin by trying to place the current broad debate, which starts from a degree of faith in the efficacy of markets that is almost unprecedented, in some historical perspective. Then, in the following section, I consider the various virtues that purportedly characterise market organisation and elevate it over other kinds of governance structures, and raise some questions about those arguments. The fourth section is concerned with 'market failure' theory, and other broad theories that point towards the desirability of a mixed economy.

In the penultimate section I return to the issues referred to above, and try to bring order to them by proposing a set of categories into which, I argue, most of them fit. Finally, a reprise.

The past as prologue

The presumption and the fact that markets play a pervasive role in the governance and organisation of economic activity are relatively recent phenomena. A significant expansion in the role of markets occurred first in Great Britain around the beginning of the eighteenth century, and later spread to continental Europe, and the United States, still later to Japan, and more recently to large portions of the world. Of course certain kinds of markets have existed from virtually the dawn of history, but until recently were central in only a small portion of human activity. It is the pervasiveness of markets and of the system that came to be called capitalism that are relatively new on the historical time scale.

With the spread of markets – of production that was largely for sale on markets, and of a context where either receipts from sales or wages garnered on labour markets largely determined the access of an individual or family to goods and services – a sphere of economic activity began to emerge in its own right, as a system that was distinct from the broader society and polity. Thus Adam Smith's (1776) *The Wealth of Nations* is about a market economy, influenced profoundly to be sure by the culture and governance of the nation containing it, but as an object in its own right, and with its own basic rules of operation. That book could not have been written a century earlier. And today, of course, the standard economics textbooks draw a picture of an economy that is quite separate from the rest of human activity.

From the time capitalism began to take on recognisable form, and students of its operation began to write about it (with time these analysts came to be called 'economists'), the system has had its proponents and its opponents. The balance of opinion about capitalism has swung back and forth over the years, and at any time has varied from country to country.

While the British 'classical school' often is thought of as comprising strong proponents of markets, as unencumbered as possible, and extended to as wide a range of human activity as possible, in fact that is not quite accurate. Adam Smith's enthusiasm for markets was nuanced, and he clearly saw a downside. John Stuart Mill did not like certain aspects he saw of the rising capitalism of mid nineteenth-century England (1961). The USA today is regarded as the locus of almost unwashed enthusiasm for unfettered markets. However, Alexander Hamilton, in his famous *Report on Manufactures* (1791), argued that protection and subsidy were needed if American industry were to survive and prosper. Many of the founders of the American Economic Association (towards the end of the nineteenth century) were much concerned about what they saw as the excesses of market capitalism, and with devising policies to tame it.

Outside of the UK and the USA, and the cultures they have strongly influenced, the enthusiasm traditionally has been even more muted, and the climate of opinion sometimes downright hostile. Indeed the socialist economic tradition was to a considerable extent basically a negative reaction to market capitalism. That tradition constituted a very roomy tent. On the one side one can find the British Fabians who did not want to abolish markets (at least not in the short run), but rather to regulate them in the public interest, and to supplement markets with a variety of other institutions to deal with the inequities they saw as inevitable in raw capitalism. On the other side stand diverse scholars who were strongly hostile to the market system and who proposed to completely replace it with something else; here one finds socialists as diverse as Robert Owen and Karl Marx.

Marx of course saw capitalism as a system of power. For him, political and economic power were intertwined. It is no coincidence that, until recently, nationalisation of heavy industry and, more generally, of the organisations that provided the basic infrastructure for economic life was at the top of the agenda for socialist parties, after they were able to attain and hold political power.

With all the enthusiasm today for market capitalism of a relatively extensive and unrestricted sort, it is easy to forget that half a century ago some of the most distinguished scholars were predicting capitalism's demise. Between 1940 and 1950 Joseph Schumpeter published his classic *Capitalism, Socialism, and Democracy*, and Karl Polanyi his *The Great Transformation*. Both saw capitalism as a system whose time had passed, the former with regret and the latter with relief. The reasons for these predictions are, interestingly, somewhat different.

For Schumpeter, the reasons were twofold. First of all, he argued that the principal economic merit of capitalism had been the rapid and radical innovation the system spurred and supported, which was the basic factor behind the great improvements in living standards that had occurred under capitalism. However, he believed that, as a result of the advance of science, rapid industrial innovation no longer required the hurly burly of competition, but could proceed in a planned and orderly way. Thus capitalist economic organisation no longer was needed for economic progress. At the same time the professional managers of industry and the scientists in R&D had little zeal for keeping competitive capitalism going as a system: their careers would be more secure and as comfortable under a different regime. This left the defenders of capitalism even more vulnerable to the attacks of intellectuals who saw many vices and few virtues in the system.

For Polanyi, market capitalism had been a disaster for the working classes and, while since the late nineteenth-century wages had risen somewhat for those who had jobs, the great depression showed that capitalism remained a pernicious system. More, (and here Polanyi's line is similar to that of Schumpeter), the depression had weakened the support of the middle classes, and even business, for the system, and was leading them to look to taming it or transforming it so that it was less brutal.

Both authors saw the economic system of market capitalism as profoundly influencing the nature of broader society and politics. Schumpeter saw the effects as largely positive, as encouraging individual creativity, freedom and independence. Indeed, he associated the institutions of modern science with capitalism, and argued that liberal democracy was a fellow traveller, a position very close to that of F. A. Hayek. For these reasons he viewed with regret what he saw as the inevitable decline of capitalism.

Polanyi's great book, on the other hand, put forth the argument that the encroachment of markets on everyday life and, in particular, the commodification of labour and land had destroyed the co-operative and communal aspects he saw as essential to a healthy civil society. He saw the defence of capitalism against the pressures of working-class interests as a fundamental aspect of political regimes under capitalism, so that a true democracy was very difficult to achieve so long as capitalism held sway. On the other hand, part of his argument as to why capitalism was dissolving involved precisely the extension of democracy despite the resistance of capitalism's defenders.

Neither author displayed any enthusiasm for the Soviet system that was taking shape at the time. But both clearly forecasted an economic system that involved far less competition among firms, and far more co-ordination, much more government regulation of firms and particularly the labour market, greater protection of the basic living standards of workers and more planning than did the system that had come to be called capitalism.

It is apparent that the strong performance after the Second World War of the European and American economies surprised many people, and changed attitudes. Unemployment was low. The economic growth rate was high and the lion's share of the population experienced rising living standards.

It was widely recognised that post-war capitalism was structurally different from that of pre-war days in a number of dimensions. The roles of government had expanded significantly. Public spending on education, particularly higher education, had increased greatly, and so had government support of R&D. There were major public investments in roads and other infrastructure. Unemployment insurance now was widespread and in many countries quite generous, as was social security. Many countries expanded the scope of national health insurance, or instituted new programmes. Both

France and the United Kingdom established an apparatus for centralised economic planning, or at least indicative planning. The United States saw the passing of a full employment act and the establishment of a President's Council of Economic Advisors.

How much these systems changes had to do with the strong performance of the economies in the quarter century after the Second World War still is an arguable matter. However, it is clear that many of the forecasts of Schumpeter and Polanyi regarding systems change had come to pass.

One could ask whether the new system still was market capitalism. C. A. R. Crosland asked that question in his 1956 opus *The Future of Socialism*, and answered that the system was very different from what it had been, and that it contained a number of elements long advocated by socialists, but still was not socialism. In *Beyond the Welfare State* (1960), Gunnar Myrdal also stressed the great change that had occurred and in effect took the position, whatever it might be called, that most of the problems of the old capitalism were resolved by the new system. Andrew Schonfield, in his *Modern Capitalism* written in 1965, took essentially the same position.

American scholars put forth a distinctively pragmatic perspective on these developments. Robert Dahl and Charles E. Lindblom in their great *Politics, Economics, and Welfare* (1953) proposed that the tasks of modern economies were complex and varied, and that different forms of governance and organisation are appropriate to different ones. The book basically layed out the wide range of different principles the United States used to organise different kinds of activities. Daniel Bell's *The End of Ideology* (1960) argued that in the United States, at least, no one was still arguing about the pluses and minuses of capitalism; rather, the discussion was about how to make it work well.

In the United States economists increasingly used the term 'mixed economy' and, when talking among themselves, 'the neoclassical synthesis'. The basic themes were well articulated in the 1960 report of the new Kennedy administration's Council of Economic Advisors, which contained a number of the country's best-known and most respected economists. Centerpiece in the formulation was the Government's role in managing the macro aspects of the economy through fiscal and monetary policy; several years later the Republican President Richard Nixon would say 'We are all Keynesians' (see US Government, 1960, 1967). Market organisation was assumed to be the basic way of governing and managing industry, broadly defined. However, the theory of 'market failures', to use a term I will unpack later, was very much part of the neoclassical synthesis. The provision of public goods, like national security and scientific knowledge, required public support and in some cases public undertaking. Externalities required regulation or a regime of taxes and subsidies. Anti-trust policies needed to be pursued and natural monopolies needed to be regulated. And the Government needed to proceed actively to assure that the workings of the economic system did not generate unrelieved poverty. There were only a few years between the Kennedy administration's first economic report and the 'war on poverty'.

These changes in economic policy or, more broadly, changes in the view of what capitalism was and what was needed to make it effective did not go unchallenged. By the middle or late 1970s there was considerable advocacy for rolling back many of the changes or, at least, blocking further moves in those directions. Mark Blyth has proposed, in his '*Great Transformations*', (2000), that there may be a natural cycle regarding popular opinion on the appropriate level and kind of government regulation, and involvement more generally, in capitalism, a cycle that involves both policies and ideologies, with overshoot of the former leading to switches in the latter.

However, it is fair to say that the seachange in ideology on these matters reflected in the rhetoric and the policies of the Margaret Thatcher and Ronald Reagan administrations caught many people by surprise. The sharp changes undoubtedly had many causes. One was the deterioration of the performance of the American and European economies that set in during the early 1970s. This was associated with a continuing rise in government spending as a fraction of GNP, and many argued that this, together with increased government regulation, was a root cause of the economic problems. And clearly the collapse of the Soviet economy bolstered the advocates of market capitalism – of a relatively simple and raw variety.

The 1980s and 1990s saw a dramatic change in intellectual writings about capitalism. Daniel Yergin and Joseph Stanislaw wrote about how the marketplace had won over government in the battle for *The Commanding Heights*, and saw the outcome as a victory for the right cause, expressing few qualms that the issues might be more complex than the ideological arguments of the victors. Francis Fukuyama proclaimed *The End of History and the Last Man* (1992), as a final victory for market capitalism (along with liberal democracy).

And yet, for all the attempts to roll back the reforms of the early post-war era and to return to a leaner and more basic capitalism, the actual systems remain extraordinarily complex and variegated. The welfare state has become a recognised part of modern capitalism, a mistaken idea in the minds of some, a necessary complement to the industrial side of modern capitalism to others, but certainly an arena of continuing policy argument. With growing recognition of the central role of technological advance in economic growth, and of science to technological advance, the old industrial policy debates have taken on new form, but the debates continue. The waves of deregulation and privatisation that marked the 1980s have not ended the debate about whether for-profit firms can be trusted in contexts where competition is problematic or the good or service being provided is crucial to the well-being of the society or polity.

In my view, however, while for the most part the contemporary discussion of issues of macroeconomic policy has broken from the ideological narrowness of the 1970s and 1980s, that is less true regarding problems of economic organisation. Too much of the current discussion of how to govern economic activity still proceeds within an intellectual frame that sees modern capitalism, and in particular market organisation of economic activity, as far simpler than it actually is. I think it very important to get the complexity and variegation of market organisation, and its limits, more clearly in view.

The case for market organisation: the perspective from economics

I have noted that, while recently there is fraying around the edges, over the last twenty years belief in the efficacy of markets has been unusually wide and deep by historical standards. Non-economists seem under the impression that economists have built a theoretically rigorous and empirically well-supported case for market organisation. In this section I argue that, in fact, the most commonly cited theoretical argument can support little weight, the empirical case is rough and ready, and the persuasive part of the argument is pragmatic and qualitative rather than rigorous and quantitative. And, in my view at least, the arguments for market organisation that are most compelling are quite different from those contained in the standard textbook formulation.

Since at least the days of Adam Smith, the Anglo Saxon tradition of economic analysis has touted the virtues of the 'hidden hand' – profit-oriented suppliers striving for customer purchasers on a competitive market. For the most part Smith's argument was qualitative, and supported by a set of empirical cases drawn from his own experiences and those of others. Also, in the present context, it is important to remember that Smith was making his case for market organisation partly as argument against a particular alternative – mercantilism.

Modern economics purports to tighten up the logic of the argument. The theoretical case made for market organisation in contemporary economics textbooks and treatises compares the performance of a stylised model market economy against a theoretical norm of Pareto optimality. Pareto optimality is a sophisticated notion of maximal economic efficiency. If the performance of an economy is Pareto optimal, it is getting the maximal value of output from the resources and technologies available, given the distribution of purchasing power. (This is not the standard definition of Pareto optimality, but it is nearly equivalent.) The textbook argument concludes that, given a package of assumptions, a competitive market economy meets that norm. However, while Nobel prizes have been awarded to economists for developing this theory, I would argue that it is a non-starter as a case for real life market organisation for several reasons.

The primary one, of course, is that the theoretical model of a market economy that satisfies the criterion of Pareto optimality is very far away from actual market organisation. Strangely, the implications of this for the whole broad argument have tended to be underplayed.

Even if one stays close to that theoretical formulation, almost all analysts would admit the presence of a variety of 'market failures', a topic I take up in the next section. Once these are taken into the model, the theoretical market economy does not achieve Pareto optimality. And from there the whole theoretical strategy of the case for markets unravels.

It unravels because, unlike Smith's discussion of the virtues of the hidden hand, which did involve an explicit comparison, the contemporary theoretical textbook argument does not compare the performance of a (highly abstracted) market-organised economy with the theoretical performance of another (highly abstracted) kind of economic system. In particular, the argument is not that another kind of economic system could not also achieve Pareto optimality. Of course, if market organisation does as well as is theoretically possible, there is no particular reason to consider an alternative. However, once the optimality argument falls away, there would seem to be no way to avoid comparing how market organisation does against alternative structures, even though this may be very hard to do.

The task is made especially difficult by the fact, which I have been stressing, that modern market capitalism (or any plausible alternative system) is very complex and variegated. The argument I am developing clearly is that it is exactly this flexibility which enables market organisation to work tolerably well in a wide variety of contexts. But then these factors absolutely need to be taken into account in any analysis which compares market capitalism against alternatives, or against some kind of an absolute scale.

There is also the question of the kind of performance attributes one should use to evaluate market organisation and its alternatives. Much of modern economic analysis is focused on economic efficiency – the value of the output (given the distribution of purchasing power) that an economy is able to achieve with given resources and technologies. While real life market economies certainly do not achieve Pareto optimality, most economists would argue that market organisation and competition often do seem to generate results that are moderately efficient. There are strong incentives for firms to produce goods and services that customers want, or can be persuaded they want, and to produce them at as low financial cost as is possible. There is a 'dynamic' version of, or supplement to, this efficiency argument. Under many circumstances competitive market-organised economic sectors seem to respond relatively quickly to changes in customer demands, input supply conditions and technological opportunities. To the extent that producing what customers value is treated as a plus, and so long as factor prices roughly measure opportunity costs, there is a strong pragmatic case for market capitalism on economic efficiency grounds, broadly defined, at least in certain domains of activity.

But the question is 'compared with what?' and 'in what context?' It is interesting that in wartime, and almost without protest, capitalist economies have adopted centrally co-ordinated mechanisms of resource allocation, procurement and rationing. The rationale has been that such economic organisation was essential if production was to be allocated to the highest priority needs, and conducted efficiently. And the experience with wartime planning sometimes has led some analysts to propose that a number of the mechanisms used then would vastly increase economic efficiency during peacetime.

On the other hand, most knowledgeable analysts have argued against that position, strongly. It is one thing to marshall an economy to concentrate on a central set of demands over a short period of time. It is something else again to have an economy behave reasonably efficiently and responsively in a context of varied and changing demands, supply conditions and technological opportunities, over a long time period. The experience with central planning in the formerly communist countries, particularly after the era when building up standard economic infrastructure sufficed as a central goal, bears out this argument.

However, I would propose that the argument behind the scenes here is much more complex, and in fact different, from the standard textbook argument that profit maximising behaviour of firms in competitive market contexts yields economically efficient results. It hinges on the multiplicity and diversity of wants, resources and technologies in modern economies that, experience shows, defy the information processing and resource allocating capabilities of centrally planned and controlled systems, and also presumes that the chances of appropriate responses to changed conditions are enhanced when there are a number of competitive actors who can respond, again a proposition consistent with experience. Many people find that case for market organisation compelling, and in accord with the evidence both about capitalist economies and about the old planned ones. That case, however, has nothing to do with a theoretical argument about the Pareto optimality of a stylised market economy, but rather rests on an empirically well-founded belief that, in a complex and changing environment, decentralised market systems work better than highly centralised ones.

Many observers have proposed that it is in dynamic long-run performance, rather than in short-run efficiency, that market capitalism reveals its greatest strength. As Marx and Schumpeter have stressed, capitalism has been a remarkably powerful engine of economic progress. And here too one can make a rather explicit comparison. Indeed a good case can be made that a central reason for the collapse of the old communist economies was their inability to keep up with and take advantage of the rapid technological progress that was going on in market economies.

But, again, the characteristics and capabilities of market organisation that contribute to technological progress are very different from those that relate to static efficiency, and those of the normative textbook model. Indeed Schumpeter made a great deal of those differences. The capitalism of his *Capitalism, Socialism, and Democracy* was an effective engine of progress because competition spurred innovation. This theory places high value on pluralism and multiple rival sources of invention and innovation. However, under this view of what socially valuable competition was all about, the presence of large firms, with R&D laboratories as well as some market power, was welcomed, despite the fact that such a market structure diverged from the purely competitive one associated with the static theorem about Pareto optimality. More, the very process of competitive innovation was itself a source of efficiency differences across firms which, from a static perspective, could be viewed as inefficiency in the system as a whole.

Earlier I noted that Schumpeter argued that as science had become more powerful, the unruly and inefficient competition of capitalist systems would no longer be needed for industrial innovation, which increasingly could be planned. History has shown him to be very wrong on that point. However, I would argue that the strong performance of market capitalist economies on this front probably has as much to do with features of modern capitalist economies which are absent from the economists' standard model, as for example public support of university research, as with those that are included in that model.

In concluding this section it is relevant to recall that not only was Schumpeter's appreciation of the economic power of capitalism different from that which was being articulated in the then-rising neoclassical economics (although not inconsistent with views of earlier economists like Smith). Schumpeter also admired the cultural, and the political, values and structures that he saw induced and supported by capitalist economic organisation. On the other hand, Polanyi detested what he thought capitalism did to people, values and politics. It is apparent that the arguments for and against market organisation, and capitalism more generally, are concerned with issues at some distance from evaluations of performance on strictly economic grounds, whatever the latter might mean. Both Schumpeter and Polanyi believed that capitalism could not survive politically, at least in its raw form, because of widespread distaste for its social consequences. Clearly many of the post Second World War reforms were attempts to mitigate those consequences.

Which brings the discussion back to the question 'What is modern capitalism?'. And what are the alternatives? Years ago it was reasonable to compare capitalism and various aspects of its performance against communist systems, but this is no longer a relevant comparison. Today no one is seriously proposing an economic system that does not make extensive use of markets. The real issues today relate to the mix of markets with other forms, in different economic activities and sectors. And here, while a number of people have in effect put forward the proposition 'The more of market and the less of other things the better', I know of no convincing argument to support that proposition.

The positive case for a mixed economy

Why is there so much in the way of non-market elements in modern capitalist economies? Contemporary advocates of a purer form of capitalism argue that it is all a mistake or partially the result of a conspiracy. My argument, of course, is that these non-market elements are essential to make the economic system work tolerably well, and to ensure the support of its basic structure under democratic institutions.

In this section I consider three bodies of theorising that provide arguments for a mixed economy. By far the best known is the economists' theory of 'market failure', in which limitations of market organisation provide reason for market supplementation or the substitution in some cases of non-market forms. Partly because it is so well known, and partly because its categories and conceptions are developed and criticised in the this section following, here I can be brief about this body of theory.

Rather, my focus is on two other bodies of theorising. One is concerned with the essential roles of the state. The orientation here is not to the need for the state or other non-market forms because markets occasionally fail, but to functions that naturally fall to government, including those that government has to perform to enable other institutions to operate tolerably well. The other body of theorising takes human society as basic, and is oriented to the rights and obligations of individuals within society. Market organisation can either help support this more fundamental structure or can be damaging to it; within this framework the question of where markets should and should not be admitted depends on how and where markets impinge on basic social structure.

Market failure theory

Without question, most of the high-level argument about how to use market organisation effectively, where market organisation needs to be supplemented by other mechanisms, and where market organisation simply works poorly, is conducted using the economists' 'market failure' language. The standard categories of market failure – public goods, externalities, monopoly problems, information impactedness, and (in some treatments) income distribution problems – serve to structure and constrain much of the policy discourse. Indeed since the 1960s, when this theory became solidly incorporated in mainline economics, almost every new president's Council of Economic Advisors has walked through basically this list in its maiden annual report to Congress and the American people, as part of its articulation of the economic policies its administration was proposing to implement.

Here I want to highlight several things about standard market failure theory that I develop in the next section. In the first place, market failure almost always is a matter of degree, not of kind. Or, from another point of view, market failure is ubiquitous: markets always 'fail' to some extent, in one way or another. This of course is an issue I flagged in the preceding section, where I also pointed out that an implication was that an explicit evaluation of organisational alternatives was needed before one could assess the implications regarding appropriate organisational form. Unfortunately, given the present state of our knowledge, economists and social scientists do not have the capability to engage in confident analysis of the likely performance of a wide range of organisational alternatives, or even to analyse the complex mixed market structures that have evolved in many sectors. But, on the other hand, a number of sophisticated advocates of market organisation have argued that the standard theory of market organisation, because it greatly oversimplifies what actually goes on in real markets, far exaggerates the extent to which markets 'fail', because in fact particular markets have evolved various procedures and structures that deal with problems which the simpler theoretical structure would see as sources of market failure. It should be clear that I have considerable sympathy for this point of view. By presenting a drastically oversimplified model of market organisation, standard economic theory blinds itself to the remarkable versatility of market organisation, broadly defined. Conventional market failure theory takes attention away from the remarkable diversity of markets.

However, by the way it is formulated, market failure theory carries a heavy normative load to the effect that markets always are to be preferred to other basic forms of organisation and governance, unless they are basically flawed in some sense. Thus the only reason why government should provide for national security and protect citizens from crime is that markets cannot do those jobs well. Parents need to take care of children because of market failure.

The functions of the state

As one reflects on it, the argument that we need government simply because markets sometimes 'fail' seems rather strange, or at least incomplete. Cannot one make a positive case for government (or families for that matter), as a form that is appropriate, even needed, in its own right?

And of course there is an ancient body of theorising that puts forward a positive case for government. In much of its early incarnation, and some of its more recent, the state is viewed as the structure through which an organic community governs itself, and values are defined at the level of the community. Reflect on Plato's discussion in *The Republic* (1961), or Hegel's discussion, where the good state is defined in terms of justice and morality and the quality of persons (1967). Under this conception of the relationships between a collection of individuals and families and their state, the good of the whole is by no means adequately judged in terms of the sum of the 'happiness' of the individuals that comprise it. This notion is very much alive in discussions about matters like the quality of justice in a society, or the aims of foreign policy. Arguments about how these activities should be governed involve beliefs about appropriate collective values, or the values of the collective, that transcend those of particular individuals. Under this theory, in these areas at least the state is the natural vehicle of governance, rather than something that is justified on grounds of market failure. In these areas the state may choose to use markets, but the purpose being served is a public purpose, and the responsibility for furthering it ultimately is a state responsibility.

It is important to keep this point of view in mind, because it plays a major role in a number of areas of contemporary dispute about governance. As I will propose shortly, in many of these areas the collective value argued to be at stake involves basic community and human rights, which I want to treat as a distinct body of theorising in its own right. Thus in the remainder of this subsection, I focus on another strand of political philosophy, particularly Anglo-American political philosophy.

From at least the times of Hobbes and Locke, theories about the importance of the state have involved, centrally, the proposition that a strong state is necessary for individuals to lead secure, decent and productive lives. Originally this body of theorising had little to do with economics, much less with the role of the state in market economies. Thus Hobbes's case for a strong state to establish and enforce a clear body of law was posed in terms of the need to avoid the 'war of every man against every man'. While this case involved security of property, that was not its central orientation. With Locke, the orientation is more towards security of property, but his great writings were before capitalism emerged as a recognisable economic system.

In *The Wealth of Nations*, Smith built on these ideas and specialised them to the market economy he saw as working in Great Britain. He ascribed the backwardness of countries like eighteenth-century China largely to the vulnerability of possessions to thieves or simply to being confiscated by those in power. To have an incentive to produce for the market, craftsmen needed to be confident that they would reap what they sowed. Trade required contracts in which the traders had confidence, and that required a body of supporting law and a tradition of law enforcement that would not simply obey the interests of the wealthy and powerful. I call this required political and legal structure 'needed infrastructure'.

In Smith's day, not much physical infrastructure was necessary to make markets work. There were roads and canals, which government could either build and maintain itself or franchise to private parties. While Smith included in his functions of government the support of education, his case assigned at least as much importance to education as a factor supporting civil society as the role he perceived formal education to play in the operation of the economic system more narrowly defined.

As technology advanced and economic systems became more complex, the physical and legal infrastructure needed for the effective operation of market economies became more complex and variegated. Establishing the telegraph and railroad systems required government action, if not necessarily government finance and operation. With the emergence of the organic chemical product industry and the industrial research laboratory in the last part of the nineteenth century, effective patent law became important as a precondition to profitable R&D in a number of industries. Education became more important economically, and in industries like those producing fine chemical products firms needed scientists with a doctoral level of expertise. Earlier I briefly discussed the legal and physical infrastructure, provided by government, that support the modern airline, pharmaceuticals and automobile industries.

Now the question of what infrastructure has to be provided for markets to work well, and what it is that markets themselves can be expected to provide, often is not easily answered. However, 'needed infrastructure' provides a point of view on some of the current argument about the role of non-market structures in market-oriented economies that is different, I propose, from the modern theory of economists about conditions of market failure. Thus consider activities like maintaining a system of contract law, building and maintaining a road system, and supporting the development of basic scientific knowledge. These activities can be viewed as public goods, in the sense of market failure theory, with the market failure stemming from the fact that their benefits are collective rather than individual, and hence that to profit firms would have great difficulty collecting for their provision on a conventional market. Or they can be considered as 'needed infrastructure', the provision of which is a function of governments. However, while the former theory sees the reason for governmental provision or overview and control in the inability of markets to do an adequate job, the latter sees provision of such goods and services as a central responsibility of government, even if they could be provided through market mechanisms. And where market mechanisms in fact are used as part of the machinery for provision, the latter perspective sees government as still responsible for overseeing the operation, at least to some degree.

Support of primary and secondary education is an interesting case in point. While many laypersons clearly consider education to provide a public good and to be a responsibility of government, economists have trouble squaring the former notion with their technical definition of a public good, and more generally tend to struggle with the reason why government should be responsible for education, in view of the large benefits to those who get the education. While the notion that education yields externalities helps along their analysis, that perspective would seem to justify some subsidy to education but hardly the major governmental responsibility in the field that is the case in most countries. It would seem that non-economists tend to place education in the 'infrastructure' category, and hence have no trouble with the notion that government is responsible for supporting it, and for governing and monitoring education at least broadly, although some would argue that private schools ought to play a significant role in provision.

Social cohesion and human rights

Education also is an example of the kind of goods and services that, under the third body of theorising identified here, is considered a basic human right, or right of citizenship, and thus which ought to be available to all, independently of their money income or wealth or social status. Thus all citizens ought to have the right to vote, to trial by jury, and to legal aid if they cannot afford it on their own. Most societies recognise a similar right to an education, up to some level at least. Access to these basics of citizenship are seen as something that should not be rationed through markets, and for which government has a fundamental responsibility.

The core arguments of modern welfare state theorists combine these venerable arguments with a set of policies designed to shield individuals, and society as a whole, from what they see as the ravages of raw capitalism. Thus a set of economic rights have been added to the older political rights. This decoupling of access to a considerable range of goods and services from normal market process is the hallmark of the modern welfare state idea.

Above I noted the overlap between theories of the state that see collective values as transcending individual values, and modern welfare state theories. There is a difference, however, in that while the former tends to see certain values as associated with the institution of the state *per se*, the latter sees collective values as based on individual values, plus a notion of a shared uncertain environment, plus extended empathy.

In any case, under this theory the governance argument is not about particular market failures but about the basic rights of humans in society, which is not the same thing. This latter point of view of course poses the challenging question of how one draws up the list of things that should be available to all, or rather how one makes the cut off. The rights to vote, to equal protection under the law and to a basic education are on everyone's list. Unemployment and disability insurance, and at least a minimal level of retirement income, have been provided to all citizens in all high-income countries, and are not now controversial. But should medical care be on that list, and if so what level of care? Adequate extra family child care? It is not clear how we are to go about answering these questions. But it is clear that the answers are not readily posed in terms of resolutions of market failures.

It also is clear that, from this perspective, the notion of a society as simply a collection of people and families who have their own independent wants and purposes misunderstands what human societies are. 'Solidarity' is a word often used by advocates of this position. From another (sometimes closely related) tradition we all are our brothers' keepers.

From that point of view, many of the market failure concepts of traditional modern economics take on a very different light. Most importantly, in my view, there is a major difference in how one conceptualises public goods. As a salient example, one can ask whether the care and well-being of children create a public good. From the standard perspective in economics, the answer certainly is no. From a more communal position, every child is one of our children. The well-being of every child is a concern of all of us. The general welfare of children in our society is something we all should be concerned about. From this point of view, child welfare certainly is a public good. More generally, from this perspective the governance and administration of economic activity need to be arranged so as to support a just and equitable society, which is the most public of public goods.

A synthetic perspective

In this section I try to bring together the three theoretical strands just discussed, to develop an analytic mapping of the kinds of activities and sectors where the appropriate role of the market and other governing structures is a matter of controversy. In developing my mapping of issues, I take two things for granted.

First, there are numerous activities and sectors where governance through market organisation is generally regarded as unproblematical. This is not to deny that there is any regulatory structure involved or, in some cases, supplementary non-market activity. However, no one seems to be suggesting that markets are an inappropriate basic governing mode, or arguing for a radically different governing structure. Textile production, automobile manufacture, restaurants, haircuts, house building, all would seem good examples. The list is long and broad.

But, second, I also take for granted that there are many activities for which markets are generally not regarded as the appropriate basic governing structure, and in fact we use alternatives. Some market activity may be involved, but in an ancillary way, and there is widespread agreement that if market principles and mechanisms became dominant, there would be a problem. The two examples I used at the start of this essay seem apt: child care by the family, and police and criminal justice more broadly. I suspect few would argue that governments do not have a basic responsibility for assuring the adequacy of national security or the regional water supply. Organised religion and little league baseball are activities where I suspect many people would reject a central role either by government or by for-profit firms. Most would agree that elections and particular pieces of legislation ought not to be for sale.

The categories I develop below are strongly influenced by the standard list in the economists' market failure theory. However, recognition of the central limitations of that theory, and the integration into the discussion of the other two strands of analysis that I introduced in the preceding section, yield (I believe) a richer characterisation of the reasons why and the arenas wherein many people are arguing that simple market structures need to be supplemented by ancillary mechanisms in order to be acceptable, or even fenced out. I focus particularly on areas and issues that seem to mark terrain that is strongly contested.

Latent public goods

Economists use the public good concept to flag a class of goods and services where the benefits are collective and communal rather than individual and private. Under this body of conceptualisation, a pure public good has two attributes. One is that, unlike a standard private good like a peanut butter sandwich, which can benefit only one consumer (although it can be split and shared), a public good provides atmospheric benefits that all can enjoy. In the language of economists, pure public goods are *non-rivalrous* in use. Your benefiting from a public good in no way diminishes my ability to so benefit. The second attribute is that, if the good or service is provided at all, there is no way to deny access to any person, or to require direct payment for access. National security is a standard example of a public good. Scientific knowledge often is used as another example. For a neighbourhood, the quality of the access roads has strong public good properties.

There are several things to note about this conceptualisation. As I have stressed on several occasions, *publicness* generally is a matter of degree, in both dimensions. A defence force may protect some regions, but not others, and given a resource constraint, defence of one area may be at the expense of another. Thus defence is not completely atmospheric or non-rivalrous in use. On the other hand, if one lives in a protected region, protection cannot be withheld if a person does not pay up, although a person can be placed in gaol for not paying taxes. In contrast, scientific knowledge does seem truly to be non-rivalrous in use; you and I can use the same fact or understanding at the same time. However, the creator of that knowledge may be able to patent it, and to sue us for using it without paying a licence fee.

Laypersons have tended to associate the concept of the public good with the impossibility or undesirability of making those who benefit pay directly for use, and to recognise that adequate provision of goods or services so characterised requires some kind of collective procurement machinery. Sometimes this can be provided through non- governmental organisations, like churches, or community voluntary organisations, which are financed through donations. Thus many suburban neighbourhoods have neighbourhood associations which collectively decide on road maintenance, and collect dues from members. But for large-scale public goods of this type we generally rely on governments.

Generally there is no real alternative. Absent some mechanism for collective decision making, or for collecting taxes, and nothing or next to nothing would be provided. There may be dispute about the magnitude and allocation of public spending, about who should pay, and about how procurement or provision should be arranged, but the principle of governmental determination of the spending on large-scale pure public goods is not in serious dispute.

However, there is a significant collection of goods and services that are non-rivalrous in use, or nearly non-rivalrous, in that the cost of making them available to additional users is very small, but where access can be denied, or users made to pay up before they gain access. I have called this class 'latent public goods'. Prominent on the list of latent public goods I would include those that are or which provide information or knowledge: science, technology, databases, TV signals. To a considerable extent these are marked by non-rivalrousness in use, but access can be barred to those who do not pay a fee. Parks and roads also have the characteristics of latent public goods. Their use is non-rivalrous, at least up to the point where they become crowded. But under appropriate institutional arrangements, for-profit suppliers can make money providing them by requiring their users pay up at a level that covers average cost plus a margin for profit. This is a real option.

For market enthusiasts, this generally is the preferred way of organising and governing these activities. However, while sometimes overlooked in the discussion, there is a downside to governing an activity with latent public good properties in this way, because some users and uses where the good or service has significant value almost surely will be shut out, even though the real incremental cost of that use is zero or close to zero. The cost of this exclusion may be, or may be deemed to be, modest, or it may be very large.

On the other hand, collective demand machinery may be put in place as part of the governance mechanism. The decision about how much and what kind to procure may be made publicly, the good or service procured using public funds, and access made free or with nominal use charge. Such a collective demand-side governance mechanism avoids the costs of limiting access to a latent good or service where the real cost of extending service is zero or small. But it does involve the real cost of putting in place and operating collective decision-making machinery, where there may be little agreement, and little objective basis for deciding, how much to provide. There also is the fractious issue of who is to pay the taxes.

I believe that a number of the current arguments about the appropriate roles of markets, and of public funding, involve latent public goods. The funding of basic science is one of the more interesting and important of these issues, and I will consider it in more detail in the next section.

Goods and services that 'ought to be public'

I return now to the remark I made earlier that many laypersons have a conception of the public good that differs significantly from the technical concept of economists. For many laypersons, public goods are what we fund publicly and make generally available. In cases like defence, this usage squares with the technical concept of public goods used by economists. But in many instances, it does not, at least not immediately. I gave primary and secondary education as an example.

Clearly there is a lot of private benefit for those who are getting an education. Some economists, therefore, have used education as an example of a 'publicly funded private good'. Most economists are comfortable with the notion that education can yield significant positive 'externalities', through enhancing the legitimate earnings' potential of people who otherwise might be tempted to crime, and in the form of the benefits to all of us of a better informed citizenry. This provides an explanation that makes economists comfortable as to why there should be public subsidy of education. But it would appear that few economists are comfortable, at least at first thought, with the notion that education provides a public good, in their technical sense of the term.

However, I want to argue that, if one broadens one's conception of the values involved, education has some strong public good properties. Thus the effects of a better informed citizenry certainly can be regarded as atmospheric. Also, in the eyes of many people a good education available to all is necessary for there to be equality, or near equality, of opportunity in a society, and hence free public education contributes to the fairness of a society. People clearly do care about the characteristics of the society in which they live. And to the extent that they do, education provides an atmospheric public good, at the same time as it provides a private good with externalities. From that same point of view, the quality of the criminal justice system can be considered a public good, with equality of access to it a necessary condition for a just society.

Modern societies fund publicly, and provide free or highly subsidised access to a variety of goods and services where extending the use to more persons and uses definitely is costly. Economists, while often strongly sympathetic to the idea of positive public policies to equalise incomes, or at least put a floor under living standards, generally have had considerable difficulty in rationalising the furthering of these objectives by selecting certain goods and services and making them 'publicly' available, in contrast with simply redistributing money income. I am proposing that the focus on particular goods and services makes sense, if certain of them can be particularly associated with the standards of justice in a society or with meeting basic human needs, and which hence should not be rationed by the market.

However, it is not at all clear just how one identifies and limits this class. The arguments for including a right to vote (but remember the old Poll Tax), a right to equality of access to the criminal justice system, to a decent education and to at least a floor level of general living standards are clear enough. So, too, the case for covering the costs of standard medical care for people who cannot afford it, and of assuring the availability of health insurance that covers very costly procedures. But why have many societies opted to remove a payment requirement for even relatively well-to-do people for even relatively low-cost and routine medical services? Should university-level education be on the list?

I believe my conceptualisation here of what the argument is all about is basically correct. But I do not see a clear way of deciding in particular cases; nor, I believe, does anyone else. That is why the debates about removing or weakening market bars to access to services like medical care or day care often are so fractious. Removing a good or service from the realm of governance through customer decisions as to whether or not to spend their own money means not only that public money is required, but that public decisions need to be made regarding who will have access at what terms. I return to this issue in the next section.

The externalities' problem: bringing broader interests to the governing structure

The notion of economists externalities is meant to refer to by-products of economic activity that have negative or positive consequences which are not reflected in the prices or other benefits and costs perceived by those who engage in the externalities-generating activity. Environmental contamination is an obvious example of a negative 'externality', and a clear case where there is a value at stake in the operations of an activity, with no one to represent and fight for it, at least in the simple model of market governance put forward in economic textbooks. In a famous article written some time ago, Ronald Coase argued that, if property rights are clear and strong, and the number of interested parties relatively small, markets can in fact deal with such problems. Those who value clean air or water can simply 'buy' behaviour that respects those values from the potential polluter. The problem arises when those who care about the values which could be neglected are dispersed. In that case some kind of collective action machinery is needed to bring them in. A good way to think about regulation, or a tax on pollution, is to see these measures as the result of governmental actions that have brought in a broader range of interests to the governing structure of an activity or sector.

But the general problem here is to delineate the range of interests which should be represented, their relative influence and the mechanisms through which they operate to make their values felt. The latter can range from public interest advertising or boycotts, which can proceed without direct access to governmental machinery, to lawsuits which involve general governmental apparatus, to particular pieces of special regulation and associated control machinery. Much of the public controversy is about the latter.

It is conventional in economics to think of the costs of an externality as objective, and in principle at least measurable, and amenable to having a market-based value placed on them. However, in many cases this is not quite the case. The concerns about the 'externality' are held by particular groups, and may be quite subjective. Consider the interests of certain groups in preserving particular species or particular wilderness areas. Or consider regulation or prohibition of the sale of drugs or guns. This can be rationalised as dealing with an externality. However, it is apparent that many people strongly believe that drugs should be prohibited not because they feel particularly threatened by drug-related crime, but because they consider drug use, by anybody, to be wrong. Or reflect on prohibitions on prostitution.

To a large extent, prohibitions on certain activities, which economists might be inclined to rationalise as attempts to deal with externalities, reflect notions on the part of some people and groups regarding what is appropriate activity and what is not. A large part of the argument in this arena is about which values, and whose values, are to count, and through what mechanisms. It is hard to identify an activity, or a sector, where there are not some values at stake that go beyond the direct interests of the customers, and of the suppliers. The question, of course, is where to draw the line.

The issue of uneven expertise and agency
Economists have become very interested recently in how asymmetric information, in particular differences in the information held by buyer and seller, complicate the workings of markets. I propose that a number of the current controversies about the efficacy of market organisation, about regulation of markets, and about alternatives to market supply, are connected with the asymmetric information problem. In particular, they are associated with difficulties that the user of a service has in assessing the quality and appropriateness of what is provided.

This problem clearly is fundamental in the arena of medical care. In view of the physician's expertise regarding diagnosis and prescription, and the obvious dependence of patients on the use of that expertise in their interests, the medical community long has professed that while physicians sell their services on the market they most emphatically do not try to maximise their profits, but rather prescribe in the patients' interests. The credibility of that claim is open to question, but professional ethics clearly can have an influence on behaviour that tends to be neglected in standard models of market governance. To further complicate matters, with the rise of insurance, third-party payers found themselves in a position of doubting whether physicians paid enough attention to costs, and worrying about whether physicians, in fact, weren't trying to maximise their own incomes. These multi-interest potential conflicts, in a context where the expertise resides largely with the physician, lies at the heart of several current controversies regarding how to govern the medical care system.

The question of how parents can assess the quality of a child-care centre, and the care their child actually is getting, is a fundamental one in the current controversies regarding regulation of day care. The question of whether parents, and children, can assess educational alternatives effectively, or whether professional teachers and education administrators know best, is a non-trivial one in the current discussion about vouchers. The question of whether for-profit companies will manage prisons effectively and humanely, or whether their interest in profits will lead them to behave in undesirable ways, is central to the controversy about the contracting-out of prison services.

In some cases the issue here shows up in debates about necessary regulation and the mechanisms for regulation enforcement. In other cases the debate is about the proposition that, in circumstances where users cannot make an effective judgement about what they are getting, market organisation, with providers having a strong interest in profits, is an inferior way to govern an activity. There is a tacit, sometimes explicit, presumption that provision by a government agency, or by a not-for-profit organisation, is a better way to go under those circumstances. Of course, whether or not this is so is an open question.

Tension between competition, and co-operation and co-ordination

Competition is an enormously energising force in many areas of human activity, but not necessarily in all. On the other hand, in some areas of activity co-operation and co-ordination among the actors providing goods and services are extremely important, and competition is undesirable or worse.

Market organisation of supply is well suited to fostering competition. Indeed, there is not much to argue for for-profit unregulated organisation of supply in contexts where competition is not desirable or is unlikely to be sustained (as in the case of natural monopolies). The other side of the coin is that, where considerable competition is desirable, there may be a strong case for opting for market supply. Thus advocates of school vouchers also tend to advocate letting for-profit schools compete for students. Much of the argument for the deregulation of public utilities, and for employing private contractors more widely to provide goods and services funded or mandated under government programmes, has been associated with the advocacy of greater competition.

Up to a point at least, market organisation of supply is not incompatible with co-operation and co-ordination among the suppliers regarding certain matters. Thus, in several manufacturing sectors where for-profit firms are the principal suppliers, various co-operative 'pre-competitive' R&D arrangements have been made. In many industries, firms that otherwise compete have managed to agree to standards of various sorts. It might be noted, however, that government agencies or other government bodies with an interest in or responsibility for the industries in question often have played a key role in organising such co-operation.

In some sectors, like those providing telephone services, or those producing and distributing electricity, the advantages of co-ordination among the different parts of the overall system are very great. Under regimes of regulated private supply, or government ownership of supply, where competition is suppressed or constrained, co-ordination was easy to achieve. Under deregulation, it clearly is a gamble whether rivalrous companies can be induced or forced to co-operate and co-ordinate on vital matters, while remaining competitors. Thus there may be a real tension between allowing local telephone companies to set up competitive long-distance phone services, on the one hand, and requiring them to grant local access to other long-distance services, on the other. Getting managed health-care organisations to share patient information when a customer shifts from one to another has not proved easy.

The question of how to make co-operation and co-ordination on certain matters compatible with competition on others is a tricky one in market-organised sectors. The need for co-operation and co-ordination, plus the proposition that competition is not needed as part of the governing structure, or is positively harmful, is often used to argue that market organisation and governance are not appropriate in a particular activity or sector.

The problem of potentially coercive power

American economists are inclined to rationalise the use of antitrust to prevent undue market power from arising, and of regulation to deal with cases where there is natural monopoly, on the grounds that monopolists tend to charge too high a price. It is clear, however, that much of the force behind the policies to break up or rein in monopolies, or regulate them closely, has to do with people's concerns that arise when private bodies gain considerable power over their lives, a matter which may involve but also may transcend being forced to pay monopoly prices. Economists are inclined to rationalise the fact that governments have responsibility for national security and the criminal justice system to the fact that these activities yield 'public goods'. But it probably is at least as relevant that there is near-consensus that it would be highly dangerous to place the power over these activities in private hands.

These propositions may strike some liberals in the Anglo-American tradition as shocking. The heart of that position has been that strong government is the dominant danger to individual freedoms, and that placing activities under market governance, therefore, serves to increase freedom. The tacit assumptions here, of course, are: first, that concentrations of private power will not in general arise under market governance; and, second, that when they do they are less threatening than government power to individual freedoms. However, I propose that, in many areas, that is just what the debate regarding the appropriate roles of market and non-market elements in the governance of an activity is all about.

Much of the current debate is proceeding in two distinct, if overlapping, arenas. There is, first, the issue of how to govern what used to be called public utilities – activities like the telephone service, electricity generation and distribution, urban water supply, the railroads' system and urban mass transport. As noted, these used to be regarded as 'natural monopolies'. In the United States traditionally they were left in private hands but tightly regulated; in other countries they often were governed as 'public enterprises'. The widespread move towards deregulation and privatisation represented a strong shift in the direction of market governance of these activities. As I noted above, where competition has emerged in these sectors, some non-trivial co-ordination problems have developed as well. And where competition has not proved sustainable, there are serious questions regarding how to control private power.

The other arena involves services for which the government still is responsible and accountable, but which under the movement towards privatisation, increasingly are provided through private contractors. Clearly it is appropriate that the police system should procure uniforms and weapons through the market. The question is whether it is appropriate for the management of activities like prisons to be contracted out, and what kind of controls there should be on private police forces.

Reprise

Many years ago, F. A. Hayek argued that economic systems are very complex, that effective ones are the result of a time-consuming evolutionary process that selected on institutions that worked, and that humans never could fully comprehend or consciously design an effective economic system. Hayek's observations were meant to warn against trying to build a communist economic system from a theoretical design, and were a forecast that any attempt to do so almost surely would fail. He proved to be correct.

Of course, the referent of Hayek's proposition about the complexity of economic systems was the capitalist system, as it had developed by the early post-Second World War period. Thus, his comments would seem to be as germane to trying to build a capitalist economic system from scratch as they are to trying to build a communist one. And history seems to bear out that proposition (see Hayek 1967, 1973).

Almost all of the economies that used to profess communism, but recently have attempted to reform towards market capitalism, continue to struggle, and some (Russia, for example) are doing very badly. The original prescription given to them for developing an effective form of market capitalism was a relatively simple one: establish a body of law that respects private property and enables transactions to proceed smoothly; privatise the organisations that produce goods and services, and encourage these new firms to seek out markets and try to make money; establish a financial system that funds companies which have promising prospects for profit making and keeps money out of the hands of others; keep government spending and involvement in the economy more generally low; and adopt macroeconomic policies that avoid inflation. There also was a reminder that government needed to ensure the provision of basic public goods and infrastructure, and to maintain some kind of a safety net for the unfortunate. However, establishing a regime of private firms and markets was assigned first priority. It is apparent that this simple prescription has proved insufficient to guide effective transformation.

Of course, it can be argued that the problem is not so much not knowing what is needed, as not having the will to do what is needed. However, following Hayek's logic, there are good reason to believe that, at their best, the economists' models of how capitalism works can provide only a very rough guide to how to design and build. They can point in the right directions, but getting it right inevitably requires a lot of trial, error, and try-again learning.

Good theories can help if they point broadly in the right directions, and provide useful interpretations for what goes right and what goes wrong. But theories can hinder efforts at reform when they point in the wrong direction, or provide misleading interpretations of the problems that arise in the course of reform. By their nature, theories simplify and abstract. But oversimplification, and abstraction that leaves out essential elements, can be a real problem.

The burden of this essay has been that the standard theory of capitalist economic organisation which today is used to guide policy is much too simplified. By missing the complexity, the variegation and the limits of markets, and the wide variety of non-market mechanisms that mark modern capitalist economies, and enable them to work as well as they do, they often hinder efforts at reform.

Of course, the focus of this essay has not been on building capitalism from scratch, as has been the challenge in the old communist states, but rather on dealing with the new challenges facing advanced and largely successful capitalist economies. A point implicit in the basic argument I have developed, that I now want to make explicit, is this. Economic systems are always evolving. They always are facing new problems, challenges and opportunities, some generated internally (as today's new technologies), some coming from external forces. Thus they always are in the process of trying to reform themselves. This reforming is never ending, but it tends to come in waves.

Thus the period after the Second World War was one of dramatic reform of capitalist systems, driven by a broadly accepted theory that raw capitalism just was not working, economically or politically, and that there was a need to build a truly mixed economy. A number of commentators argued that the wave of reform overshot. We went through another wave of reform in the 1980s under the theory that a purer and simpler form of capitalism would work much better. We may have overshot here too.

In any case, I think we need a better conceptualisation of what modern capitalist economic organisation is and how it works than today is common currency to guide our reforms in the early twenty-first century. A good part of that understanding, I am arguing, involves an appreciation of the complexities and limits of markets.

References

Bell, D. (1960), *The End of Ideology*, Cambridge, MA, Harvard University Press.

Blyth, M. (2000), 'Great transformations', Manuscript.

Coase, R. (1960), 'The problem of social cost', *Journal of Law and Economics*, 3, pp. 1–44.

Crosland, C. A. R. (1956), *The Future of Socialism*, London, Jonathan Cape.

Dahl, R. and Lindblom, C. E. (1953), *Politics, Economics, and Welfare*, New York, Harper.

Fukuyama, F. (1992), *The End of History and the Last Man*, New York, Avon Books.

Hamilton, A. (1791), *Report on Manufactures*, reprinted in Cooke, J. (1964), *The Reports of Alexander Hamilton*, New York, Harper Torchbooks.

Hayek, F. (1967), *Studies in Philosophy, Politics, and Economics*, London, Routledge & Kegan Paul.

Hayek, F. (1973), *Law, Legislation and Liberty*, London, Routledge & Kegan Paul, Vol. 1.

Hegel, G. (1967), *Hegel's Philosophy of Right*, trans. F. M. Knox, London, Oxford University Press.

Marx, K. (1932), *Capital*, New York, Modern Library.

Mill, J. S. (1961 [1848]), *Principles of Political Economy*, New York, Augustus Kelley.

Myrdal, G. (1960), *Beyond the Welfare State*, London, Duckworth.

Owen, R. (1991), *A New View of Society and Other Writings*, Harmondsworth, Penguin.

Plato (1961), *The Republic*, New York, Pantheon Books.

Polanyi, K. (1944), *The Great Transformation*, Boston, MA, Beacon Press.

Schonfield, A. (1965), *Modern Capitalism*, London, Oxford University Press.

Schumpeter, J. (1950), *Capitalism, Socialism, and Democracy*, New York, Harper.

Smith, A. (1937 [1776]), *The Wealth of Nations*, New York, Modern Library.

US Government (1960, 1967), *Economic Report of the President*, Washington, DC, January.

Yergen, D. and Stanislaw, J. (1998), *The Commanding Height*, New York, Simon & Schuster.

2

Markets, embeddedness and trust: problems of polysemy and idealism

Andrew Sayer

Introduction

In this paper I develop a critique of certain approaches to markets and firm behaviour in economics and economic sociology. There are two main targets of the critique. The first concerns some common approaches to markets and the nature of firms in relation to them. Here I argue that the diverse uses of the term 'market' in contemporary lay and academic discourse cause confusion. Also problematic in both mainstream and institutional economics is the tendency to treat market exchange as the atomic structure of all economic processes, and as the default form of economic co-ordination, so that any other forms of organisation are either marginalised or treated as problematic exceptions. The second target of critique concerns literature on the socially embedded character of economic processes, on the nature of networks, and the role of trust. While largely endorsing the importance attached to these factors in recent literature, I argue that their treatment has suffered frequently from being idealist, both in the sense of underestimating material aspects of economic life and in presenting an overly benign view which underestimates the instrumentality of most economic relations. Finally, I conclude with a reminder of the political significance of explanations of markets and competition.

The multiple meanings of 'market'[1]

If we are to discuss market relations and competition, we need to be clear on what the former involve. However, such is the variety of uses of the term 'market' that it is important to distinguish them if we are not to talk at crossed purposes. As Maureen Mackintosh observes, these are rarely distinguished, so that people regularly slide unknowingly between quite different uses of the term, sometimes within one sentence, while imagining that they are talking about the same thing (Mackintosh, 1990; see also White, 1993). These conceptual slides are a feature of both lay and academic–scientific usages of the term, and are found in both liberal and radical economic theory. In everyday usage the shifts are often innocuous. Polysemy is not necessarily a problem, and the scope and subtleties of everyday usage are worth treating with respect. By comparison, attempts to analyse and codify the tacit understandings involved are bound to seem lumbering and unsubtle. Nevertheless, the ideological influence of the discourse of markets in the shape of 'neo-liberal fatalism' is too important for the conceptual slides to be ignored. While the variety of different uses of 'market' and 'markets' is confusing, many of the uses have contexts in which they identify something significant. The problems come when authors apply them outside those contexts, particularly where explanatory weight is transferred unknowingly from one referent of 'market' to another. On occasion, the conceptual confusion can have disastrous effects; Mackintosh found a World Bank report offering diagnoses and prescriptions for poor countries to have 'at least three different meanings floating in the text' (Mackintosh, 1990).[2] I shall attempt to take further her strategy of distinguishing different senses.

A 'core definition'

One of the few theorists to problematise the definition of markets is Geoffrey Hodgson (1988). For him, a market is 'a set of social institutions in which a large number of commodity exchanges of a specific type regularly take place, and to some extent are facilitated by those institutions' (p. 174). A market therefore includes not only commodity exchanges themselves and the associated transfers of money and property rights, but the practices and setting which enable such exchanges to be made in a regular and organised fashion. One might add that markets are also normally competitive to some degree. I take this as a core definition of a market, while noting that other uses may have some validity.

The *institutionalisation* of commodity exchanges, referred to by Hodgson, emphasises that markets are not spontaneous products of exchange activity but are socially constructed – and as Abolafia (1996) adds, constructed by skilled and specialised actors. Hodgson further distinguishes market exchanges from exchanges of commodities made outside markets through some other sphere of activity – or *non-market exchanges* (1988, p. 177). An example of the latter would be occasional commodity exchanges between firms linked together by complementary asset specificities that have developed over long periods. Such exchanges are a significant feature of market economies, though highly elastic concepts of markets allow the difference between them and market exchanges to pass unnoticed.[3]

Inclusiveness

Concepts of 'the market' differ in their degree of inclusiveness. Markets may be defined narrowly in terms of routinised buying and selling under competitive conditions, or inclusively to embrace not only exchange but the production and consumption of the exchanged goods, and the particular property relations that hold therein. Accordingly, for a fruit and vegetable market we could adopt a restricted focus, ignoring what buyers and sellers do outside of the moment of exchange, or we could take a more inclusive view, examining how the sellers get their produce, how the supply chain is organised, even going back into production, and on the other side, how customers are differentiated into individual and institutional buyers and how their purchasing behaviour is related to things like income and ability to save.

Many abstract discussions of 'the market' slide between restricted and inclusive versions (Hodgson, 1999, p. 177). The basis for the powers or forms of behaviour commonly attributed to markets are consequently often ambiguous: is it markets in the restricted sense that give rise to the effects of interest, or markets when mediating between particular kinds of producers, with certain kinds of property relations, and particular kinds of consumers? Since markets can co-exist with different property relations and systems of production, we cannot expect to read off an inclusive account from a restricted focus. This is of critical importance in political economy for understanding and evaluating market economies, and for identifying the sources of competitiveness. Restricted accounts of markets exclude major contextual influences which explain behaviour. On the other hand, a more inclusive view which takes in those influences is going beyond exchange into production and consumption. Thus price competition in buying and selling, identifiable in the restricted view, differs from competition through product and process innovation, identifiable in the inclusive view. (These correspond to 'weak' and 'strong' competition, respectively, to use Storper and Walker's 1989 distinction.) The dynamism of capitalist economies is not a consequence simply of markets in the restricted sense, but of capital, obliged to accumulate in order to survive, and liberated from the ties which bind petty commodity producers. Hence this slide from a restricted to an inclusive sense of 'market' also enables the term 'market economy' to serve as a euphemism for capitalism.

Marshallian demand–supply diagrams provide restricted views of markets, marginalising the social relations of production and the processes of production and consumption on which demand and supply depend. As Maurice Dobb pointed out in 1937, this treats production and consumption as the creature of price rather than vice versa. Moreover, the static equilibrium approach, with its conflation of *ex-ante* and *ex-post* quantities, treats markets as closed systems. Instead of tracing the aetiology of actual markets in an inclusive sense, taking into account the semi-autonomous evolutionary dynamics of production and consumption, this approach attributes change either to an exogenous black box (technologies and preferences) or to the endogenous variable of price signals.

Production and market 'optics'

The problems regarding inclusiveness are frequently combined with those of broader conceptual frameworks. In practice, decisions about what is included are largely determined on the Left by a 'production optic', in which production and capital are generally treated as prior to exchange, thereby marginalising markets, and on the Right by a 'market optic' which swallows up production in exchange. In the market optic of mainstream economics, the whole economy becomes 'the market' in the singular, or 'market system'.[4] Moreover, this positive prioritising of markets is coupled with and frequently slides into a normative preference for markets as a form of economic organisation.

Economies are about the provisioning of societies, and hence are necessarily about production. While they necessarily involve production as a transhistorical feature, they only contingently involve market exchange as a specific mode of co-ordination of divisions of labour. Arguably markets in the restricted sense may be good at stimulating production, but certainly they produce nothing themselves. The illusion that they can is further present in the assertion that firms can either make things or get them from the market (the 'make or buy' decision). While this is true, in fact the existence of a market for inputs is, of course, dependent on the existence of other producers making those inputs. Markets are not an alternative to production or to firms or 'hierarachies' but a mode of co-ordination of the division of labour. Enterprises or hierarchies are usually involved not only in co-ordination but in production; they are therefore not merely an alternative mode of co-ordination, as is often assumed.

Production and exchange are therefore not alternatives such that more of one means less of the other: a vertically disintegrated form of industrial organisation involves no less production than a vertically integrated one, even though it involves more market co-ordination. Nor should markets and firms be seen simply as alternative forms of economic organisation where one can be substituted for another. In fact, they are generally mutually dependent in their development: a developed market economy requires large-scale commodity *production*, and *firms themselves are leading constructors of markets* (and of non-market exchange)[5] (Auerbach, 1988). Market and authoritative co-ordination therefore develop together and it is their combination which is the important thing to explain (Hodgson, 1999).

However, numerous theorists adopt a market optic in which firms represent a problem to be explained whereas markets are a natural phenomenon. While Coase's much celebrated question regarding why firms exist identifies a difficulty for those within the market optic, it is itself also thoroughly trapped within it. For Coase and followers, the firm is defined negatively in relation to the market, being distinguished and defined by the absence of the price mechanism, where the latter's absence becomes a problem to be explained. The popularity of negative definitions of firms reveals the strength of normative and positive presumptions in favour of market co-ordination, a presumption which of course is also implicitly against state or collective control. There is also something else that is strange about emphasising negative definitions of firms: it is rather like saying that the difference between cooking and eating is that cooking is defined by the absence of eating, and to understand cooking it is that absence which we must explain. True, the negative definition is accompanied by a positive one: firms co-ordinate by means of authority rather than the price mechanism. But this is not all that most firms do: what is distinctive is that, like cooks, they are co-ordinating production rather than exchange. And of course, without production for exchange, there would be little need for markets.

Indeed it is the fact of being involved in production that makes firms require non-market co-ordination; insofar as production is always of specific commodities – whether goods or services – whose use-value properties require specific inputs and production processes, where that specificity is in use-value, or engineering terms; for example, involving getting the ingredients of the cake right and the temperatures used in production right. Thus even though the goal of capitalist production is exchange-value, the firm's co-ordination and planning have to take strict account of use-value constraints. Whatever the prices of the inputs, the good to be sold cannot be successfully made unless those ratios and processes are correct. Of course, producers of commodities have to be responsive to the exchange-value of their inputs and outputs, and the sufficient conditions of successful business are set in exchange-value terms, but for producers of goods and services the means to those ends have to satisfy use-value constraints.

The market optic has not only a presumption in favour of market co-ordination but also a market individualist presumption. The fact that production is not generally carried out by individual producers, but by producers acting in concert, therefore becomes an awkward one. (Coase reflected on both possibilities.) But provisioning requires production, and as social beings we quite naturally co-operate in production; while examples of primitive communism have been widely recorded, instances of primitive individualism have not, for of course the latter would be too precarious to be sustainable. It is entirely unsurprising that, throughout history, humans, as social animals, have co-operated in their productive activities. It is also entirely unsurprising that given the specific historical origins of capitalism in competition in early markets and expropriation of land there arose a class of people unable to produce for themselves and hence obliged to produce under the direction of others. The existence of firms is not a puzzle. What would be deeply puzzling would be precisely a market economy of individual commodity producers instead of firms.

(It could be objected that it is naive to take the idea of markets producing things as anything more than a shorthand: no one seriously imagines that exchanging things actually produces anything and it is *obviously* the whole 'market system' that is meant here, including producers – or rather, 'hierarchies'. However, the concept of 'the market' or 'the market system' here is not merely an inclusive one which already encompasses production, for as we have seen the market optic barely acknowledges production, reducing it to 'supply' or 'transactions', and has difficulty conceptualising anything that does not involve or approximate exchange. The shorthand would not be suspect if liberal economists took production seriously and if the belief that exchange, or change in ownership, actually created anything new were not so common in actual economic behaviour. The illusion is particularly strong in the more liberalised capitalist economies, where it is evident in the pursuit and celebration of takeovers. In such cases we have markets without production – the buying and selling of existing commodities or property, including companies, without adding anything to the existing stock of goods and services. Treating this as equivalent to productive activity is a disastrous error, though it might facilitate – or inhibit – *subsequent* production, and *might* affect efficiency. The confusion is echoed further in the Thatcherite practice of encouraging share ownership – i.e. rentiers – as a way of encouraging entrepreneurship: whereas entrepreneurs are celebrated precisely for producing something which didn't already exist, rentiers can earn an income without producing anything. There are important arguments about the benefits of market exchange in terms of their effect on production and the efficient allocation of resources, but it remains the case that exchange itself produces nothing. There is a curious fetishisation of the power of markets here, which attributes to a mode of co-ordination a power which is actually dependent on another sphere of the economy. It is the liberal celebrants of 'the market' who are fooled by their own shorthand.)

Further grounds for concern over the difference between inclusive and restricted analyses of markets relate to the ideological uses which can be made by slides between the two or attempts to pass off one as the other. For liberal economics, the market optic and the use of a restricted analysis of markets as if it were actually an inclusive analysis marginalise social relations and present capitalism in neutral guise, merely as a market economy, as if it were not significantly different from non-capitalist market economies of petty commodity production. In Marxism, matters are reversed, with the behaviour of market forces under capitalism being taken as condemning markets operating outside capitalism.

In the Marxist account, commodities are merely 'thrown' on the market, and the role of exchange is limited to realising the value of commodities and completing the circuit of capital. Allocational effects are of no interest. By contrast, the market optic focuses on the allocational effects, and either ignores production and its social relations or conceives of them as a sphere of transactions or exchanges; or else it reduces production to 'supply' (which fails to distinguish between produced goods and unproduced goods such as land).

The market as ether: imaginary and latent markets

Concepts of imaginary, latent or implicit markets figure prominently in mainstream economics. It should be noted that these are not the same as abstract (i.e. one-sided, selective) concepts of real markets (in which commodities and property rights are traded) for whereas the latter already exist, imaginary markets are only a possibility. Hodgson (1988, p. 81) notes how Arrow and Debreu assume 'that a market exists for the exchange of every possible commodity on every possible date in every possible state of nature'. This is an extraordinary usage, for it means almost the opposite of what it says: namely that such a market hardly exists and can only be imagined. What this concept of market seems to involve is a representation of economies as consisting of a vast array of opportunity costs, where the goods whose use or non-use have those opportunity costs could be exchanged for money in markets. In this kind of view the market 'is seen as an ether in which individual and subjective preferences relate to each other, leading to the physical exchange of goods and services' (Hodgson, 1988, pp. 177–8). The ether is the latent or imaginary market, and again actual markets are seen as their natural consequence, unless somehow blocked.

Once everything is seen as having a price, notional or real, then it is tempting to look upon the range of resources and projects in society as one big market. A loaf of bread, a picture, a house, a field, a letter, a haircut, a motorway, a worker, a conversation – all these things and countless others might be thought of as having a price which someone might possibly be prepared to pay for them, though even under capitalism, some of them may never be offered for sale. In some economies few or no goods are exchanged in real markets at all, and, as many have pointed out, including Marx, it is absurdly ahistorical (and often ethnocentric) to project the concept of 'the market' onto non-market economies, and therefore quite accurate to term that kind of economics 'bourgeois'.[6]

However, while Marxism's critique of this way of thinking is still powerful, it does not excuse its failure to note that, even if there are no real markets, there is an array of opportunity costs regarding the use of resources, including labour power. That there are always opportunity costs is a non-trivial transhistorical fact about all economies. In simple economies, and in many situations in advanced economies, opportunity costs are transparent enough to be estimated and be evaluated in real terms (i.e. in terms of use-values through practical judgement; see O'Neill, 1994), without the aid of money and prices. The notion of an economy as an array of opportunity costs is a useful one, but since the existence of such an array is only contingently related to real markets, it is both absurd and tendentious to refer to it as 'the market'. Real markets are just one form in which those opportunity costs sometimes get reflected.

We could say that the notion of the market as ether refers to 'implicit markets', but this still tendentiously suggests that real markets are the normal form of economic organisation, and, if absent, are held back by pre-modern conventions and practices, ill-defined property rights and state restrictions, and are just waiting to be 'freed', whereupon economic benefits are supposed to follow. In this way, the conceptual slide from imaginary to actual markets is closely associated with negative judgements of non-market production and modes of co-ordination as causes of economic backwardness, and it has the effect of legitimising policies for the development of actual markets. Thus commodity production is assumed by the World Bank to be superior to subsistence production and state regulation, despite the plentiful evidence that marketisation in developing countries offers no guarantees of development (Sen, 1987; Mackintosh, 1990). In liberal economics, 'the market' is privileged both normatively as the best form of economic organisation and positively as the key to how actual economies work, indeed the image of the former colours its vision of the latter. Economies which lack markets or have only a few are judged negatively, not only because they lack mechanisms which allegedly bring benefits, but because they do not fit with mainstream economics' market optic. Further, 'the market' or 'markets' are given powers and authority of their own and treated as if they were unitary actors. In a sense markets do condense all the demands and offers made, not only in a single market but in others in which the same and other actors participate, and across which resources are allocated. Yet, as noted earlier, market prices are not merely neutral reflections of demand and supply but reflect the balances of power in many arenas. 'You cannot buck the market', a slogan beloved of Margaret Thatcher, was another way of saying that 'might is right', regardless of how the might is distributed.

The ideological notion of latent or implicit markets which only need freeing figures strongly in neo-liberal rhetoric, and contrasts strikingly with the view, associated with Polanyi and others, that markets are social constructions whose birth is difficult and requires considerable regulation and involvement by the state and other institutions to achieve (Polanyi, 1944; Marquand, 1988). The experience of the post-communist countries weighs heavily in support of Polanyi. The liberal underestimation or denial of this institutional support is partly derived from the elision of the difference between the potential or imaginary and the actual in its concept of 'the market'.

Through its fetishisation of markets, the market optic attributes to markets in the root sense powers which are contingently rather than necessarily associated with them, such as responsibility for competitiveness. While markets do indeed provide incentives and sanctions which encourage competitive behaviour, whether the latter occurs depends on other features, such as technological possibilities, spatial monopolies and organisational learning and strategy, which take us into the spheres of production and use/consumption.

Economic discourse – including radical political economy – is plagued by elisions among these different concepts of market. Uses of 'the market' in the singular are particularly slippery, referring either to a specific real market, or to the whole system of such markets throughout the economy, or sometimes to the allegedly latent 'market' discussed above. The second of these three uses – the system of real markets – has some logic in that markets are interdependent, such that changes in a particular market (for example, the oil market or the mortgage market) have effects – 'market forces' – which ripple through entire economies, indeed round the world. This notion of 'the market' in the singular, as a pervasive system of particular interlinked markets, fits better with the perspective of the final consumer, having money and able to spend it on anything, than the seller who is stuck in a particular market with the particular commodities he or she has to sell (Offe and Heinze, 1992). The holder of money can roam across many markets, as if they were one big market;[7] indeed many retail markets have coalesced to such an extent that they offer thousands of products in a single location and institutional setting. Once again, while the many meanings of 'market' can cause considerable confusion, there are often contexts in which particular uses contain a valuable insight. In developing a critique of the discourse of markets we have to recognise these insights as well as attack the conceptual elisions.[8]

Embeddedness, trust, networks and markets

'Embeddedness', 'trust' and 'networks' are perhaps the most distinctive terms in the new economic sociology. They identify dimensions of economic organisation which most economists have chosen to ignore. Insofar as these dimensions are necessary conditions for economic activity rather than merely contingent associations, abstracting from them is likely to mislead. Moreover, the argument is not only that these dimensions are universal features of economic activity, but that in their more highly developed forms they can benefit economic performance, and that, conversely, where they are limited, performance suffers. This, as Ronald Dore argued in 1983, posed a fundamental challenge to the liberal individualist view of capitalism, which regarded the narrow pursuit of individual self-interest as sufficient for success and embeddedness and networks as frictions, or 'conspiracies against the public'. Dore (1983) argued that the success of Japanese capitalism, with its strongly embedded economic relations, involving long-term commitments among firms and between large firms and their key workers, demonstrated that the liberal model of capitalism was faulty. There was not one capitalism but several kinds, none of which was to be regarded as the norm, and the more embedded and regulated Rhenish and Japanese capitalisms were looking stronger than the Anglo-American neo-liberal versions. This, of course, has been music to the ears of social democrats. Now, however, since the bursting of Japan's bubble economy in the early 1990s, the alternative model is under threat from more liberalised economic pressures and may yet give way to the liberal model.

My argument is that while embeddedness, networks and trust are indeed important aspects of economic organisation, theorising about them has tended to idealise them somewhat. The focus on embeddedness can inadvertently produce an overly benign view of economic relations and processes, in showing that practices hitherto seen as governed purely by narrow self-interest, or 'the icy waters of egotistical calculation' as Marx put it, are actually embedded in relations of trust, in which there are shared norms and various forms of reciprocity. While this is true, Marx and the other theorists of self-interest, economic power and impersonal system mechanisms were not wrong either. Such embedding is often strongly adapted to the system pressures of market forces, and indeed may be cultivated to enhance the pursuit of self-interest. As authors such as Massey *et al.* (1996) and McDowell (1997) point out, the social embedding of economic activity often involves relations of domination, some of them based on gender, class or race. The metaphor of em*bed*dedness sounds soft and comforting, and possibly sends our critical faculties to sleep, but what it describes can, on occasion, be harsh and oppressive. Further, at the same time as it highlights apparently softer versions of capitalism, it has little or nothing to say about issues of distribution and inequality, and the literature on embeddedness and networks often amounts to merely a sophisticated form of boosterism.

The comforting view of embedding is reinforced by the enthusiasm of cultural political economy for networks. As Ash Amin and Jerzy Hausner (1997, p. 13) note:

> There is a creeping tendency in the socio-economics literature to privilege the qualities of networks over those of markets and hierarchies. Relations within and across networks are seen to be somehow more reciprocal and more egalitarian, because they rely on interaction. Nothing could be further from the truth. Not all networks are non-hierarchical, mutually beneficial or discursive . . . .⁹

Further, it is not only that strongly embedded economic systems are not necessarily benign, but that they may also prove to be less robust than is commonly supposed. The embedded character of economies refers to their incorporation into the subjective and informal relations of the lifeworld. But modern economies have also developed 'systems', in Habermas's sense – particularly markets and bureaucracies – which have mechanisms that go beyond those of the lifeworld and that produce unintended effects which operate 'behind actors backs' (Habermas, 1987). A strongly embedded capitalist economy may involve more negotiation and collaboration than a minimally embedded one, but the former is not immune to market forces. When a system crisis strikes – like that experienced recently in East Asia – the local forms of embedding may provide some resistance, but they also form some of the conduits along which market pressures – such as those that follow from a collapse of the currency – flow. Sometimes the pressures can sweep the networks away.

Furthermore, stable forms of embedding, including networks and regulations, are not necessarily the product of a free consensus. They may represent an uneasy compromise between interests which would interact differently, given the chance. Consequently, agents such as companies may sometimes use a crisis as an opportunity to escape onerous conventions and commitments – most typically with reference to organised labour – which arose in the context of the balance of power obtaining in more prosperous times. In other words, we need to remember the dialectic of regime of accumulation and mode of regulation, or forces and relations of production. As may turn out to be the case in Japan or Europe, forms of embedding of economic relations which hitherto worked successfully may not survive severe system crises.

Thus networks do not necessarily fuse the self-interest of different actors into a harmonious and egalitarian whole but may be characterised by inequalities of power, strategic coalitions, dissembling and opportunistic collaboration. However good the networking, however strong the reliance on information and trust, economic survival for capitalist firms depends on costs and cash, though extraordinarily this literature says remarkably little about these factors: the bottom line remains the bottom line.

We can amplify these points in relation to *trust*. Recent social and political economic theory has been very taken with the role of trust in economic relations, often in reaction against neo-liberal exaggerations of the sufficiency of self-interest and contract in producing successful economic performance (for example, Fox, 1974; Luhmann, 1979; Baier, 1994; Fukuyama, 1995; Misztal, 1996; Sztompka, 1999). While mainstream economic theory's emphasis on self-interest has led it to ignore or overlook the role of trust in economic relationships, the significance of trust can also be overestimated, especially where markets and competitive economic behaviour are concerned.

Trust differs from mere confidence or expectations of consistency in that it involves social relations and has a moral dimension.[10] Trust is relational: it is always dependent on trustworthiness, and the latter involves a sense of moral obligation. In most of the literature trustworthiness is mentioned only rarely or in passing, as if trust were dependent only on a unilateral act of will by people in the role of trustors. But the relational character of trust is one of the features which distinguishes it from mere confidence or expectation. I expect my computer to continue working, but it does do so not because it knows it ought to behave properly – it is simply reliable. However, I trust the service engineer to make every effort to repair it not only because s/he is competent to do so but because s/he has a sense of obligation towards me as a customer, or at least as a person, who, other things being equal, should be treated properly. It would only be a slight exaggeration to say that trust is the dependent variable, and trustworthiness or probity the independent variable. Hence the overwhelming emphasis on the former rather than the latter is peculiar, especially as trust relations can be initiated by the trustee ('trust me').[11]

Exaggerating the importance of trust produces analyses which are idealist in both senses of the term – i.e. attributing to ideas powers which often have more to do with material circumstances, and exaggerating the role of moral influences on economic behaviour relative to power and interest. Here we note two cautions – derived from Durkheim and Marx – against idealist accounts.

While Durkheim famously demonstrated the moral presuppositions of contractual relationships, he rightly treated these as conditions or material causes rather than as efficient causes; and he acknowledged that contractual relationships arise because the parties to them *need* each other (1933, p. 160). Co-operation occurs among firms in similar or related lines of business not simply because they trust one another but because they recognise that it is sometimes in their self-interest to do so. For example, among competing suppliers, there may be times when orders outstrip the capabilities of any single supplier and so the suppliers must either co-operate and share the order or risk losing out altogether. At another time, those same firms may compete directly for the same business. A certain amount of competition for business among such firms is tolerated, provided it is not deemed to be unfair. Especially among small businesses, there may be more or less tacit agreement to take turns in getting contracts (see Whitaker, 1994, for analyses of examples of such behaviour in Japanese industrial districts).

The more firms need each other the more they are likely to develop trust relations beyond a base level of generalised probity to a level where they put considerable trust in each other. Though 'high trust relations' may result, they have an instrumental rationale. They also have a material basis as they do not arise independently of series of acts and investments that tie the fortunes of the parties together through complementary asset specificities and mutual lock-in. Such long-term relations between firms may even include, at least on a small scale, elements of gift relationships, insofar as each party takes its turn to invest time and money in the relationship. However, such practices are always instrumental – directed to economic goals rather than to the relationship itself – and subject to the discipline of the bottom line. The threat of exit may even be used to develop a long-term relationship.

It is therefore probably an exaggeration to argue, as Granovetter (1998) does, that members of industrial groups see themselves as belonging to a particular moral community; rather, they recognise the overlaps in their self-interest, reinforced as they usually are by various forms of interlocking shareholding and directorships.[12] Even where industrial groups originate from kinship networks, as many do, these are likely to be characterised by power asymmetries as well as by a sense of moral obligation.

Marx's comments on trust and economic behaviour in market economies (in the Notes on James Mill's *Elements of Political Economy*) are generally compatible with these remarks, though he does make the typically caustic comment that 'the basis of trust in economics is mistrust' (Marx, 1975, p. 265).

This is provocative of course, but not so different from the tendency to assume universal malfeasance on the part of actors in some of the more Hobbesian contemporary mainstream economic literature, except that Marx saw mistrust as context-dependent and historically specific rather than a transhistorical feature of the human condition. What Marx had in mind here in particular were credit relations. In simple market exchange involving straightforward one-off transactions, obligations among people are settled the instant the transaction is done, and it is the value of the money (and the goods) rather than the people that has to be trusted to last into the future. While market actors have the option of exit according to their self-interest, in non-market economies reciprocity is the norm and individuals have to trust one another and/or find ways of making the recalcitrant reciprocate. Reciprocity and gift relations are extended in time: as the alternating obligations between actors stretch into the future, so they have to trust one another to act responsibly in the future. (This implies that trust is backed up by implied resort to sanctions in the event of malfeasance.) Of course, not all commodity exchanges in capitalism are simple. Since credit relations extend over time, collateral or the assurances of others with appropriate capital are needed. When we trust someone, by definition we do not have to calculate the risks of them defaulting; but where credit relations are concerned, such calculations are standard and a condition of credit being extended. The debtor is mistrusted unless she has money or collateral. For example, legal requirements regarding banks' cash reserves are based on mistrust, but are intended to ensure the trustworthiness of the banking system.

Combining the insights of Durkheim and Marx, we need to avoid the extremes of both assuming a universal propensity for malfeasance, and of underestimating the extent to which trust (and trustworthiness) is limited by self-interest and opportunism. Aside from trust, dissembling and wheeling and dealing are common in both markets and networks; within certain limits, they are expected and excused. In a market situation, trust, by definition, does not extend to trusting customers or suppliers never to use the option of exit. It is generally understood that any mutual commitments are always conditional upon an ability to maintain quality, profitability and competitiveness. In view of the general recognition of the need to economise and remain profitable, a certain level of dissembling is expected and excused (for example, buyer A dissembles to keep the goodwill of supplier B while secretly negotiating to buy from C instead). Networks, too, allow for exit, and need be underpinned by no assumptions of loyalty beyond what self-interest requires.

Further, what appears to indicate trust and trustworthiness may in fact be largely a consequence of domination or lack of alternatives, or simple mutual dependence. As Annette Baier (1994[13]) points out, trust can be part of relations of domination instead of relations among equals, for the dominant trust the subaltern to behave as their status befits them. This is a common situation in both inter-firm and employment relations. Similarly, where certain economic relations are concentrated within particular ethnic groups, that may itself be a product of domination within the group or within-group asset specificities rather than simply trust (Sanghera, 1998).

Trust or lack of trust may sometimes be mistakenly invoked to explain situations which have more to do with material circumstances. As philosophers note, *ought* implies *can*. Someone may fail to engage in an economic relationship not because they lack trust or are themselves untrustworthy, but because they lack the material resources to do so. Thus, lack of success in developing markets, as is being experienced in some post-communist countries, may have less to do with lack of trust than a lack of material preconditions for the development of firms and markets.[14]

Idealist accounts of trust in economic life need also to be tempered by reference to the way in which high-trust and low-trust relations have different institutional supports. Long-term high-trust relationships tend to be associated not merely with certain cultural traditions such as forms of kinship relations (*pace* Granovetter, 1998, for example), but are backed up with institutional, legal and financial circumstances that influence the timescale over which rates of profit matter and the degree to which firms are exposed to short-term pressures, and the scope for voice relative to exit. Moreover, while culture influences economic behaviour, it is itself subject to economic influences, and of course not just any cultural influences can survive in a capitalist context. For example, while Japanese 'company familism' corresponds to certain traditional cultural forms favouring 'groupism', many observers argue that it was cultivated instrumentally as a way of controlling labour in the 1950s onwards, following earlier industrial unrest and high rates of labour turnover (Ichiyo, 1984; Cusumano, 1985; Eccleston, 1989). Moreover, the vertically-disintegrated *keiretsu* groups owe their success in large part to their ability to take advantage of the wage gradient between large and small firms, thereby lowering costs below those of their more vertically integrated foreign competitors, and to the way in which they allow large firms to dominate suppliers without being tied to them by ownership (Williams *et al.*, 1994). Again, this is not to deny cultural differences and their influence over economic behaviour, but rather to argue that, equally, they are not themselves immune to capitalist instrumental influences.

Conclusion

'Disciplinary imperialism' drives sociologists to emphasise culture, embedding, trust and voice at the expense of choice, self-interest and exit, and it drives economists to do the opposite. To do justice to the range of influences present in economic life we need to refuse the temptations of disciplinary imperialism and to adopt instead a post-disciplinary standpoint where explanations are evaluated on their own merits, not according to whether they advance the ambitions and preoccupations of one's favoured discipline (Sayer, 2000).

Although the foregoing critique is very much an academic one in its concern for the adequacy of explanations, it is certainly not without social and political significance. The market optic and its positive and normative presumption in favour of markets both mystifies and promotes unfettered capitalist dynamics and social relations. These issues are especially significant given the prevalence of neo-liberal dogmatism and fatalism, which are driving a particular model of economic development liable to increase insecurity by strengthening disembedding effects, while passing it off as the only workable model. At the same time, while recent literature in economic sociology and institutional and evolutionary economics has noted how more strongly embedded and regulated forms of capitalism moderate those effects, we must avoid an overly benign view of embedding which allows us to overlook the persistence of forces creating inequality and insecurity.

Notes

1 This section (pp. 41–9) is a development of earlier work (chapter 4 of Sayer, 1995) which comes to conclusions similar to those of Boyer's 1997 essay on markets. See also the 1997 collection edited by Carrier.
2 These are: 'the market', denoting exchange of goods and services, including labour power, for-profit and private ownership; secondly, abstract models of markets constructed by economists; and, thirdly, different ways of buying or selling, i.e. the concrete or real markets studied mostly by anthropologists and geographers.

3 Since in practice there is usually a possibility of the buyer choosing to exit and 'go to the market', there is a continuum between non-market, or non-competitive, exchanges and market exchanges.

4 Thus even Teece and Pisano, who are critical of neo-classical economics' silence on firms, write: 'While the price system supposedly co-ordinates the economy, managers co-ordinate or integrate inside the firm' (1998, p. 198), which implies that the economy is just the market, and firms are somehow outside the economy! This is not to deny that some parts of their essay do indeed escape from the market optic, but their deference to Coase prevents the escape from being complete.

5 To be sure, when they do construct them, by persuading others to buy their products and setting up the means of regularised exchange for them to do so, they create something which goes beyond their control. This is, first, because other firms also help to construct them, usually in competition and hence often in ways which challenge the original firm's interests, and, second, since the new market becomes linked to others between which money can be switched and substitutions of products made. The market is not necessarily already 'out there'.

6 The exchange model of social action is also congenial to those who want to make individual 'choice' the organising principle of economic behaviour, rather than production or social organisation. For example, J. Buchanan defines the market as an institutional process 'within which individuals interact, one with another, in pursuit of their separate individual objectives, whatever these may be' (cited in Brown and Harrison, 1978, p. 87). Insofar as this need not involve the exchange of money for commodities and the exchange of property rights, the 'market' here is imaginary and metaphorical.

7 However, buyers employed by firms generally have far more constraints on what they buy, being limited by the use-value requirements of their firm's line of business.

8 These senses of 'market' do not exhaust the range of uses. Others include 'the market' as referring to actual and potential demand for a particular product, as in 'the market for mobile phones is vast'. Another is the restriction of the term 'the market(s)' to refer specifically to certain capital markets and markets in other financial products, rather than just any market.

9 See Amin and Thrift (1995) for further reflections on the political implications of networks.

10 As Maclagan points out, while trust may appear to be related primarily to moral behaviour rather than competence, sometimes lack of competence may be seen as morally reprehensible (Maclagan, 1998, p. 57).

11 It is an exaggeration to the extent that it overlooks the fact that the act of placing trust in others encourages the behaviour on which it depends, and vice versa. Mistrusting others who in fact are trustworthy is insulting – a refusal to recognise their integrity and potential. It can therefore be argued that from a moral point of view, we have a responsibility not only to be trustworthy, but to respect others' moral qualities by trusting them (Fox, 1974).

12 Granovetter (1998) draws a parallel between industrial groups and the concept of 'moral economy', but the former are primarily about interlocked self-interest, not obligations according to what is morally right or wrong. All economies are in some respects moral economies, but this is not one of those respects.

13 As Baier also points out, while the term 'trust' connotes goodness and reciprocity, in practice it is possible for trust to be placed in individuals and institutions which do not deserve it (Baier, 1994). Also, production in a sector may become

more efficient when it moves from a position of rough equality among producers to one of domination of the many by the few through the organisation of supply chains. The replacement of trust by domination may improve rather than damage economic performance.

14 I am grateful to Ivaylo Vassilev for contributing to discussions on this point. Ironically, some of the most successful business people may be the least trustworthy members of such societies, Also, insofar as trust is a problem, the post-communist societies may be suffering less from a lack of trust in market situations, than from a lack of trust in the state, for example in its ability to collect and use taxes efficiently and without corruption (Rothstein, no date). Again it is the extent of trustworthiness that creates the problem.

References

Abolafia, M. Y. (1996), *Making Markets: Opportunism and Restraint on Wall Street*, Cambridge, MA, Harvard University Press.

Amin, A. and Hausner, J. (eds) (1997), *Beyond Market and Hierarchy: Interactive Governance and Social Complexity*, Cheltenham, Edward Elgar.

Amin, A. and Thrift, N. (1995), 'Institutional issues for the European regions: from markets and plans to socioeconomics and powers of association', *Economy and Society*, 24(1), pp. 41–66.

Auerbach, P. (1988), *Competition*, Oxford, Blackwell.

Baier, A. (1994), *Moral Prejudices*, London, Routledge.

Boyer, R. (1997), 'The variety and unequal performance of really existing markets', in Hollingsworth, J. R. and Boyer, R. (eds), *Contemporary Capitalism: The Embeddedness of Institutions*, Cambridge, Cambridge University Press, pp. 55–93.

Brown, D. and Harrison, M. J. (1978), *A Sociology of Industrialisation*, London, Macmillan.

Carrier, J. G. (ed.) (1997), *Meanings of the Market*, Oxford, Berg.

Cusumano, M. (1985), *The Japanese Automobile Industry*, Cambridge, MA, Harvard University Press.

Dobb, M. (1937), 'The trend in modern economics', reprinted in Hunt, E. K. and Schwartz, J. (eds) (1973), *A Critique of Economic Theory*, Harmondsworth, Penguin, pp. 39–82.

Dore, R. (1983), 'Good will and the spirit of market capitalism', *The British Journal of Sociology*, 34(4), pp. 459–82.

Durkheim, E. (1933 [1984]), *The Division of Labour in Society*, London, Macmillan.

Eccleston, B. (1989), *The State and Capital in Japan*, Cambridge, Polity.

Fox, A. (1974), *Beyond Contract: Work, Power and Trust Relations*, London, Faber & Faber.

Fukuyama, F. (1995), *Trust: The Social Virtues and the Creation of Prosperity*, New York, Free Press.

Granovetter, M. (1998), 'Coase revisited: business groups in the modern economy', in Dosi, G., Teece, D. J. and Chytry, J. (eds), *Technology, Organisation and Competitiveness*, Oxford, Oxford University Press.

Habermas, J. (1987), *The Theory of Communicative Action*, Vol. 2, trans. T. McCarthy, Cambridge, Polity.

Hodgson, G. M. (1988), *Economics and Institutions*, Cambridge, Polity.

Hodgson, G. M. (1999), *Economics and Utopia*, London, Routledge.

Ichiyo, M. (1984), 'Class struggle on the shopfloor – the Japanese case', *Ampo: Japan–Asia Quarterly Review*, 16(3), pp. 38–49.

Luhmann, N. (1979), *Trust and Power*, New York, John Wiley.

Massey, D., Quintas, P. and Wield, D. (1992), *High-Tech Fantasies: Science Parks in Society, Science and Space* (London: Routledge).

McDowell, L. (1997), *Capital Culture: Gender at Work in the City*, Oxford, Blackwell.

Mackintosh, M. (1990), 'Abstract markets and real needs', in Bernstein, H., Crow, G., Mackintosh, M. and Martin, C. (eds), *The Food Question: Profits versus People*, London, Earthscan, pp. 43–53.

Maclagan, P. (1998), *Management and Morality*, London, Sage.

Marquand, D (1988), *The Unprincipled Society*, London, Fontana.

Marx, K. (1975), *Early Writings* (Harmondsworth: Penguin).

Misztal, B. A. (1996), *Trust in Modern Societies*, Cambridge, Polity.

Offe, C. and Heinz, R. G. (1992), *Beyond Employment*, trans. A. Braley, Cambridge, Polity.

O'Neill, J. (1994), *Ecology, Policy and Politics*, London, Routledge.

Polanyi, K. (1944), *The Great Transformation*, New York, Beacon Press.

Rothstein, B. (no date), 'Trust, social dilemmas and collective memories', mimeo.

Sanghera, B. S. (1998), 'The social embeddedness of markets: the case of fruit and vegetable market traders', PhD thesis, Lancaster University.

Sayer, A. (1995), *Radical Political Economy: A Critique*, Oxford, Blackwell.

Sayer, A. (2000), 'For postdisciplinary studies: sociology and the curse of disciplinary parochialism and imperialism', in Eldridge, J., MacInnes, J., Scott, S., Warhurst, C. and Witz, A. (eds), *For Sociology: Legacies and Prospects*, Durham, Sociologypress, pp. 83–91.

Sen, A. (1987) *Ethics and Economics* (Oxford, Blackwell).

Storper, M. and Walker, R. A. (1989), *The Capitalist Imperative*, Oxford, Blackwell.

Sztompa, P. (1999), *Trust: A Sociological Theory*, Cambridge, Cambridge University Press.

Teece, D. J. and Pisano, G. (1998), 'The dynamic capabilities of firms: an introduction', in Dosi, G., Teece, D. J. and Chytry, J. (eds), *Technology, Organisation and Competitiveness*, Oxford, Oxford University Press, pp. 193–214.

Whitaker, J. (1994), *Small Firms in Japan*, London, Routledge.

White, G. (1993) 'Towards a political analysis of markets', *IDS Bulletin*, 24(3), pp. 4–11.

Williams, K., Haslam, C., Williams, J. and Johal, S. (eds) (1994), *Cars: Analysis, History, Cases* , (Oxford, Berghahn).

3
Cognition and markets

Brian J. Loasby

Introduction

Whether as an explanation of decision making or as a guide to making decisions, rational choice theory is not very interesting. What is called 'a decision' is merely the logical precipitate of the premisses: everything that might be regarded as a determinant of choice is already in place, and assumed to be known (if only as a probability distribution) to the chooser. Within choice theory agents make no decisions. Now this should not be a source of complaint, for, paradoxical as it may seem, choice theory is not about decision making. Its purpose is to provide an essential element in constructing theories of equilibrium, and equilibrium in economics is routinely defined as a state of affairs in which there are no decisions to be made. In fact, analysis often proceeds – notably in the Arrow–Debreu model – directly from basic data to equilibrium allocations.

When choices are deduced, only the premisses matter; and so it is the explanation of those determinants – and why they, and only they, are determinants – that deserves attention. One might therefore have expected economists to have shared Herbert Simon's view (1976: xii) that the premisses should be the unit of analysis; but even though it is standard practice to explain differences in behaviour, including changes in behaviour over time, by differences in the premisses from which behaviour is deduced – usually differences in opportunity sets, and often with specific emphasis on incentive structures – these differences are not themselves investigated. The reason is that decision premisses are assumed to reflect precisely the fundamentals of economic analysis; they are therefore innocuous. (There are a few exceptions, such as the theory of speculative bubbles.) Consequently it is not accidental that few economists pay specific attention to organisational forms, because in equilibrium models any organisational structure must be transparent to the basic data; and it is notable that orthodox and quasi-orthodox economists who have tried to explain why firms, as organisations, exist have taken care to isolate their explanations from the theory of production, which continues to be directly based on the supposedly fundamental data of the economy. As Coase (1991, p. 65) has pointed out, this has led economists 'to neglect the main activity of a firm, running a business'. In a rational choice equilibrium, running a business is a trivial activity: production functions are public knowledge, and productive skills are incorporated in the specification of inputs.

Simon, however, believes that decision premises are problematical and yet capable of investigation by observation and experiment, and furthermore that organisational design is a significant influence on the premises that are used in various parts of an organisation. To understand organisational behaviour, therefore, it is not sufficient to postulate rationality in the peculiarly restricted sense that is used in much economic theory (though it is normally appropriate to postulate intelligent and purposive behaviour); one needs to investigate the procedures by which occasions for decision are identified, options are sought and examined, and choices made; and this investigation should pay particular attention to the premises which guide these procedures.

In this chapter my primary concern is not the firm but the individual, though there is a need to consider the activities of firms. But this brief excursion into organisational design is not irrelevant, because in considering the individual as decision maker particular attention has to be paid to the ways in which individual knowledge is organised, and to the decision premises which shape both the development and use of that individual knowledge. In accordance with the title, I give some emphasis to the influence of markets on the growth and use of individual knowledge and also note how knowledge within firms may benefit from market relationships. I begin by identifying some basic elements of human cognition to provide a credible psychological basis for economic reasoning.

Cognition and the growth of knowledge

The principle of biological evolution is genetic selection for features which contribute to inclusive fitness. These features include both physical and behavioural characteristics in a sorting process which necessarily extends over very many generations. The standard biological model therefore assumes a stable selection environment, and implies the possibility of extinction if there is an unfavourable environmental change; we should not therefore be surprised that only a very small proportion of the species which have appeared on earth have survived, or that species are disappearing at a high rate in the present era of environmental change, much of it the result, sometimes intended and sometimes not, of human activity. Our own species is not exempt from the possibility of extinction; but it does have a biological advantage in our distinctive, though limited, capability to recognise significant change and to develop new behaviours in response. This potential for learning may itself be interpreted as a biological adaptation to environments in which change is too rapid or too transitory to allow adequate genetic response through mutation and selection (Schlicht, 2000); it provides some real options to cope with the unexpected.

This capability is not well represented by the economic concept of rationality, because its crucial feature is the cognitive potential to create new localised structures of classification and premises for decision making, which in relation to the economic concept is pre-rational. The possibility of individual adaptation does not arise from the presence within the brain of a general purpose programme for system-wide optimisation or a universal strategy set in the game-theoretic sense of sequences of conditional actions that can be applied to all situations – which seems to be the conception tacitly underlying rational choice theory, especially when extended to rational expectations; instead an architecture of the brain which is appropriate for distributed programming allows sensory inputs to be assembled into distinctive patterns, each of which triggers effective actions, in the process of interaction with specific environments.

There are two linked evolutionary reasons for this architecture. The first is that genetic evolution proceeds by successive adaptations, each step of which has to be compatible with survival, and the step-by-step construction of a general problem-solving programme would entail many stages in which the use of the incomplete system would be likely to lead to disastrous mistakes. The second reason is that brain tissue has particularly high energy requirements, and the emergence of *homo sapiens* has been marked by a very substantial increase in brain size, and a consequent need to economise on energy demands. We should not therefore be surprised that a potential for multiple cognitive systems, each adapted to a limited function, and switched on only when required, was the naturally selected pathway to improved cognition, rather than a central processing system which would need to be permanently engaged. The division of labour is a fundamental principle of development, in the brain as well as in society; and the evolved network architecture of the brain made such a division possible.

These capabilities for adaptation were well advanced before the development of consciousness; and consciousness appears to have emerged, as one might expect, from this architecture and the functions that it supports. If the unconscious brain collects impressions into categories, and associates each category with a particular action, it is natural that consciousness should begin with awareness of some of these categories, and in particular with a perception that one of the categories presently employed is inadequate or linked to actions which are not effective. (The resemblance to the Carnegie language of aspirations and achievements is not accidental.) The response to dissatisfaction is then a search for better ways of ordering sensory impressions or for better connections between impressions and actions. We consciously try to make sense of our environment by imposing patterns upon it, seeking to improve upon tacit skills by codification, or by giving conscious direction to a process which remains beyond any detailed conscious control; and it is one of the most remarkable features of modern formal economics that its models of human behaviour make no reference to this characteristic activity of pattern making, both conscious and unconscious – even though modern formal economics is itself an impressive example of the drive to impose patterns. Consequently what is called 'rationality' within modern economics is a rather small, if important, part of human cognition, and makes a limited, if important, contribution to the explanation of human behaviour.

The two stages of development of human cognition which have just been outlined were presented as an evolutionary hypothesis in an early paper written by Alfred Marshall (1994) for a Cambridge discussion group. The significance of that paper for both the content and method of Marshall's subsequent work as an economist was identified by Tiziano Raffaelli (1994); and it has been suggested (Butler, 1991) that the motivation for writing it was supplied by a double crisis of religious and mathematical faith, the common feature of which was the perceived failure of axiomatic reasoning to guarantee empirical truth. The mathematical crisis was precipitated by the invention of non-Euclidean geometry: the point was not that Euclidean reasoning was wrong, or even inapplicable, but that its applicability was not ensured by the irrefutability of its logic. As Ziman (1978, p. 99) warns us, 'scientific knowledge cannot be justified or validated by logic alone'. This was also the lesson of Marshall's later encounter with Cournot's argument that falling costs entail monopoly – a lesson that was entirely lost amid the reinvention of Cournot's logic in the 1930s. Marshall's response was to apply Darwin's principles to sketch an evolutionary account of the growth of knowledge as structures of relationships. Caution in applying the patterns of axiomatic reasoning which had proved inadequate, and use of the evolutionary principles of the organisation of knowledge are persistent characteristics of his work as an economist.

More than a century earlier, David Hume had shown that it is impossible to prove any general empirical proposition, and turned to the question of how people acquired what we call knowledge. Marshall appears not to have read Hume's philosophical work – though he had studied Kant's response to it – nor Adam Smith's remarkable development of it in his psychological theory of the growth of science (1980), but he was later to make the connection with Smith's best-known application of his theory. As I have observed, the basic, and very powerful, skill of human cognition is the creation and application of patterns (of which logical reasoning is a special case); and Smith characterises scientific activity as the invention of 'connecting principles' which provide a credible account of relationships between phenomena. For this cognitive skill to be put to effective use it is important that people should be both sensitive to patterns and motivated to seek out or manufacture patterns. Not the least of the merits of Smith's analysis is the attention he gives to motivation, and what that motivation is. The driving force is the link between cognition and emotion.

Smith begins by identifying three human emotions: surprise, wonder (what we might now call perplexity) and admiration. An event or impression which does not conform to our expectations is surprising, and surprise causes discomfort. If we can find no way of accommodating it to our cognitive categories we are conscious of a failure to understand, which is at least disconcerting and may be dangerous; we therefore feel an urgent need to find a new way of making sense of our environment. 'Wonder, therefore, and not any expectation of advantage from its discoveries, is the first principle which prompts mankind to the study of Philosophy, of that science which pretends to lay open the concealed connections that unite the various appearances of nature' (Smith, 1980, p. 51). From an evolutionary perspective, we can easily see that the emotive power of 'wonder', in Smith's sense, might sometimes be much more effective than 'an expectation of advantage' in promoting fitness-enhancing cognitive activity and thus improving adaptation to novel circumstances.

If we are successful, either through our own efforts or by adapting means which are already being used by someone else, in creating a new cognitive structure that seems to make sense, then our feeling of relief produces admiration in proportion to the discomfort, providing reinforcement to our new cognitive skill. Thus 'the repose and tranquillity of the imagination is the ultimate end of Philosophy' (Smith, 1980, p. 61); and because this repose and tranquillity rests on human inventions, rather than revelations of the principles that are actually in operation – even, Smith observes, when the invention has been made by Newton – it is always liable to further disturbance, which stimulates further invention. Hayek (1952) was later to note that the categories we use to order sensory impressions may differ substantially from the categories which have been developed to accommodate the development of corresponding scientific knowledge, and suggested an evolutionary explanation which is compatible with the argument of this section.

In a recent paper, Ekkehard Schlicht (2000) has associated both the motivation to resolve difficulties by inventing new patterns, and the criteria by which possible new patterns are assessed, with an aesthetic sense which, he suggests, often seems to take priority over more strictly instrumental concerns; as in Smith's analysis, an emotive drive may be more powerful than the prospect of practical benefits. Indeed, when people are consciously searching for a theory which will account for some puzzling phenomenon, or for an effective product design, they often work on the principle that 'if it looks right, it is right'. Schlicht provides some examples from modern science; and Smith's detailed account of the succession of cosmological theories incorporates repeated attention to the significance of aesthetic criteria, for example in the desire of Copernicus to incorporate the heavenly bodies within 'a new system, that these, the noblest works of nature, might no longer appear devoid of that harmony and proportion which discover themselves in her meanest productions' (Smith, 1980, p. 71). In explaining the triumph of Newtonian physics, Smith (p. 105) recognised the rhetorical power of its aesthetic appeal; and in his *Lectures on Rhetoric* he used this appeal in recommending that, in giving an account of some system, one should 'lay down certain principles . . . from which we account for the several phenomena, connecting all together by the same chain' because 'the Newtonian method is undoubtedly the more philosophical, and in every science . . . is vastly more ingenious and engaging' (Smith, 1983, p. 146). The incentives which both Smith and Schlicht emphasise do not coincide with the incentives to which economists typically give priority, though the latter may complement them; but they still appear to be important incentives to scientific investigation. In this, as in other aspects of its practice, science is still an art.

Smith went on to observe that as science progresses it tends to divide into specialisms, and these specialisms encourage attention to details which would otherwise not be noticed. Closer observation increases the chance of perceiving anomalies which provoke efforts to modify or replace patterns that would be acceptable to the non-expert; thus the division of labour within science leads to increases in scientific knowledge. Smith (1976a) founded his theory of economic development on this principle, in an exemplary demonstration of 'the Newtonian method'. We can now see that what underlies the unique potential of the division of labour within human society, in comparison with specialisation within any other species, is the architecture of the evolved human brain, which is capable in principle of forming any of an enormous variety of networks, far more than any single brain can actually sustain. By appropriate specialisation, therefore, a human community can generate far more knowledge than any single person is capable of. Marshall combined Smith's principle of the division of labour with Darwin's emphasis on variation in response to environmental differences, which had already been incorporated in Marshall's evolutionary hypothesis and underlay his insistence on the importance of variety among the firms in each industry. Economic development is the result of the division of labour, supplemented by variation within each field of knowledge, exploiting the capacity of the human brain to develop new cognitive networks and motivated by the human desire to make sense (and not just money) by imposing patterns. Marshall (1920, pp. 138–9) not only insisted on the importance of organisation as an aid to knowledge: he insisted on the distinctive contributions of different forms of organisation, for different connections are appropriate for different purposes.

Institutions

A necessary consequence of this process is the increasing interdependence of human society. Most of the knowledge and the skill that each person needs is held by others; and knowledge and skills are rarely re-usable without cost by those who do not already possess them. The lowest costs are typically incurred in acquiring knowledge within familiar fields from those who seem to be more knowledgeable, or by adopting the practices of those who seem to perform better. Willingness to borrow ideas and methods from others is a familiar human characteristic, explicable by its survival value (Schlicht, 2000). Nor is it difficult to understand why we should so often converge on a few models, as Smith realised; his psychological theory of science gives due attention to the factors affecting the diffusion of each cosmological system.

Our cognitive limitations provide the incentives to borrow; the cognitive limitations of others, by impelling them to make and use patterns rather than attempting to optimise by using information that we cannot observe, make it easier to understand their rules of behaviour (Heiner, 1983); and our shared characteristics help us to imagine ourselves in someone else's situation and to tailor actions and communications to their perceptions, as Smith showed in both his *Theory of Moral Sentiments* (1976b) and his *Lectures on Rhetoric* (1983).

When we converge on rules for deciding how to behave, the shared conventions and procedures may be called 'institutions'; and our understanding of institutions is enhanced if we begin with an appreciation of human cognition, and the consequent advantages of adopting other people's procedures that seem to work for them, even when our actions have no effect on anyone else (Choi, 1993), rather than by postulating games between people without cognitive limitations. Schlicht's focus is on the conventions that facilitate interaction, and in particular on the criteria for a good rule, and this leads him to emphasise the importance of 'evaluations of an aesthetic kind, relating to formal features like symmetry, analogy, or good continuity' (Schlicht, 2000, p. 35). Such aesthetic evaluations are also important in choosing good rules for our private procedural rationality. As Schlicht points out, these features are not relevant to anyone who is deemed capable of optimising everything except the use of scant cognitive resources, but in a changing environment optimisation on each separate occasion is not a sensible objective, even by the criterion of overall optimisation. We may recall Schumpeter's proposition (1943, p. 83) that '[a] system . . . that at *every* given point of time fully utilizes its possibilities to the best advantage may yet in the long run be inferior to a system that does so at *no* given point of time, because the latter's failure to do so may be a condition for the level or speed of long-run performance'. Schumpeter applied this proposition to 'any system, economic or other'; it is a proposition about uncertainty and discovery, which is as applicable to the individual as to the economy; indeed it is its applicability to the individual that underlies its application to the economy.

Schlicht identifies imitation (which is rarely a precise copy) as an effective mechanism for coping with changes which do not last long enough to permit adaptation at the genetic level, but long enough for knowledge which has been acquired by individual pattern making to be re-usable by others at relatively moderate cost. Sometimes this re-use may be formally organised. Frank Knight (1921), having defined 'uncertainty' as a situation in which no existing pattern or procedure is sufficient, and 'the entrepreneur' as someone who is willing to impose an interpretative framework on that situation, then suggests that an entrepreneur may find it quite easy to persuade people to accept his offer of employment rather than attempt to cope with uncertainty on their own. (Their motivation may well correspond to that on which Smith based his theory of scientific development.) The entrepreneur therefore exercises authority within his firm precisely in Barnard's sense (1938,

p. 163), which locates the decision about which communications are author-itative with the recipient, not the source.

However, our analysis should indicate that authority is by no means restricted to hierarchical relationships, or even to relationships within for-mal organisations. Anyone whose instructions, advice, or example we accept in any particular context is a figure of authority within that context; and we would find it very hard to manage our lives without many such authorities. It is important to recognise the source of both institutions and authority in individual efforts to cope with individual cognitive problems and the urge to make sense of the complexity of our environment, because it provides a basis for understanding why the emergence of institutions which serve to co-ordinate interactions is often much easier than would be suggested by the multiplicity of equilibria in many game-theoretic models, and why people should be much readier to accept subordinate roles in organisations than might be expected from a model populated by cogni-tively self-sufficient agents. It also explains the effectiveness of marketing institutions which match cognitive needs.

Markets

A great deal of effort has been devoted by economists to examining the effi-ciency of exchange. However, it is not often that this examination begins by posing the question in an appropriately cognitive form: to what extent can the problems of differentiated knowledge be resolved through the exchange of knowledge which is embodied in goods and services? To do so immedi-ately raises questions about the design of goods and services and also about the arrangements for exchange – or, in other words, about the working of markets. These are not necessarily distinct questions, for as Marshall (1919, p. 181) observed,

> [p]roduction and marketing are parts of the single process of adjustment of sup-ply to demand. The division between them is on lines which are seldom sharply defined: the lines vary from one class of business to another, and each is liable to modification by any large change in the resources of production, transport or the communication of intelligence.

New products may require the creation of new market institutions, and the possibility of creating new market institutions may suggest product redesign. I adopt Ménard's definition of a market as 'a specific institutional arrange-ment consisting of rules or conventions that make possible a large number of voluntary transfers of property rights on a regular basis' (1995, p. 170); and my focus is on the ways that these rules or conventions reduce the costs of transactions by simplifying cognitive tasks. We should also recognise the importance of transfers of knowledge that is not embodied in goods or serv-ices, and of arrangements for the development of knowledge, for these aspects of co-ordination are also often dependent on the working of markets.

The markets to be considered are not, of course, the unanalysed markets of so much microeconomic – and of almost all macroeconomic – theory.

The failure to analyse markets as institutional arrangements which structure processes is a natural, and almost inevitable, consequence of choosing to start the analysis of exchange with perfect competition, for competition cannot be perfect unless every potential buyer has equal and costless access to every seller, and vice versa. The moment that one provides any structure to these market relationships competition is no longer perfect. The methodological necessity of avoiding structure accounts for the extraordinary status of the 'auctioneer' as the organiser of the perfect market (for which Walras has received undeserved blame): the auctioneer has neither preferences nor motivation, consumes no resources, is able to communicate with everyone without ever establishing any kind of personal contact and without cost to either party, and never makes a mistake; most extraordinary of all, the auctioneer is a monopolist who is trusted by everyone never to exploit his position, and always justifies this trust. Exactly the same characteristics are attributed to the 'social planner', who is subject to the same methodological necessity. Walrasian models are therefore dangerous guides to policy.

Since these perfect markets deliver efficient allocations without cost, it is not surprising that economists found some difficulty in explaining the existence of firms, which used resources in doing what the auctioneer did for nothing; nor is it surprising that Coase found it necessary to assume that economic agents, if not the auctioneer, incurred some costs in using markets. If Coase had been better trained in economic theory, he might have realised that costs of using markets would be difficult to reconcile with perfect competition, and responded by following Joan Robinson (1933) into her world of monopolies; if, however, he had been less well trained, or alternatively had been more familiar with the work of earlier economists, he might have addressed to markets the question that he posed about firms: if they cost something to operate, why are people willing to incur these costs? Markets should be explained, not assumed.

The route to an explanation was provided by Carl Menger (1976), who set out to analyse the structure of an economy as an increasingly complex system for meeting human needs. Beginning with goods which can be directly applied to their owners' needs, he introduced what was to become a characteristically Austrian concern with indirect ways of meeting these needs, such as making machines to make tools for growing crops which can then be turned into food. In this analytical system, the exchange of what one already possesses for something which can be used in the production chain is itself an indirect way of meeting needs. It is therefore not surprising, though it is significant, that Menger introduced exchange at the opposite end of the range from what had become the standard practice, with simple bilateral deals, and that he also recognised that making a deal incurs costs. A model of isolated exchanges but no market creates the possibility of explaining markets as a means for reducing the costs of exchange when there is a demand for multiple exchanges.

In Menger's theoretical sequence it is the next step that is crucial. Rather than exchanging what they already have, some people may begin to use what they already have in the production of goods which are intended to be exchanged; and if that plan is successful, it may be worth while acquiring additional goods, not for use, but as inputs into regular production. Exchange now becomes an essential part of the business of improving one's condition, and the efficiency of the exchange process itself becomes a constraint on this improvement, and therefore a matter for attention. If the creation of a market can improve the efficiency of exchange, it is, in Menger's terms, a good of higher order, and its value is derived, in the first instance, from the value of the exchanges that it makes possible through this improvement in efficiency – and ultimately by the value of the indirect contribution that it makes to satisfying human needs.

The most obvious means of improving the efficiency of exchange is through the development of a generally accepted medium of exchange, which removes the need for direct barter. Menger concentrates on money, because it exemplifies the emergence of a pervasive institution as a result of individual initiative and the readiness of people to copy behaviour that seems to work effectively for others. In the course of developing this argument, he does, however, point out that goods differ substantially in their marketability – that is, in the costs which must be incurred in the process of exchange. Unless the producer has some special advantage, commodity production will be concentrated on goods with relatively high marketability, though, in accordance with Marshall's observation, a change in product design or production methods may be undertaken in order to improve marketability (canning and refrigeration provide two important examples). However, there are always some costs of exchange. Here the importance of indirect methods again comes to the fore, because the costs of achieving a single sale can often be substantially reduced by appropriate investment – by creating a set of institutions which constitute a market. The customer might pay for this investment, but would naturally need to be compensated by a lower price; and it is usually the producer who expects to be most dependent on particular categories of exchange who has the greater incentive to develop procedures which will facilitate exchange within those particular categories – in other words, to create a special market. Casson (1982, p. 163), who has given particular attention to the firm as market maker, provides a convenient summary of the obstacles to trade, and of the ways in which the producer may seek to overcome them: all these ways reduce the customer's cost of making a single transaction (and often the producer's cost of a single transaction) by a substantial initial commitment of resources.

The obstacles to trade discussed by Casson are primarily the result of deficiencies of knowledge; and so are the costs invoked by Coase (1937) to explain the creation of firms – though Coase did not see that firms make markets as well as goods. Both require knowledge to be organised; this is a cognitive issue, to be handled by procedural, not substantive, rationality.

Costs per transaction are reduced by the development of a set of conventions about the way in which that transaction is to be carried out, including, for example, the location, the provision of information, opportunities to inspect or try out the product, standards for product characteristics, methods of payment, provision for servicing, and the commitments that are implicit in the deal. Because of the standard use of preference functions in consumer theory, it is important to mention that the use of money prices simplifies the assessment of each potential purchase; the 'measuring rod of money' is among the most important of conventions. The effect of these institutions is to ease the cognitive task of making a satisfactory purchase (and also the cognitive task of making a satisfactory sale). This cannot be achieved without a cognitive investment, and though the cost of this may fall mainly on the producer, customers must develop their own new routines. Everyone has to learn how to shop in a supermarket, how to buy through mail order, how to buy PEPs or ISAs, and now how to use the Internet effectively. This learning produces potentially re-usable knowledge; consequently everyone who makes this cognitive investment experiences the equivalent of what Penrose (1959) called 'the receding managerial limit' as new capabilities become embedded in new patterns of behaviour which release cognitive resources for other tasks, especially tasks that can incorporate the new routines. On the other hand, significant changes in institutional arrangements, such as the replacement of PEPs by ISAs and, on a much larger scale, the development of internet markets, impose new cognitive burdens.

The importance of simplifying the customer's cognitive task is illustrated by considering those markets in which many customers are willing to go to a good deal of trouble to get what they want, and where the common practice of supplier-fixed price does not apply. Three outstanding examples are the markets for houses, cars and many collectables. Here there are two powerful incentives for the customer to incur substantial transaction costs: purchases typically involve a substantial outlay, and they have substantial implications for the customer's style of living, and even for self-image. Such cognitive structures as lifestyle and self-image are a natural consequence of the pattern-making characteristics of the human brain which have been considered earlier, and the maintenance of these structures will normally be a major objective. It is therefore worth taking a good deal of trouble to ensure that any major purchase is compatible with the relevant patterns – or, occasionally, that an available purchase has sufficient appeal to justify some modification of those patterns. Rules for making such decisions have a substantial aesthetic component, even when the opinions of family, friends, colleagues, or neighbours are not of direct concern.

When there is substantial diversity among customers, the greatest reduction in transaction costs for a particular group may be achieved by the creation of sub-markets in which the rules and conventions, as well as the products, are precisely adapted to that group. This is yet another instance of the effects of the division of labour, which as always is limited by the extent of the market;

but the extent of the market is influenced by the incremental cost of transacting in it. Firms, like individuals, differ in their capabilities, including their capabilities in devising institutional arrangements that are appropriate for particular groups of potential customers, and these differences are reflected in what they attempt and (even more) in what they achieve. But thinking of the ways in which firms can develop arrangements that enable them to sell more easily should not distract our attention from the contribution of these arrangements to the firm's knowledge about its business. They are an important part of what Marshall called its external organisation; and we have already drawn attention to the pervasive importance of externally organised knowledge to augment our own cognitive skills.

Market institutions are an important part of consumers' external organisation: the rules and conventions form part of their interpretative system and their framework for decision making. How we decide is not without influence on what we decide; and the power of market-making firms to shape the way that we decide seems to be well appreciated in many businesses, as is manifest in a brief observation of marketing strategy. This power is often attenuated by the efforts of rivals; as Hayek (1948, p. 106) pointed out, competition is a 'process of formation of opinion', or, in the language used earlier, a means of deciding whose communications will be provisionally accepted as authoritative. There is no choice without a framework, and as in Penrose's theory, the routinisation of procedures makes possible the acquisition or creation of new knowledge and new skills. If the process of transacting is easy, we can concentrate on what to transact, and how to develop new skills as consumers – or indeed as humans. Our cognitive resources, like the productive and managerial resources of the Penrosian firm, are capable of development, and when developed may deliver new productive services; we have therefore an incentive to learn about the possibilities and the opportunities (Penrose 1959, p. 77) – what we might call their 'option value'. We may be encouraged to do so by the recognition that the array of markets which we can use without much effort also has an option value for us: they allow us relatively easy access to a wide range of other people's capabilities.

We should not forget that the greater part of the value of transactions within a modern economy has no direct reference to final customers at all; and the same incentive to reduce the costs of individual transactions by substantial investment in developing appropriate institutions applies here. Business customers may have stronger incentives than do their suppliers to simplify the process of transacting, and this may not merely be a matter for the purchasing department, for production is closely linked with purchasing as well as marketing. Arrangements with suppliers may reduce the costs associated with production, and modifications to product and process may simplify relationships with suppliers. Amid the flurry of excitement about e-commerce, there have been several predictions that its impact may be greater on relations between businesses than on retailing; if this is so, it will be because of changes in the handling of transactions and also because of associated changes in the internal operations of firms.

Conclusion

We make sense of our situation by constructing order; the quality and applicability of our knowledge capital, as of physical capital, depend on its structure. But even in our private lives we are not dependent on our own resources: our common mental architecture makes it possible to connect to external knowledge capital, though by no means to all of it. Market relationships provide links that make possible the construction of additional knowledge and, by allowing many activities to be guided by rules and conventions, provide scope for imagination. Co-ordination by institutional arrangements defines boundaries, which should not lightly be assumed to match the fundamental data – this is not known anyway; but from a cognitive perspective it also defines a space to think within those boundaries, and even to make selective forays across them. The history of human development is one of discovering ways of circumventing the limits apparently imposed by the cognitive capacity of each individual, by an increasing division of cognitive labour and by developing procedures which enable us to make new combinations from the results of that division.

Market institutions not only release cognitive resources for the development of both consumer and organisational capital and therefore of new consumer demands and new productive opportunities which create new contexts for competition: particular institutional structures will encourage these developments to take particular forms. A study of the competitive process requires a study of the institutions within which it is channelled, and also of attempts to modify those institutions in ways that will favour the modifiers, not always with the effects intended. (Co-operative retail societies pioneered the development of supermarkets.) Indeed, we should not forget that much economic activity is devoted to the provision of market institutions and to the extension of market institutions to new classes of goods and services, illustrated by the diverse histories of Marks & Spencer, Tesco and many providers of financial services, and also to the creation of new markets based on new institutional arrangements. The latter has recently appeared so important in its scale and possible effects that it has often been labelled 'the new economy'. We now have clear evidence that the creation of new institutions to gain competitive advantage may be very costly and that success is problematic; the new economy has not produced a new economics.

As with any innovation, acceptance depends on a combination of continuity and novelty that matches the perception of the customer, and it is easy to get this combination wrong. The competitive process combines *ex-ante* selection of what to offer and how to provide it by each competitor, based on premises which are not a simple reflection of the basic data, but are defined from 'the imagined deemed possible' (Shackle, 1979, p. 26), and *ex-post* selection by customers who have their own notions about what will fit their own perceived needs. These notions are the product of cognitive, emotional and aesthetic factors, and change over time; the study of 'the active consumer' (Bianchi, 1998) is closely complementary to the study of competitive markets.

References

Barnard, C. A. (1938), *The Functions of the Executive*, Cambridge, MA, Harvard University Press.

Bianchi, M. (ed.) (1998), *The Active Consumer*, London, Routledge.

Butler, R. W. (1991), 'The historical context of the early Marshallian work', *Quaderni di Storia dell'Economia Politica*, 9(2–3), pp. 269–86.

Casson, M. (1982), *The Entrepreneur: An Economic Theory*, Oxford, Martin Robertson.

Choi, Y. B. (1993), *Paradigms and Conventions: Uncertainty, Decision Making, and Entrepreneurship*, Ann Arbor, University of Michigan Press.

Coase, R. H. (1937), 'The nature of the firm', *Economica*, new series, 4, pp. 386–405.

Coase, R. H. (1991), 'The nature of the firm: influence', in Williamson, O. E. and Winter, S. G. (eds), *The Nature of the Firm: Origins, Evolution and Development*, Oxford, Oxford University Press, pp. 61–74.

Hayek, F. A. (1948), 'The meaning of competition', in *Individualism and Economic Order*, Chicago, University of Chicago Press, pp. 92–106.

Hayek, F. A. (1952), *The Sensory Order*, Chicago, University of Chicago Press.

Heiner, R. A. (1983), 'The origin of predictable behavior', *American Economic Review*, 73(4), pp. 560–95.

Knight, F. H. (1921), *Risk, Uncertainty and Profit*, Boston, MA, Houghton Mifflin. Reprinted Chicago, University of Chicago Press, 1971.

Marshall, A. (1919), *Industry and Trade*, London, Macmillan.

Marshall, A. (1920), *Principles of Economics*, London, Macmillan.

Marshall, A. (1994), 'Ye machine', *Research in the History of Economic Thought and Methodology*, Archival Supplement 4, Greenwich, CT, JAI Press, pp. 116–32.

Ménard, C. (1995), 'Markets as institutions versus organizations as markets? Disentangling some fundamental concepts', *Journal of Economic Behavior and Organization*, 28(2), pp. 161–82.

Menger, C. (1976 [1871]), *Principles of Economics*, trans. Dingwall, J. and Hoselitz, B. F., New York, New York University Press.

Penrose, E. T. (1959), *The Theory of the Growth of the Firm*, Oxford, Basil Blackwell; 3rd edn, Oxford, Oxford University Press, 1995.

Raffaelli, T. (1994), 'The early philosophical writings of Alfred Marshall', *Research in the History of Economic Thought and Methodology*, Archival Supplement 4, Greenwich, CT: JAI Press, pp. 53–159.

Robinson, J. V. (1933), *The Economics of Imperfect Competition*, London, Macmillan.

Schlicht, E. (2000), 'Aestheticism in the theory of custom', *Journal des Economistes et des Etudes Humaines*, 10(1), pp. 33–51.

Schumpeter, J. A. (1943), *Capitalism, Socialism and Democracy*, London, Allen & Unwin.

Shackle, G. L. S. (1979), *Imagination and the Nature of Choice*, Edinburgh, Edinburgh University Press.

Simon, H. A. (1976), *Administrative Behaviours*, 3rd edn (New York: Free Press).

Smith, A. (1976a), *An Inquiry into the Nature and Causes of the Wealth of Nations*, ed. Campbell, R. H., Skinner, A. S. and Todd, W. B., 2 vols, Oxford, Oxford University Press.

Smith, A. (1976b), *The Theory of Moral Sentiments*, ed. Raphael, D. D. and Macfie, A. L., Oxford, Oxford University Press.

Smith, A. (1980), 'The principles which lead and direct philosophical enquiries; illustrated by the history of astronomy', in *Essays on Philosophical Subjects*, ed. Wightman, W. P. D. and Bryce, J.C., Oxford, Oxford University Press, pp. 33–105.

Smith, A. (1983), *Lectures on Rhetoric and Belles Lettres*, ed. Bryce, J. C., Oxford, Oxford University Press.

Ziman, J. M. (1978), *Reliable Knowledge*, Cambridge, Cambridge University Press.

4

Competition as instituted economic process

Mark Harvey

Introduction

A challenge to the new economic sociology is that central *economic* processes should become the focus of theoretical and empirical sociological analysis. This chapter makes some steps towards analysing competition in that light, partly because competition is often assumed to be the market force of all market forces. The central argument made is both that competition processes are co-instituted with markets (including end markets), and that market processes are in turn co-instituted with industrial divisions of labour. Thus, it is suggested that an excessive burden of explanatory expectation is placed on competitive processes within markets, as *the* dynamic of capitalist economies. Indeed, I argue here that many conceptions of competition suffer from this 'tilt towards the market' as the sole or primary dynamic force behind economic growth, to the exclusion or at least sidelining of complementary but at least equally significant dynamics within the realm of production, such as capital accumulation. After all, to put it at its weakest, competition may stimulate but cannot deliver growth, and in some models of competition, the outcome is merely the efficient allocation of existing resources through transparent price setting, a static equilibrium model.

The chapter begins with an examination of some of the few empirically based studies of competition, suggesting that they often are developed for overtly normative or prescriptive purposes. It then returns to analyse some of the early Weberian conceptions of competition, upon which to build an economic sociology of competitive processes. After contrasting the seminal concept of 'instituted economic process' with the other and more widely adopted Polanyan legacy of 'embeddedness', the chapter explores competition as an instituted economic process in five dimensions: the co-institution of competitive processes and markets; relations of power and mutual dependence between classes of economic agent; the formation of units of competition; the formation of scales of competition; and the development of formal and informal norms of competition. The chapter then provides an exemplification of this analytical framework through a schematic analysis of changing forms of competition in the historical development of UK food supermarkets. The conclusion drawn from this analysis is that competitive processes are a result of processes of transformation wider than intra-market dynamics.

Empirico-normative views of competition

Leaving aside neo-classical views of 'perfect competition', this much acclaimed market force has attracted surprisingly few empirical 'competition studies' to complement those in the field of innovation. There is a wide range of conceptions of what constitutes competition: static efficiency of resource allocation: dynamic efficiency of innovation and adaptation; and Schumpeterian creative destruction. But many of these conceptions are what might be called 'empirico-normative', stating as much what ought to be as what is. A classic instance of this is the work of Porter, which comprises the more overtly prescriptive (1985) with empirico-normative analysis (1998a, b). 'Competition is dynamic and rests on innovation and the search for strategic difference' (Porter, 1998a, p. 209) is a proposition that rolls together statements about what competition is, empirically and optimally, into what amounts to a definition. Clusters of interconnected firms are seen to provide optimal competitive conditions for strategic differentiation, with the Porter diamond being used as a strategic tool for achieving the best combination of its four facets: factor inputs, supply chain networks, demand conditions, and regulatory frameworks and infrastructure. In this way, clusters are seen as being capable of going beyond static efficiency competition, beyond cost-reduction competition, and onwards and upwards to optimal forms of competition based on strategic differentiation.[1] Low barriers to entry into clusters, levels of 'social capital' ensuring free flows of information, absence of formal contractual requirements resulting from a level of common purpose, combined with an exactly right dose of rivalry in the cluster,[2] are thus empirical characteristics, ones given the normative seal of approval. Empirical cases, such as the birth of the Medtronics' pacemaker cluster in Minneapolis, are thus woven into the narrative as 'exemplary' events as much as evidential demonstration.

Cartels are bad (they 'undermine economic value') while clusters are good ('open', 'facilitating', 1998a, p. 227). The best kinds of clusters are to be found mostly in the USA, where the greatest number provide the greatest synergies arising from overlapping clusters, whereas in developing countries clusters tend to be too centralised around a few dominant players, are often state supported, and are 'hub-and-spoke networks' (1998a, p. 231). Japan is castigated for following such a model, exacerbated by a metropol-centric and overdirected bias. Given this fusion of the empirical and the normative '[c]luster theory emphasises not market share but dynamic improvement. This results in a positive sum underlying view of competition, in which productivity improvements and trade expand the market' (1998a, p. 249). There exists empirically an optimal kind of competition and its effects are unreservedly benign.

Two examples of theorisation of competition which are clearly empirically based but nonetheless attached to an advocacy of particular forms of competition can be found in the work of Best (1990), on the one hand, and in a network of researchers clustered around the Applied Economics Department and the ESRC Centre for Business Research at Cambridge University, on the other. In an historical analysis of different forms of competition, Best argues that changing forms of competition are the outcome of complex interactions between industrial divisions and productive organisation, on the one hand, and formal competition regulatory systems, on the other. Thus, in the USA the multi-divisional Chandlerian corporation involved a form of competition in which Big Business mass production responded to conditions of oversupply by further increasing supply to achieve greater market share in shrinking market conditions, and by market expansion, 'democratic consumption', in growth conditions. The regulatory framework provided by corporation law and Sherman's Anti-Trust Law had the unintended consequence of accelerating acquisition and consolidation by criminalising inter-firm co-operation.

By contrast the 'New Competition', which involves strategic differentiation, organisational superiority and continuous innovation in a shifting competitive environment, emerges when inter-firm relationships across the production chain are facilitated by consultative co-ordination. A balance is struck between sectoral inter-firm co-operation on prices to enable competition for innovation potential. And there is an enabling and supportive policy framework and infrastructure subverting the dichotomy between market and hierarchy which sustains a 'balance between co-operation and competition' (Best, 1990, p. 267). The particular form of the *keiretsu* in Japan as they evolved during the 1970s was thus once more an industrial and productive organisation in interaction with a competition regulatory environment. Best argues strongly that this development was an unintended consequence of an institutional countervailance between MITI and the Free Trade Commission, preventing either the dominance of centralised and directive planning or the imposition of US-style competition law.

> United States industrial regulatory policy had presumed the idea of perfect markets and defined inter-firm co-operation as collusion against the public interest. Japanese industrial policy, in contrast, has been based on the presupposition that a mix of inter-firm competition and co-operation can promote international competitiveness. (Best, 1990, p. 201)

The 'Third Italy' provides another example of a complex interaction between trade associations, consortia and municipally sustained tax and 'social capital' infrastructure facilitating collective Schumpeterian competition for strategic sectoral advantage, also balancing competition and co-operation. It is clear, from this account, that for Best 'the purpose of strategic industrial policy is to promote Schumpeterian competition and (collective) entrepreneurial firms', and that '[t]his means, in part, shaping competition and affecting the form that competition takes in order to enhance economic performance'

(1990, pp. 265–6). The empirical analysis is one in which particular historical forms of industrial division and organisation generate distinctive forms of competition (focusing on productivity cost reduction, on market share, or on strategic differentiation, innovation and comparative organisational advantage). These forms of industrial organisation and competition are then sustained by and, in their turn influence formal institutional competition regulation. In Best's work there is a strong sense, too, that the New Competition is both historically and normatively superior to an antecedent and moribund Big Business corporation form of competition.[3]

The 'Cambridge network' has likewise produced a number of comparative studies of competitive and co-operative behaviour, combining legal, economic, sociological and management perspectives. Lane (1997) demonstrated how different technical and quality norms operating in markets in Germany and Britain effectively provide a distinctive basis for collaboration and competition in the former by establishing industry-wide common standards. In Britain, in contrast, in the absence of specified quality and technical standards, quality and cost can more easily become *opposing* objectives of competition. Likewise, contractual law, a propensity to litigate, and the fostering of trust have been analysed as being central to different forms of inter-firm relations which fundamentally affect the nature and focus of competitive forces in Britain, Germany and Italy. Institutional and legal infrastructures thus form part of the essential basis for co-operative productive systems which enhance their innovation capacity and hence their competitiveness (Deakin and Wilkinson, 1995; Arighetti *et al.*, 1997; Deakin, Lane and Wilkinson, 1997). Complementary to Best's analysis of the role of competition regulation, these authors also demonstrate how regulation policy in the USA followed economic fashion, first the Chicago School, then game-theoretical and principal-agent theories, to shape a particular kind of competition environment through key legal cases. They contrast this with the regulatory environments in the UK and at the European Commission levels (Deakin, Goodwin and Hughes, 1997), and suggest ways in which these differently affect competitive behaviour.[4] This body of work, which places a central emphasis on formal and contractual institutions and the way they shape competitive and interfirm relations, also shares a common normative standpoint, both by providing an effective critique of regulatory models assuming atomistic competition, and in promoting a view that '*co-operation* between firms is a necessary productive feature of productive innovation and competitive success' (Deakin *et al.*, 1997, p. 339). The comparative study, therefore, provides an important lever of judgement for critiquing 'the broad orientation of systems of competition law which continue to privilege models of industry based on atomistic competition' (p. 362).

Drawing this introductory discussion to a close, it is clear that in this field of empirical analysis, some important if partial analyses have been made. These far surpass the prescriptive and normatively motivated account of competition by Porter, and even more so the formal models of 'perfect competition'. Best gives the most comprehensive theoretical basis for an analysis, embracing the historical development of industrial organisation, in parallel with formal institutional regulatory regimes. But that analysis leads towards a more normative account of the virtues of Schumpeterian collective entrepreneurship of the New Competition. The 'Cambridge network' provides significant additional perspectives, emphasising especially formal institutional conditions for co-operatively based competition. But, lacking Best's perspective on industrial organisation and, especially, consideration of power relations in vertically organised supply chains, the analysis of co-operation also tends to be normatively laden.

Towards an instituted economic process approach

If one looks hard enough, it is generally possible to find antecedents for most ideas, and the early formulations of a synthetic discipline of economic sociology do provide some initial pointers to an instituted economic process view of competition. 'A market may be said to exist wherever there is competition, even if only unilateral, for opportunities of exchange among a plurality of potential parties' (Weber 1968, p. 635).

Swedberg (1994, 1998) has argued that Weber enlarges a conception of markets beyond their status as simple vehicles for exchange by distinctively pairing exchange with competition as a prerequisite for the existence of markets, but he still leaves much to be done analytically. In particular, competition is here defined fairly restrictively in terms of a struggle over opportunities for exchange. That struggle is one into which power directly enters. Indeed, for Weber economic competition is a form of 'peaceful conflict', whereby attempts are made to 'gain control over opportunities and advantages which are also desired by others' and which take place 'in exchange relationships, bound . . . by the order governing the market' (Weber, 1968, p. 38). Although not clearly stated, Weber clearly intends that competition here involves winners and losers, and thereby a process of 'social selection' (1968, pp. 38–40). In this view of competition as a pacific power struggle, however, it appears that the power exercised within the market and through the exchange process is not explicable by the market or exchange relations alone. To found a notion of relative powers, it is necessary to include the sphere of production and the differential capacities to create and own wealth.[5] Moreover, Weber's action-oriented approach is undoubtedly an obstacle to an analysis of the power relations that arise from industrial divisions, such as those between capital and labour, between primary and secondary producers, or between retailers and manufacturers, retailers and consumers. The 'elemental' description of a market as a plurality of buyers confronting a plurality of sellers (Weber, 1968, p. 635; Swedberg, 1998, pp. 42–3) already makes important assumptions about their separation into two classes of economic agent which is difficult to account for in terms of actor-oriented agency.

Nonetheless, Weber's ideas of economic competition as 'pacified' struggle and of exchange as one that obeys rules of calculation embodied in market organisation anticipate some notion of normalised or instituted competitive process. Moreover, as Swedberg has commented, Weber hesitated in *Economy and Society* to take this view of economic competition in exchange to develop a theory of price, restrained by fear of transgression into the field of economics and marginal utility theory. But he privately acknowledged that the logic of his position would be to view real price formation as an empirical process resulting from the economic struggles between actors (Swedberg, 1998, p. 44). This, were it to be developed further, provides intimations of an instituted economic process (IEP) account of price and price formation, through 'economically normalised' competitive struggle. What this significantly shares with an IEP approach is that core economic processes, such as price and competition, as well as markets, are seen as 'normalised' *ipso facto* for being economic, and that the 'rationality' of markets and market agents is itself a consequence of normalisation.

The notion of economic processes as instituted was first explicitly formulated by Karl Polanyi, and in order to weigh its full significance it is first necessary to disentangle it from the concept of *embeddedness* for which Polanyi is much better known, as well as from its pair *dis-embeddedness* which, equally, has found less favour. It should be emphasised that this is an attempt to develop the notion of IEP from the rather confused and, tangled usage within Polanyi's own work, on the one hand, and on the other, to suggest that Polanyi had in embryo a much more radical agenda than the subsequent appropriation of embeddedness, notably by Granovetter (1985, 1992 and with McGuire, 1998), has given it. The concept of embeddedness carries with it the idea that economic relations are moulded and shaped by the social relations and contexts within which those relations occur (Polanyi, 1944, pp. 46, 49; 1957, p. 250).[6] Thus, in the terms of the above discussion of legal and contractual institutions, the concept might be used to say that transactions are 'embedded' in such a societal framework. Granovetter, however, appropriated the concept for the purpose of developing a more actor-oriented approach, with embeddedness referring to 'dense and stable networks of relations, shared understandings, and political coalitions' (Granovetter, 1985, p. 501). And he argued that trust and co-operative relations developed through 'concrete personal relations and the obligations inherent in them . . . quite apart from institutional arrangements' (1985, p. 495). In more recent work, this type of analysis is taken to an extreme in which, at a more macro level than in his previous work, small-scale interpersonal networks, even conspiracy between a handful of people, were seen as constructing the overall industrial structure, including the competitive relations, of the electricity supply industry in the USA.[7] Moreover, this perspective is applied to industrial organisation more generally, by arguing that

> processes and relationships once shaped by individuals became institutionalised
> in more formal organisations, institutional alliances, standardised practices, and

industry norms. As in other industries . . . such patterns become embedded as norms, unless and until an industry-wide crisis occurs. (Granovetter and McGuire, 1998, p. 168)

Callon (1998) extends this notion in an actor network context, suggesting that the idea of embeddedness is one which means, firstly, that all levels of analysis are reduced to 'the network of interactions' in which individuals are involved,[8] and, secondly, that as such networks bind economic, social, political, cultural, technological and material aspects together, there is in principle no distinct sphere of the economic that can be analysed as such. Indeed, in this conception of embeddedness, Callon argues that we are now increasingly living in 'hot' situations where it becomes difficult to 'frame' the economic into a distinct sphere of economic calculation, and there is a continuous 'overflowing' into networks too fluid for economic calculation.[9] Only in 'cold' situations, when markets are discrete, framed, and immune from excessive externalities, are Coasian or other economically rational calculations possible. Thus, the idea of embeddedness here invoked suggests the continuous and overwhelmingly invasive presence of incalculable externalities in market interactions.

In tracing this lineage of the concept of embeddedness, its latent potential for sociologising the economy out of existence, and of dissolving institutions of price, capital, competition, industrial division of labour, supply, demand, market, etc., into emergent networks of interpersonal relations becomes manifest. This seems quite remote from Polanyi's original intention and usage. Indeed, analysing the development of the 'self-regulating market' in *The Great Transformation*, Polanyi suggested very forcefully that during the industrial revolution *all* factors became commodities (including, notably, land, labour and money). That was a key historical moment when economic institutions became *dis-embedded* or even entailed a *reverse* embedding of society into the economy. It is that formulation which gives such a different reading to the concept of embeddedness:

> Instead of economy being embedded in social relations, social relations are embedded in the economic system . . . For once the economic system is organised in separate institutions, based on specific motives and conferring special status, society must be shaped in such a manner as to allow that system to function according to its own laws . . . A market economy can function only in a market society. (Polanyi, 1944, p. 57)

The commodification of labour, in particular its separation from preceding modes of subsistence living, and the development of urbanisation, meant that many more social interactions were mediated by money exchanges and price, and as such became *economically* instituted. That was the intent of the more general formulations Polanyi later gave (1957, p. 250) where he stated:

> The instituting of the economic process vests that process with unity and stability; it produces a structure with a definite function in society; it shifts the place of the process in society, thus adding significance to its history; it centres interest on

values, motives and policy . . . The study of the shifting place occupied by the
economy in society is therefore no other than the study of the manner in which
the economic process is instituted at different times and places.

When speaking of motives, values and policy as also instituted, he adopts for-
mulae akin to a notion of *habitus* where 'no individual economic motives
need come into play' (Polanyi, 1944, p. 49), because social organisation 'runs
in its ruts', and the motive for gain, in becoming generalised in tandem with
a commodified economy, is one of those ruts (Polanyi, 1944, pp. 41–2).

The central consequences that can be drawn out of this approach are three-
fold. First, given that economic process is an instituted process, open to de-
and re-institution, it is socially, comparatively and historically variable. That
applies to capital, labour, price mechanisms, markets – as well as to economic
motives. It fundamentally underpins a notion of varieties of capitalism. Second, rather than talking of instituted economic processes and their context as
socially 'embedding', the specificity of economic instituted processes can be
seen to find their 'place' in different articulations with legal, political and civic
institutions. So there is no question of the economic being dissolved in the
social, or vice versa, as with an over-sociologised view of embeddedness.
Rather there is mutual conditioning between, for example, competition law
and industrial organisation (as with Best). Third, and likewise, an IEP
approach opens up the possibility of running through from micro to macro,
from the motive for gain to the Gold Standard, and the articulation between
different scales of instituted process. Thus, for Polanyi, both the motive for
gain and the Gold Standard are prime examples of the instituted economic
process, the former very likely being articulated with all kinds of networks
of interdependences at the micro-social level (in the manner of Granovetter);
the latter being a transnational, trans-societal, instituted economic process,
relatively dis-embedded from such micro-social networks.

Competition as instituted economic process

Developing an IEP approach in relation to competition will involve looking
at a number of different dimensions, under the basic assumption that
competition, far from being a universal or natural law of the market, is instituted differently in different historical and comparative circumstances. The
focus becomes the study of competition in its varied modes of institution,
and competition, being multi-dimensional, needs to be analysed as a complex
phenomenon. In many ways, this section is programmatic, to be followed by
the next, where the rise of UK supermarkets will be used as an illustrative
example of a multi-dimensional reconfiguration of competition.

Markets and forms of competition are mutually instituted
The starting point for an understanding of competition as an instituted economic process is that it is manifest in market exchanges, as indeed we saw

Weber suggest. So even empirical examples of 'perfect competition' *à la* Samuelson can be discovered, as Garcia (1986) has demonstrated for a strawberry market, near Paris, in Sologne. She showed that in this market there was relative equality between buyers and sellers; unrestricted entry into the market; homogeneity of the product; and transparency or near perfect information. But unlike a view of embeddedness,[10] this market was the effect of a quite distinct process of institution which involved a number of different preconditions. First, it required the elimination of one form of trading institution (the itinerant merchant–grower) and its replacement by a computerised local auction. Second, the growers' association attracted the assistance of the central and the local state in the funding of the market institutions, such as the central collection hall for display of produce and an electronic terminal and screen system. Third, homogeneity of product was ensured through collective quality regulation and a common grading system, adopted by the growers. And, last but not least, a balance of power with purchasers was achieved as a result of the formation of a growers' association. Buyer–supplier equality was, somewhat precariously, facilitated by the particular patterns of land ownership among growers, and relatively small-scale retailers or market traders coming from Paris. In other words, the balance of power, or equality between buyers and sellers, pre-supposed special social and economic characteristics of both sets of agents. In short, the form of competition, so-called 'perfect competition', was instituted – but only under quite special social and historical circumstances.

In a more general way, it can be seen that the formation of the broad categories of labour, product and capital markets, each with its own distinctive competitive processes,[11] is itself the outcome of instituted economic process. The institutions of a stockmarket, for example, involve quite distinct, and historically changing, processes of competition, as can be seen from various developments and possibilities of European or cross-Atlantic merger, alongside distinctive rules for trading, and formal regulation.

Comparing distinct European labour markets, it is clear that different quality and pricing institutions for labour, and different frameworks for regulating long-term, short-term, temporary and part time contracts, fundamentally condition the forms of competition within labour markets (Harvey, 2000; Harvey *et al.*, forthcoming). A conclusion from these works is that the labour contract, the commodity purchased and hence the exchange between capital and labour are radically differently instituted in differing countries. Moreover, such differences have led to major political debates about the competitiveness of 'high social cost' and 'low social cost' labour. However, given the radical incommensurability between what is being purchased in two disparate labour markets; given the 'indirect' competition via product markets; and given exchange-rate fluctuations, it is clear that there an absence of 'normalised' competition at this level. There are no overarching instituted measures in the absence of a common currency. So, from an IEP perspective, the *indirect* competition between diverse labour markets via product markets and institutional forms of fluctuating exchange rates and monetary institutions exemplifies the institutedness of competition. I return to this point in considering different instituted scales of competition.

Asymmetric power and mutual dependence

Competition generally takes place *within* the same class of economic agent, but not *between* classes of economic agent, and the formation of such classes is itself a result of instituted economic process. Thus, to continue with labour markets, the focus of competition is *among* employers (capital) and *among* employees (labour), across an exchange relationship, as a consequence of the formation of two distinct classes of economic agent performing distinct economic functions.[12] But competition does not occur *between* labour and capital.[13] The exchange relation is characterised by mutual dependence (owners of capital need labour; people are, in varying ways, obliged to sell their labour) and asymmetrical power relations. The kind of power wielded by capital (degree of concentration, domination in the market, etc.) is different from the kind of power wielded by labour (from individual sale through to various forms of countervailing association). In this exchange relation, the nature of competition as affected by concentration or organisation of capital on one side of this power equation affects the opportunities of exchange, just as the nature of competition on the other side of the equation can be affected by forms of association and by labour market institutions of the kind suggested above.

But the more general proposition that competition applies within and not between classes of economic agent is also applicable to exchange relations between retailers and consumers, retailers and manufacturers, manufacturers and primary producers, and so on. Each of these pairs can be seen as classes of economic agent, historically instituted, and performing distinct economic functions. New classes, still in the process of institutionalisation as is the case with the emergence of e-commerce, can fundamentally restructure the configuration of existing exchange relations, thereby instituting new forms of competition. I explain later how the emergence of powerful supermarkets has affected the structure of exchange relations, and hence of forms of competition.

Thus, as with capital and labour, retailers as one class of economic agent can be seen to compete with retailers, but not with farmers or manufacturers or consumers, as other classes of economic agent. Vertical exchange relations along a supply chain are significantly affected by the shifts in asymmetrical power relations, as will be seen. But those power relations must be distinguished from competitive relations. Consequently, in so far as retailers and manufacturers, for example, are mutually dependent and in asymmetrical power relations, it is important to consider that *if competition does not occur across classes of economic agent, nor does co-operation in the sense of unconstrained mutual co-operation between similar equals*. It becomes important to distinguish co-operation between members of the same class of economic agent (trade associations, employers federations, trades unions, etc.) from forms of concertation that occur within exchange relations characterised by mutual dependence and power asymmetry, a form of economic constraint (retailers have to acquire goods from manufacturers, manufacturers have to find a way to market). For co-operation between economic agents of the same class, Richardsonian notions of complementarity of dissimilar capabilities (Richardson, 1972) may be appropriate, and Marshallian districts can be taken as empirical examples (Best, 1990;[14] Dei Ottati, 1994).

It should be stressed that there are two aspects to power asymmetry: on the one side, relative balance or position as a consequence of size and levels of concentration within one of two economic classes party to the exchanges, and, on the other, the nature of the power wielded. Thus, as a result of concentration, retailers may control and shape access to market. But this is a very different type of power or capacity from that involved in the productive capacity of manufacturers. In terms of instituted economic process, therefore, one could contrast the power of food retailers in the UK in relation to food manufacturers with the power of motor manufacturers and franchised retail outlets. These two instituted exchange relations affect fundamentally the nature of the competition, the pricing mechanisms – and also the power of consumers in relation to either of those two arrangements.

Referring back to Best's historical analysis of changing forms of competition with changing patterns of industrial organisation, that can now be reformulated in an IEP perspective where the development and differentiation of classes of economic agent, within a given sector of production, affect the nature of competition within those classes, not least because differentiation affects the nature of power asymmetries and mutual dependences between classes of economic agent. To return also to Weber, the way power enters into economic exchanges is centrally through the asymmetry and mutual dependences of trading relations between differently constituted classes of economic agent.

Units of competition and the 'channelling' of competition

If competition is variously instituted by the formation of markets and by the configuration of different classes of economic agent, then a further dimension of the shaping of competition arises from the institution of different units of competition, from individuals to firms, supply chains, or clusters of firms. The formation of different units of competition should be distinguished from the formation of different scales of competition, which are discussed below, the former concerning primarily the competitive entities *within* a given market, the latter the *scale of the markets* themselves – local, regional, national or global. So, to emphasise the distinction, transnational corporations can compete with each other, but at various different scales of competition in different markets.[15] The assumption of much competition regulation is that the firm is the only unit of competition, and the objective of such regulation is to institute norms of competition for firm behaviour, in specified markets. Indeed, in many instituted markets, firms can be the central and dominant units of competition, and there are degrees of 'atomism' in this respect, depending on the levels of repeat trading or formal and informal partner relations between firms within different economic classes (Fulconis, 1999).

But, in many contemporary product markets, the competing units are integrated supply chains, networks or clusters, each of which can be orchestrated by the dominant power within it. The locus of power within the supply chain, and the degree of integration of the supply chain, fundamentally affect where the competition is channelled, and, as I argue below, what form the competition takes in terms of cost reduction, product differentiation, innovation capability, logistical efficiency, or whatever. Thus Nike has been seen as exemplifying a 'buyer-driven' supply chain, where the design and marketing node of the supply chain and its associated brand marque form the dominant power. This in turn affects the nature of the competition and its locus and focus in relation to other competitors, such as Reebok and Adidas (Gereffi and Korzenewiecz, 1994). But power can equally be situated upstream, as in the case of Monsanto and the biotechnology of seed manufacturing, 'mid-stream' as in the case of motor-manufacturers, or downstream, as in the case of UK food supermarkets or many clothing retailers. Thus, in as much as supply chains, or other less linear inter-firm entities, produce outputs for given product markets, they can become in Polanyan terms relatively normal and stabilised forms of industrial organisation, reflecting also a normalisation over periods of time of power asymmetries within them in the markets in which they operate. There is a consequent channelling of competition and also a focus of competition on different product aspects (novelty, style, marque, quality, freshness, convenience, price, reliability, etc.). Equally, such inter-firm organisations create a halo of competition, again at certain loci of the supply chain, between insiders and outsiders.

Scales of competition

From an IEP perspective different scales of markets can be seen to be the results of historical processes of institution,[16] rather than any pre-given frameworks, and as a consequence are intimately connected with the development of the sizes of firms, the lengths of supply chains, as well as with national and supranational organisations such as NAFTA or the European Union. Moreover, different scales overlay each other, rather than necessarily replacing each other, so that competition, as it were, plays in different registers at the same time. When Krugman (1994, p. 44) argues that 'competitiveness is a meaningless word when applied to national economies' he is in effect arguing that the kind of competition which occurs between firms does not occur between nations or at different scales. That seems to be self-evident. It does appear to be meaningless if a nation is treated as a mega-firm producing a bundle of commodities traded in a multitude of markets at all different scales competing with other such mega-firms. But in so far as nations, in their capacity to set incentives for foreign direct investment or regulatory environments for trading, or infrastructural support for education, or any number of other distinctive and formative institutional measures,[17] can affect the ensemble of nationally active economic agents, it is clear that there is a form of competition distinctive to nations as a class of economic agent. Similarly the formation of supranational scales, such as NAFTA or the EU involve distinctive competitive regulatory frameworks which can accentuate market integration over other competitive criteria such as market share, inter-firm vertical constraint, or cartelisation (Anderman, 1997; Deakin, Goodwin and Hughes, 1997). So the institution of different overlaying scales of markets is a historical process which generates new forms of competition at different registers. To continue the musical metaphor, there is no presumption of harmony between scales, and the emergence of new scales can be discordant in relation to 'normal' forms of competition at other scales.

Norms and formal institutions of competition
The arguments of Best (1990) and Deakin, Goodwin and Hughes (1997) that formal normative institutions regulating competition evolve in relation to organisations of units of competition as they in turn evolve,[18] suggest a complex interaction between formal frameworks and informal norms of competitive process. Regulation can thus stimulate vertical integration at the expense of inter-firm co-operation, but in circumstances where stockmarkets as a main feature of capital markets can also lead to more predatory merger and acquisition processes than in economies where long-term banking finance plays a greater role. Particular firm–market structures can become normalised over quite long periods, and thereby establish norms of competition. During processes of restructuration of industrial organisation, or, for example, shifts in the location of power along supply chains, these norms become destabilised, and as the market is re-formed 'abnormal' or market destabilising turbulence occurs. Examples of how one competitive configuration replaces another are given below, but there is a sense in which such processes of institution involve the supersession of one mode of competition by another, rather than competition between one productive system and another. But, equally, different and conflicting modes of competition can continue to exist side by side: 'New Competition' is far from having driven out 'Old Competition'. In speaking of 'norms' of competition, therefore, and of the co-evolution of formal regulatory and non-formal norms of competition, there is no presumption of a functionalist process of mutual adaptation.

From the above discussion of different dimensions of competition as instituted economic process, it is clear that competition is complex, multi-dimensional and variable, both historically and comparatively. Changes in the nature of the competitive process in terms of how 'atomistic' or firm-oriented it is co-varies often with changes in the object or focus of the competitive process. Under specific, possibly unusual, empirical conditions, purely narrow price competition for homogenous products and high levels of transparency, under conditions of relative equality, may occur. But to do so, infrastructural conditions, and particular market rules, need to be instituted. There is indirect competition between labour markets and product markets, product markets and capital markets, and the relationship between these different markets is open to variable historical processes of institution and reconfiguration. Different forms of competition operate at different scales of competition, so that competition is operating in several registers simultaneously. And, finally, there is a complex interaction between formal norms of competition enshrined in competition regulation and the non-formal norms of competition occurring in relatively stable, often quite long-term, market formations. To illustrate this multi-dimensionality, and the process of de-institution and re-institution of different forms of competition, discussion now turns to the effects of the changes in the UK food retailing market.

UK supermarkets and changing forms of competition[19]

During the course of the twentieth century, UK multiple retailers have grown from having roughly ten per cent of the market share of the food market to over 85 per cent. In a first phase, multiple retailers established an integrated national market for food retailing (Jefferys, 1954). In a second phase, from the early 1970s, but accelerating through the 1980s, the small handful of major retailers established a commanding share, and two, Tesco and Sainsbury, contested for market leadership (Wrigley and Lowe, 1996). As a mark of their power, these two market the highest supermarket own-label proportion of goods of any food retailers – in many product ranges well over 50 per cent and in key ranges up to 100 per cent. This is a story of growth as much as of competition, and competition between these rivals alone would be insufficient to explain the structural changes that have taken place.

In terms of the IEP approach developed above, this rise to power of supermarkets can be seen to have fundamentally altered all dimensions of competition, and the forms of competition, within this sector, by

- instituting new market forms for consumer markets and intermediate markets;
- altering the asymmetrical power relations, changing the structure of mutual dependences and forming new units of competition between supply chains;
- re-channelling competition, giving it a new locus and focus;
- changing the distributed nature of innovation, and also the innovation process and style; and
- provoking a conflict between an 'old-style' regulatory regime relating to earlier forms of competition and the new norms of competition.

The significance of this change arises from the combination of all of these processes, but, for analytical purposes, each will be briefly separately discussed below.

The institution of new markets

The new supermarkets fundamentally restructured the end market, by creating the comprehensive one-stop-shop food and household provisions' retailing outlet. The essential characteristic of these retail outlets is that they trade in total ranges of commodities. The competition is between traders in the totality of the ranges and services they have on offer, rather than in specific product to product competition. Consequently, through either out-of-town or town-based superstores, they aggregate demand over distinctive catchment areas, and adapt product ranges to the socio-economic characteristics of those areas. They also effectively eliminated wholesale markets as intermediary markets, and thus eradicated the forms of competition typical of those markets by bypassing them. The typical instituted form of those wholesale markets was to operate as spot markets, with very short-term, price-focused and market-clearing competition. The structure of trading had been for a large plurality of primary producers to supply a relatively small number of wholesalers who traded with a large plurality of retailers on a commission basis. From the mid-1980s, supermarkets centralised their purchasing activities, bought direct from primary producers, with whom they established relatively long-term, often exclusive, trading relations.

New asymmetric power relations of mutual dependence, new units of competition

The concentration of power in the hands of two or three major multiples has resulted in a radical shift in power in relation to at least three other classes of economic agent: consumers, primary producers, and food manufacturers and processors. In relation to consumers, the operation of catchment areas, in which one major store is locationally strongly advantaged in respect of a large number of consumers can create a quasi-monopoly position. Reinforced through various 'loyalty card' electronic point of sale (Eftpos) schemes, the result is that 70 per cent of the majority of shoppers' grocery purchases is undertaken regularly in one store.

In relation to brand manufacturers, major international companies, with global presence, are constrained to produce own-label products under supermarket specification. In short, where competition does occur between own-label and branded goods, retailers are in a powerful position to set the terms of that competition.

But perhaps it is in relation to own-label producers that the most conspicuous changes have taken place. As a consequence of the development of own-label manufacture, five or six major own-label manufacturers supply the bulk of all own label produce to a similar number of retail multiples, creating a complex interlocking matrix of exclusive trade in relation to particular products and product ranges. Typically, one of the large own-label manufacturers will have a number of factory units, each dedicated to the exclusive supply to one of the major multiples. For example, one company provides all the lasagne, each under a different specification and design, to the top five retailers. Or, for pizzas, two manufacturers supply one retailer with different segments of the pizza market, also on an exclusive basis. This type of 'multiple and criss-crossing monopsony' between relatively low numbers of trading partners on either side of the exchange, means that competition is reduced significantly between own-label manufacturers, and orchestrated at the retail–consumer end through the retailers' integration of the ranges of products that they obtain from manufacturers. Moreover, retailers audit and specify the suppliers used by the own-label manufacturers and, in cases of long-term relations, operate on the basis of 'open accounts'. This 'monopsonistic matrix' is not easily described in terms of vertical constraint or quasi-vertical integration, in as much as they any given own-label manufacturer has a *number* of exclusive relations with retailers, and vice versa.

In relation to primary producers of fresh produce, direct purchase has led to a massive concentration of the supply base, and long-term, often exclusive, trading relationships between retailers and primary producers. The effect of this is to relocate competition from a process occurring between large numbers of primary producers, to competition within a periphery of contingent suppliers striving to become established in the core of long-term stable suppliers. The competition thus changes in nature, from a focus essentially on price to a focus on the *capacity* to produce consistently to the specification of supermarkets, across a differentiated product range and quality, over the long term.

Overall the effect of this shift in asymmetrical power is to create new forms of mutual dependence, of locked-in long-term trading relationships. It is clear that this is not a form of co-operation between similar economic agents under conditions of complementarity, but a form of co-ordination, often involving high levels of trust and also of mutual recognition of where the power lies. As a result, new units of competition have been developed which have displaced the old. In terms of definition of the market, there is a sense in which the residual independent small retailers are not being eliminated through competition with supermarkets (Competition Commission, 2000), *strictu sensu*, but are being superseded by a different form of retail organisation, with competition now occurring between superstore companies each with its particular supply chain, logistical system and productive innovation capabilities.

The re-channelling of competition
As a result of the formation of new market organisation and new units of competition, it can be seen that competition is squeezed to the ends and the peripheries of the supply chains, on the one hand, and between rival supermarket chains at a national scale, on the other. Within the supply chains, competition is replaced by the power to transmit and displace competitive pressures downwards from the 'front end'. So, *within* the units there is not so much direct competition between equivalent economic agents (own-label manufacturers, primary core exclusive suppliers), as an exercise in relative power to displace competitive pressure from the front end, *subject to the constraints of maintaining trust and partnership*.

New forms of innovation and distributed innovation process

The development of these new units of competition has involved, *pari passu*, the development of both new forms of organisation and innovation process, distributed across different agents within, and intersecting with, the supply chain. A striking example of such a process might be the way in which a major supermarket orchestrated the development and introduction of biological pest controls in southern Spain with a biotechnology company, which produced the beneficial pests, the tomato growers, and the training and technical support bodies in the region. It is obvious that such an innovation process requiring co-ordination between a number of diverse agents *by a retailer* involves a quite different form of trading relationship between those agents than in earlier retailing epochs. An equally striking example is the way in which retailers combine with an exclusive own-label manufacturer, TV chefs, and *chic* metropolitan restaurants, to deliver a constant stream of fashion-following-and-setting products onto the supermarket shelf. The own-label exclusive trading relationship, by giving secure market access to the manufacturers, and rapid lines of communication, reduces the time from concept to market from about two years to as little as four weeks. Consequently, compared to the typical innovation style of a major branded manufacturer normally launching four or five new products per year, who has to secure market access and presence through advertising and many other sunken costs, the own-label manufacturer normally launches over 1,000 products, many of them with a short lifecycle. In this latter style of innovation, the new products are effectively creating a new consumer food market, of different demand characteristics, rather than simply copying and undercutting branded products within the same market segment.

Conflict between formal and non-formal norms of competition

In 1999 the Office of Fair Trading referred the grocery retailing sector to the Competition Commission, to determine whether a monopoly existed within the sector, whether a monopoly situation was being exploited, and whether the monopoly, if it existed, operated against the public interest. The terms and formal norms of the competition inquiry were based on assumptions about the nature of competition which belong to a different structure of markets and organisation of economic agents, still largely concerned with price competition, measured by 'the shopping basket' (Office of Fair Trading, 1997). Thus, the problem was identified in terms of whether competition existed 'in catchment areas where consumers have little choice of supermarkets' and that their 'power may become exploitative' in relation to their suppliers (in reference to the Competition Commission, November 1999). Yet, on the one hand, superstores require catchment areas, which, if not exclusive, provide a secure breadth and depth of aggregate demand. Clusters of small independent retailers offering similar products in close proximity in a given highstreet reflects a particular organisation of the retail market, and a similar geographical arrangement for superstores would be unsustainable.

On the other, supply chains dominated and orchestrated by retailers, with long-term insiders and contingent outsiders, comprise the basis on which supermarkets have developed the distributed capacity to deliver an entirely new product range and style of product innovation. We have seen how the perhaps bizarre matrix of trade between own-label manufacturers and large retail multiples defies normal categories of cartelisation, vertical constraint or integration. Thus, we are witnessing a conflict between new instituted non-formal norms of competition and existing, 'anachronistic' formal norms of competition (Competition Commission, 2000). That is not to say, of course, that the outcome of the conflict is one in which the 'new' will prevail over the 'anachronistic', especially if the latter facilitates the entry into the market of a new discount-oriented, price-focused, retail model following Wal-Mart's acquisition of Asda.

Conclusion

The rise in the relative power of UK supermarkets has been given as an example of how the restructuration of a sector has resulted in new forms of competition as an instituted economic process. This analysis of forms of competition in terms of a number of interrelated dimensions has focused on the *processes* of the institution of competition, rather than classifying or defining types of competition. The interest of the case of UK supermarkets is not so much that it represents the result of a particular historical institution of competition (which may or may not last, spread or contract), as that it reveals processes of transformation from one form of competition to another, and the dynamics of that transformation. Perhaps the most significant aspect of this analysis is that a particular norm of instituted competitive process is the outcome of this multi-dimensional restructuring, rather than *the outcome of competition itself*. A process of competition is the historical *result* of the transformations of markets, the formation of new units of competition and of new scales of markets, the re-shaping and creating of new classes of economic agent with new asymmetries of power and mutual dependence, and an interaction between formal and non-formal norms of competition, rather than an independent, *sui generis*, dynamic force. With varieties of capitalism go varieties of competition, and explanations must look to dynamics and processes of variation.

Notes

1 'Ultimately, rivalry must evolve beyond cost to include differentiation' (Porter, 1998a, p. 213).
2 'Viewing a group of companies and institutions as a cluster highlights opportunities for co-ordination and mutual improvement in areas of common concern without threatening or distorting competition or limiting the intensity of rivalry' (Porter, 1998a, p. 205).
3 This view has been further developed in an analysis of the historical comparative

advantage held by regionally developed capabilities, and new modes of productive organisation exemplified by Boston's Route 128 (Best, 2001). See also chapter 9, this volume.

4 The focus is also on vertical constraint in supply chains, the subject of further discussion below.

5 To take another classical sociologist, Simmel, it is possible to envisage forms of competition which, far from acting to the detriment of others, simply spur others to produce greater variety (Swedberg 1994, p. 272). That conception is one which almost presupposes growth, an expanding market, which does not reside in efficient allocation of existing resources, with some losers and some gainers. In ways which seem to foreshadow Porter's 'positive sum' world of potential winners, this 'benign' and 'emulatory' competition in exchange relies on productive capacities for growth lying outside exchange.

6 'The human economy, then, is embedded and enmeshed in institutions economic and non-economic' (Polanyi, 1957, p. 250). Note here the ambiguity of human economy being embedded in *economic* institutions.

7 'The electric utility industry was born not out of Benthamite Equations or optimising rationality, but longstanding friendships, similar experiences, common dependencies, corporate interlocks, and active creation of new social relations. Samuel Insull and his circle of collaborators socially constructed their firms in similar ways, and then promoted a system of industry governance and template diffusion. They drew upon their local and national contacts to re-frame the market and the political system in ways that pressured utility firms toward technical, organisational, economic and legal conformity' (Granovetter and McGuire, 1998, p. 167).

8 'The actor's ontology is variable: his or her objectives, interests, will and thus identity are caught up in a process of continual reconfiguration, a process that is intimately related to the constant reconfiguration of the network of interactions in which he or she is involved' (Callon, 1998, pp. 252–3).

9 'In this "hot" world, which is becoming increasingly difficult to cool down, the work of economists is becoming ever more arduous because the actors they are tracking are faced by non-calculable decisions' (Callon, 1998, p. 263). He argues that societies are increasingly 'hot' in this sense, because of the role of rapid innovation, and in a quite technoscientific deterministic fashion suggests that what makes societies 'hot' is that 'technosciences . . . cause entanglements and networks of interdependencies to proliferate at their leisure – the market must be constantly reformed and built up from scratch' (*ibid.*, p. 266).

10 'The anonymous market of neo-classical models is virtually non-existent . . . Transactions of all kinds are rife with social connections . . . ' (Granovetter, 1985, p. 495).

11 As suggested in a preliminary way by Swedberg (1994, pp. 273–4)

12 Most notably analysed by Marx, *Capital*, Vol. 1.

13 This is not to say, of course, that capital and labour factor inputs cannot be substituted for one another on occasions, depending on the relative costs of such factor inputs.

14 Best characterises the Marshallian district as one of static complementarities, as against New Competition dynamic complementarities arising from continual mutual enhancement of dissimilar but complementary capabilities (1990, p. 235).

15 To stress the multi-dimensional aspect of such competition, there can be different scales of product, labour, and capital market competition at play simultaneously.

16 Braudel's 1982 work exemplifies a long duration approach to the historical formation of different scales of market formation.

17 For example the International Institute of Management Development's *World Competitiveness Yearbook* (2000) uses a battery of different measures to rank nations in terms of how nations provide 'firms with an environment that sustains the domestic and global competitiveness of the firms operating in their borders'.

18 And indeed as a response to shifts in dominant economic orthodoxies.

19 This illustrative example is based on research undertaken between 1997 and 2000 which used the tomato as an empirical probe to explore the relationships occurring in supply chains and markets, and the way these shaped innovation processes. Interviews were conducted along the length of the chain, and in the networks surrounding different nodes of the chain. Seed manufacturers, biotechnology companies, scientists, own label and brand manufacturers, supermarkets, wholesale markets, logistics companies, importers, and a number of other key players were interviewed during the course of this research.

References

Anderman, S. (1997), 'Commercial co-operation, international competitiveness and EC competition policy', in Deakin, S. and Michie, J. (eds), *Contracts, Co-operation and Competition. Studies in Economics, Management and Law*, Oxford, Oxford University Press.

Arighetti, A., Bachmann, R. and Deakin, S. (1997), 'Contract law, social norms and inter-firm co-operation', *The Cambridge Journal of Economics*, 21(2), pp. 171–96.

Best, M. H. (1990), *The New Competition. Institutions of Industrial Restructuring.* Cambridge, MA, Harvard University Press.

Best, M. H. (2001), *The New Competitive Advantage. The Renewal of American Industry*, Oxford Oxford University Press.

Braudel, F. (1982), *The Wheels of Commerce. Civilisation and Capitalism*, London, Fontana, Vol. 2.

Callon, M. (1998), 'An essay on framing and overflowing: economic externalities revisited by sociology', in Callon, M. (ed.), *The Laws of the Markets*, Oxford, Blackwell, pp. 244–69.

Competition Commission (2000), *Supermarkets. A Report on the Supply of Groceries from Multiple Stores in the United Kingdom*, London, HMSO.

Deakin, S., Goodwin, T. and Hughes, A. (1997), 'Co-operation and trust in inter-firm relations: beyond competition policy?', in Deakin, S. and Michie, J. (eds), *Contracts, Co-operation and Competition. Studies in Economics, Management and Law*, Oxford, Oxford University Press.

Deakin, S., Lane, C. and Wilkinson, F, (1997), 'Contract law, trust relations, and incentives for co-operation: a comparative study', in Deakin, S. and Michie, J. (eds) *Contracts, Co-operation and Competition. Studies in Economics, Management and Law*, Oxford, Oxford University Press.

Deakin, S. and Michie, J. (eds) (1997), *Contracts, Co-operation and Competition. Studies in Economics, Management and Law*, Oxford, Oxford University Press.

Deakin, S. and Wilkinson, F. (1995), *Contracts, Co-operation and Trust: The Role of the Institutional Framework*, Working Paper No. 10, ESRC Centre for Business Research, University of Cambridge.

Dei Ottati, G. (1994), 'Co-operation and competition in the industrial district as an organisation model', *European Planning Studies*, 2, pp. 463–83.

Fulconis, F. (1999), 'Les "structures en réseau": nouvelle forme de concurrence', in Krafft, J. (ed.), *Le Processus de Concurrence*, Paris, Economica, pp. 202–19

Garcia, M.-F. (1986), 'La construction sociale d'un marché parfait: le marché au cadran de Fontaines-en-Sologne', *Actes de Recherche*, 65, pp. 2–13.

Gereffi, G. and Korzenewecz, M. (1994), *Commodity Chains and Global Capitalism*, Westport, CT, Praeger.

Granovetter, M. (1985), 'Economic action and social structure: the problem of embeddedness', *The American Journal of Sociology*, 91(3), pp. 481–510.

Granovetter, M. (1992), 'The sociological and economic approaches to labour market analysis: a social structural view', in Granovetter, M. and Swedberg, R. (eds), *The Sociology of Economic Life*, San Francisco, Westview Press.

Granovetter, M. and McGuire, P. (1998), 'The making of an industry: electricity in the United States', in Callon, M. (ed.), *The Laws of the Markets*, Oxford, Blackwell, pp. 147–73.

Harvey, M. (2000), 'Systemic competition between high and low "social cost" labour: a case study of the UK construction industry', in Clarke, L., de Gijsel, P. and Janssen, J. (eds), *The Dynamics of Wage Relations in the New Europe*, Boston, MA, Kluwer Academic Publishers.

Harvey, M., Beynon, H. and Quilley, S. (forthcoming), 'Processes of variation: how capitalism appropriated the tomato', in Harvey, M. and Beynon, H. (eds), *Capitalism or Capitalisms? Approaches to Varieties of Capitalism*, Manchester University Press.

International Institute for Management Development (2000), *World Competitiveness Yearbook*, available online: www.02.ind.ch/wcy.

Jefferys, J. B. (1954), *Retailing Trading in Britain 1850–1950*, Cambridge, Cambridge University Press.

Krugman, P. (1994), 'Competitiveness: a dangerous obsession', *Foreign Affairs*, 73(2), pp. 28–44.

Lane, C. (1997), 'The social regulation of inter-firm relations in Britain and Germany: market rules, legal norms and technical standards', *The Cambridge Journal of Economics*, 21(2), pp. 197–217.

Office of Fair Trading (1997), *Competition in Retailing*, prepared by London Economics, Research Paper 13, London, HMSO.

Polanyi, K. (1944), *The Great Transformation. The Political and Economic Origins of Our Time*, Boston, MA, Beacon.

Polanyi, K. (1957), 'The economy as instituted process', in Polanyi, K., Arensberg, C. M. and Pearson, H. W. (eds), *Trade and Market in the Early Empires*, New York, Free Press, pp. 243–70.

Porter, M. E. (1985), *Competitive Advantage: Creating and Sustaining Superior Performance*, New York, Free Press.

Porter, M. E. (1998a), 'Clusters and competition', in *On Competition*, Boston, MA, Harvard Business Review, pp. 197–288.

Porter, M. E. (1998b), 'Competing across locations', in *On Competition*, Boston, MA,, Harvard Business Review, pp. 309–47.

Richardson, G. B. (1972), 'The organisation of industry', *Economic Journal*, 82, pp. 883–96.

Swedberg, R. (1994), 'Markets as social structures', in Smelser, N. and Swedberg, R.

(eds), *The Handbook of Economic Sociology*, New Jersey, Princeton University Press, pp. 255–82.

Swedberg, R. (1998), *Max Weber and the Idea of Economic Sociology*, New Jersey, Princeton University Press.

Swedberg, R. (forthcoming), 'Max Weber's sociology of capitalisms', in Harvey, M. and Beynon, H. (eds), *Capitalism or Capitalisms? Approaches to Varieties of Capitalism*, Manchester University Press.

Weber, M. (1968 [1922]), *Economy and Society. An Outline of Interpretive Sociology*, ed. Roth, G. and Wittich, C., New York, Bedminster Press.

Wrigley, N. and Lowe, M. (eds) (1996), *Retailing, Consumption and Capital. Towards the New Retail Geography*, Harlow, Longman.

5
Markets, materiality and the 'new economy'

Don Slater

Introduction

The contemporary 'cultural turn' in thinking about economic processes has been deeply bound up with narratives of 'dematerialisation'. We might start from Veblenesque stories of status symbols, and proceed through semiotic stories of ideologies and codes, through tales of post-industrial societies and service economies, through post-Fordist segmentation and lifestyling and finally on to knowledge, information or 'weightless' economies, 'new economies', global brands and digital commodities. Indeed, Mark Poster's *What's the Matter with the Internet?* (2001) declares a turn into 'linguistic capitalism', and his title clearly identifies the issue at hand: the dubious materiality of contemporary social reality. The story is always the same: the processes, factors and outputs of economic processes are to be understood – increasingly – in terms of meanings, signs and cultural processes.

'Dematerialisation', however, rests on a dubious distinction that has plagued much social theory: the distinction between objects and signs. This distinction equates 'materiality' with the physicality, or physical properties, of goods and social objects. It then contrasts this physicality with a 'something else' – meanings, signs, culture, desires, identities, services, information or knowledge. These are then regarded, firstly, as non-physical (hence having quite different kinds of social properties); secondly, as additive (a later accretion or layering of physical reality); and, finally, as historical (things have become *more* immaterial, or immaterial things have become *more* socio-economically central today).

The argument proposed in this chapter is that characterisations of 'new economy' that are based on the idea of dematerialisation are problematic because the distinction on which they are based misrepresents the issue of materiality. A historical account of socio-economic change which argues that 'things' have become 'less material' assumes that they were somehow more, or more transparently, material in the past, an argument that is contested by most research in areas such as sociology of consumption, material culture and science and technology studies. Indeed, as the next section argues, notions of materiality based in the object–sign distinction are generally not properly social or historical accounts at all: they are propounded in relation to ethical, philosophical and methodological concerns. What is required is a more adequate social ontology: an account of what I will call 'processes of materialisation', of the social processes by which things come to be treated as things in the social world – whether they are commodities, brands, technologies, or information.

From this perspective, 'materiality' is not a matter of physicality but rather of what might be called 'social thingness', rather close to the Durkheimian notion of 'social facts': under what conditions are we able to treat things in the world as objects – durable, stable, external to individuals, with determinate properties and relations to other objects? In answering this kind of question, we cannot look to the *a priori* physicality of things to guarantee their social materiality; nor does the meaningfulness of things necessarily render them unstable or immaterial. To the contrary, this question points us to the social processes and conditions through which things are stabilised as social materialities, or destabilised, reconfigured, problematised. If 'dematerialisation' has any meaning it is not as a condition of becoming 'merely a sign'; rather it is a condition in which the social agencies and processes that previously held an object stable – held it together as both physical entity and as meaning, inseparably – no longer do so. And it is the reasons for the changes in these conditions – not supposed changes in the nature of social objects themselves – that needs to be understood.

Hence, the third section of the chapter tries to think through current socio-economic changes – such as the idea of a 'new economy' – in terms of transformations in these conditions of stability and instability, in the processes of materialisation that characterise the contemporary landscape. This might be called an exercise in 'commercial ontology': how might we understand the changing materialisations of transactable objects? How might we understand the conditions of their materialisation in terms of stability and destabilisation? The conclusion will be that many widespread claims about 'new economy' may well be correct, but only if we abandon the notion of dematerialisation that arises from the object–sign distinction. Indeed, we can give better accounts of these developments through the filter of stabilisation–destabilisation: it is not that commercial objects have become more like signs, but that things in general have become sites of intense social and economic contestation such that they have become increasingly provisional and incipiently unstable as materialities.

Materiality, physicality and stability

The first task is to understand the various strategies used to 'black box' goods as stable objects within economic and cultural theory, and to understand what kind of game is being played through those strategies. In both economic and cultural theory, the social object oscillates wildly between an absolute, pregiven 'thingness' and an equally absolute indeterminacy, when it is treated as a sign. It is as if objects have to be 'black boxed' for fear that, once opened, they will behave more like a Pandora's box, issuing formless spectres.

Goods and markets in economic thought

It is in relation to markets that goods are most obviously conceptually stabilised within economic thought. (For a full discussion of the argument presented in this section, see Slater, 2002.) In everyday language, we define markets as markets *for* particular goods: there are markets *for* consumer electronics, or cars, or clothes. Similarly, marketing directors or financial analysts are concerned with futures markets or housing markets. And this is fundamental to both conventional economics and critical economic dis-courses: markets are delineated by virtue of their containing goods that are considered similar enough to be substitutable for each other and hence can be understood as competing with each other. The very notion of a market therefore depends on an anthropology of goods – the boundaries of markets follow the categorisations of things. But it is a frozen anthropology. Within economic analysis categorisation is not a process but a presumed background that provides a stable framework within which market analyses can be carried out. To some extent, this is a methodological manoeuvre that is sup-ported by a variety of methodological devices which allow the analyst to take 'things' for granted. 'Utility', for example, abstracts from cultural processes to a quantitative common denominator. Demand curves, frozen in time, erase all changes in the properties of goods and in the nature of needs and desires (Lancaster, 1971). The conceptual and disciplinary distinction between formal and substantive rationality permits economics to detach formal analysis from any knowledge of changing consumption cultures, and allocates the latter to external disciplines such as sociology, psychology and anthropology (Fine and Leopold, 1993; Slater, 1997).

At the same time, however, such manoeuvres are clearly tied to an underly-ing ontology, even a cosmology: the conventional approach is to regard the commercial object as an entity defined by a bundle of need-satisfying proper-ties, glossed as 'utilities' or 'use-value'. It is therefore part of an essentially rela-tional formulation – a relationship of 'use' – and therefore something that only makes sense as a subject–object relationship. Indeed, the framework of eco-nomics is more akin to epistemology than ontology: it concerns the use of informed reason to manage an object world. It is hardly surprising that an issue which has fatally dogged Western philosophy – the separation and then attempted reconciliation of subjects and objects – is not going to be resolved by economists. They instead veer between two unsatisfactory alternatives both of which bracket processes of materialisation. Firstly, *naturalisation* – needs and goods are effectively treated as natural, rational, given or taken-for-granted; assumed needs are associated with the assumed properties of things. Secondly, *subjectification* – needs and objects are both matters of perception and opinion.

Social materiality is detached from social process, either by taking it as given or by rendering it arbitrary. Each strategy achieves a stabilisation of goods as things that establishes the market as a stable methodological object of knowledge and a presumed framework of normative social action. And yet this assumption of stable homogenous goods runs counter both to common sense and to actual economic practice. Firstly, we know not only that goods change over time in a physical sense (innovation), but that perception of goods changes, and along with this our sense of 'what is the same as what'. Hence markets are not stable structures if only because our anthropology of things is not a stable structure but an evolving and conflictual cultural dynamic. Moreover, economic actors – today functionally differentiated into institutions such as advertising, brand consultancy, design – may place the conjoint redefinition of goods and markets at the very centre of market practices: marketing, for example, is specifically dedicated to altering relations of sameness and difference for competitive advantage. Far from competition presuming the stability of things, destabilisation is central to conceptualising and conducting competitive strategies.

Secondly, aggregation is a fiction: only if there was an exact fit between every individual need and every good could we regard any collection of goods to be *the same* for every consumer (Klein and Leiss, 1978). This is anthropological nonsense: people need to interpret goods (and usually do so collectively, not individually) in order to assimilate them into their consumption. To the extent that economic actors – producers or consumers – are indeed able to aggregate things, it is precisely on the basis of the cultural reasoning through which they establish (and dispute) provisionally stable categorisations.

This is not to say that goods and their categorisations are always unstable and that therefore market structures, enduring competitive relations and meaningful aggregation are impossible. There are everyday reifications that fit economic analysis reasonably well (for example, a financial analyst looking at the car market in global terms; or a consumer negotiating a category such as chewing gum). We need to understand both stability and destabilisation, and the conditions, processes and agencies that structure their relationship. The point rather is that the instability of goods is always an inherent property of their social being, and can be mobilised by economic actors as a resource in their production, exchange and consumption. The problem is that the assumption of stable goods and stable markets – inscribed in the very definition of a market – blind us to the dynamics of stabilisation and destabilisation.

Cultural theory
The stabilisation of things, therefore, needs to be understood as a conceptual and practical strategy rather than in terms of stable physicality, or the loss of stability through loss of physicality. Analysts and actors are engaged in strategic games of constituting and deconstructing social materialities. The objectifications that arise are always provisional and contestable; their durability resides in a broad range of social conditions and balances of social powers. It cannot be guaranteed by physicality; but neither does 'culturalness' necessarily entail destabilisation or the loss of social materiality.

The relationship of physicality to object stability in cultural theory parallels moves along the axis of the distinction between 'objects' and 'signs'. Like the distinction between naturalisation and subjectivisation strategies in economic thought, 'object' and 'sign' denote two different ways of fleshing out, or filling up, the empty space left by the qualitative indeterminacy of objects and needs. However, the object–sign distinction also emerges out of a longer and relatively autonomous history of thinking about social objects. It is generally bound up with moral and philosophical critiques rather than analyses of social processes. On one side of the object–sign distinction there is the presumption that both things and needs *can* arise from a natural order, in which they directly and transparently correlate with one another. This posits a Gold Standard in object relations – usually located in a romanticised organic community of the past – in which objects could be construed as natural entities (or humanly produced ones with natural properties) that functionally or rationally answer to needs which are themselves regarded as natural. If these needs are not defined as actually physical (food, shelter, clothing), they are defined as if they were (for example, a natural need for love, security, specific social skills). This view begins with a long pre-modern moral–religious tradition of asceticism and restraint (for example, critiques of 'luxury': see Sekora, 1977; Berry, 1994). It is continued into a Romantic tradition that posits a past or future harmony of objects and needs outside of the diremptions of capitalist modernity (for example, Marx's 'natural metabolism' between man and nature posits an ideal social formation based on use value). We can similarly cite what Veblen (1898–99, 1990) termed the 'instinct for workmanship' (a functional transformation of nature in relation to real needs that constitutes his ultimate critical standpoint on the 'invidious' sociocultural system of industrial manufacture and consumption); Marcuse's 1964 critique of false needs that arise from the commodity form; or Bourdieu's 1984 appeal to a 'taste for necessity' that sentimentally stands the poor in opposition to the symbolic violence of bourgeois culture. (Barthes 1986 uses the same argument in the postscript to *Mythologies*.)

It is against this backdrop that 'signifying properties' of goods (and that motility of needs) might be regarded as both separable and relatively disreputable: as signifying, needs and goods lose their anchorage in a moral–existential objectivity, and become the playthings of commodity forms, status competition, ideology, ethical relativism. The common denominator is invariably a charge of arbitrariness. The stability of objects and needs is not studied as a social outcome but is asserted as a normative standard; the presumed dematerialisation of contemporary objects and needs, on the other hand, is investigated as a pathology. Even in relatively neutral constructions of this distinction (for example, Douglas and Isherwood, 1979) the informational uses of goods can be analysed entirely separately from their functional order.

Of the many problems with the object–sign distinction, the one that most concerns me here is that it presupposes the answer to the very question it is meant to be asking: what counts as an 'object' or a 'thing' or a 'function'

under specific social conditions? It is not simply that the very notion of a
'function' has to be meaningfully constructed (Sahlins 1976 still provides the
most comprehensive statement of that position); or that 'cultural' entities are
capable of both highly durable and objectified materiality. The basic problem
is that adopting the standard of brute physicality produces an oscillation
between crude things and hyper-sophisticated signs. Baudrillard is probably
the most extreme exemplar of that analytical structure: his rigorous critique
of the mythology of use-value results in the loss of all materiality from the
social world and the reduction of all sociality to the arbitrary play of signification. The infamous result is a vortex of signs, or an ecstasy of communication, that precludes any object stability, any possibility of social materiality in
the sense employed here.

What is lost in-between objects and signs are the socio-cultural practices
by which things are constituted and recognised as things in the first place.
Much like the subject–object relations that characterise economic thinking,
the object–sign distinction is essentially epistemological. The questions that
concern it are not about the processes by which we make our world but those
by which we can guarantee correct knowledge of it: to what extent are object
relations governed by a correspondence between the real properties of physical things and the real needs of humans? To what extent are people capable
– in pre-modern times, or within consumer cultures, or 'after the revolution'
– of functionally subordinating the things of the world to their human projects? (See Lash 1999 for a call to move from epistemology to an ontological
perspective concerned with how things are 'grounded' in lifeworlds.)

Black boxes: conceptual and practical stabilisation

As we have seen, there are diverse of motives for treating social objects as
'black boxes'. This bounding of the object has a philosophical status (it marks
off subjects and objects, and identifies objects in terms of their 'bundles of
properties'); it has an ethical status (it is a way of thinking about correct and
incorrect objects, needs and uses); and it has a clear economic function (it
marks off objects as discrete, singularised and therefore transactable entities
[Callon, 1998, 1999, 2002]).

We might contrast this situation with alternative frameworks such as the
perspective of material culture and objectification within anthropology and
consumption studies (for example, Miller, 1987; Strathern, 1990), and science and technology studies derived from Latour and Callon. What science
and technology studies has been particularly good at demonstrating is the
complexity and heterogeneity of elements that hold together these black
boxes (and which spring out when we open them), and their clear irre-
ducibility to an object–sign distinction. 'Black boxing' means treating social
objects as finalised entities with fixed boundaries that cut them off cleanly
from other objects and social processes on their outside and that endow them
with a taken-for-granted 'inside' that is assumed to account for their shape
and stability. However, when we open the black box, or crack the shell that

seemingly contains the object as a physical entity, we do not suddenly find signs and meanings (they were always there) but rather the heterogenous social networks that held the object in shape. For example, when we talk unproblematically about everyday objects like cars or pens or utilities (water or gas or electricity as reliable 'objects'), we 'black box' a social entity in a physical form. The example of utilities indicates how dubious this physicality is: we know that in turning on the cooker, we are not simply consuming a physical entity but rather we set in motion a socio-technical device (Callon, 2002) that stretches from, say, the North Sea through pipelines, regulatory bodies, market structures, ownership structures, retail practices, advertising, expert discourses, and much more. We also know that there is a liklihood that complicated definitional issues will arise at the boundaries of these objects and their uses. The idea of black boxing indicates that complex interwoven social systems of provision (which mix the physical and the non-physical indiscriminately) and potentially disputable categorisations of social things can be crystallised in the form of stable objects and needs. A car is not a car because of its physicality but because systems of provision and categories of things are 'materialised' in a stable form. Conversely, these stable forms can be destabilised in various ways, which does not mean they become somehow less physical but that they might be put together differently.

A useful analogy might be made with the semiotic concept of *découpage*: the idea of a stable object – like that of a stable signifier – involves making a cut or incision in the world, cutting out a set of relations and oppositions that are in reality continuous, and could be divided up quite differently. Destabil-isation (for example, coming up with the idea that electricity companies can sell gas) means returning to the continuity of systems and relationships and trying out alternative *découpages*. The problem with black boxing – as the analogy with *découpages* should suggest – is not that things and signs are never stabilised. As already suggested, they very definitely are. The problem is in hiding the process of production, and assuming that this stability arises from the object itself rather than from the agencies that cut it out and bind it together in particular forms. The further problem is that we have to understand the way in which actors use the possibilities and conditions of stabilising and destabilising things in structuring their actions, such as their competitive behaviour.

As already noted, this does not mean that social objects are always unsta-ble. We are constantly able to black box them in using or buying them on often quite stable markets. The move of opening or closing black boxes is a matter of the actor's perspective, intentions and projects, not the nature of objects. This is evident within corporate practice. An advertising or market-ing executive may spend a great deal of time thinking through the definition of an object and the structures that stabilise it precisely in order to destabilise the good and re-stabilise it in an optimal position within competitive and consumption relations. What should this mobile phone, for example, be sold as? A gadget, a status symbol, a practical necessity, an integral part of mobile information systems comprising PDAs, Internet and integrated messaging services? Sales staff may reconfigure the object in relation to each prospective customer.

Yet looked at from the perceptive of the corporate boardroom, or of a management consultancy, the mobile phone and its market may be considered relatively stable entities – indeed, as one part of an even broader context of continuity, the consumer electronics market. That is to say, there are real processes of abstraction as we move to higher levels of strategic planning at which specific markets – and the products they contain – can be regarded as stable and self-evident for all practical purposes. At that level, markets are also held stable by broad structures which are resistant to the interventions of single-market actors, and are therefore treated as given environments: for example, distribution and retail infrastructures, or the market categories of finance capital. We could in fact isolate a series of market levels – from corporate planning through brand management (dealing with broad markets) to product management (dealing with market segments), each of which treats the lower levels as givens. And yet the black box may be opened at the most global of levels, too. For example, we are currently witnessing the deconstruction of the very idea of a telecommunications market at the most global and macro of levels, a process through which even the most strategic players must question both objects and market structures. The convergence of mobile phones with PDAs (personal digital assistants) potentially creates new objects that realign older ones; new wireless interconnections between objects (for example, Bluetooth) potentially reconfigure systems in which they are embedded; unforeseen technical potentialities reconfigure competition, pricing and market frameworks (for example, Internet telephony, empowered by broadband, potentially merges all communications within a single information flow). Finally, we need to recognise that the 'black boxing' of, say, the mobile phone market by a financial analyst is not a neutral conceptual move: it has a determinate effect on the stabilisation of that market, of the individual products it 'contains' (i.e. which define it), and on retail structures and consumer practices.

Old and new economies: opening Pandora's Box

The preceding argument has aimed to show how current commercial ontologies bracket processes of materialisation. However, the issue of materialisation – or of stability–destabilisation – is not specific to any particular period or society. It cannot ground a historical argument. Trobriand islanders participating in a *kula* ring are as exercised by the materialisation of objects as stable social entities as are dot.com capitalists. They both have to deploy a total social repertoire of practices and institutions to ensure the *objectness* of what they transact. Moreover, we cannot distinguish *kula* rings from dot.coms on the basis of increasing role of signification or culture: the materiality of all their objects involves the same heterogeneity of elements and regulatory structures, in which physicality and meaning are not usefully separated out.

If we want to return to the issue of 'new economies', what we might look for – instead of an altered social ontology – are new forces and principles of stabilisation and destabilisation, and new ways in which issues of stabilisation–destabilisation are understood and reflexively incorporated into social and economic action. What is 'new' today, I want to suggest, concerns the extent to which the process of materialisation, and hence the dynamics of stability–destabilisation of objects, has become reflexively institutionalised and instrumentalised as a premiss of economic action and organisation. We can re-describe vast areas of corporate and consumer behaviour in terms of the opening and closing of black boxes in the interests of either competitive gain or cultural reproduction. Put this way, we open up the historical question of what new social conditions have opened up that historical path. I want to put forward three developments – not exhaustive but illustrative – that might answer this question. None of these is a new idea, to say the least: they are the stock-in-trade of numerous theories of late modernity, post-modernity or new economy. The point of this discussion, rather, is to show that these developments build up a plausible picture of new conditions of social materialisation but do so without reference to 'dematerialisation' or the object–sign distinction.

Detraditionalisation and pluralisation of styles of life

We commonly characterise modernity in terms of the loosening of social and cultural structures that – in pre-modern times – were fixed by juridical, religious and traditional structures. For example, studies of emergent consumer culture emphasise a destabilisation of both status and lifestyle: there is a new fluidity to material culture, as well as a new pluralism that requires 'choice' and problematises the taken-for-grantedness of the objects, lifestyles and relationships that fill everyday life (for example, Giddens, 1991). Critics of post-modern and late modernity perspectives (for example, Warde, 1994, 1997; Gronow and Warde, 2001) have been correct in pointing to enduring continuities and routinisations of consumption, commodities and status/class in everyday life, and even to a lack of anxiety or even reflexivity in much mundane consumption. Nonetheless, even that takes place against a backdrop of flux and destabilisation. The situation is probably best described in terms of Simmel's dynamics of objective and subjective culture: modern subjects, confronting an explosive objective culture under conditions of increasing atomisation and impersonality, oscillate between enervation and indifference, or between reflection and habit, or even modernity and tradition; nonetheless indifference, habit and tradition all take on different meanings – and instability – under modern conditions. At the same time, this unfixing and pluralising opens up commercial opportunities, which further ratchet up the new dynamism. For example, there is a routinisation and spectacularisation of innovation – not just the shock of the new, but the routine expectation of the new – in commercial as much as in cultural modernism.

The destabilisation of commodities that is part of these developments has nothing to do with a change in the nature of goods. There could, of course, be nothing more 'signifying' than a pre-modern sumptuary regulation such as the sanctity of the king's deer or the reservation of certain colours and cuts of clothing to guild orders or aristocracies; but equally there could be nothing less fixed – either in itself or in relation to status distinctions – than the material range of foods or clothing today. We can use a simple historical example to relate detraditionalisation to commercial ontology and market structures. Political economists like Adam Smith, Ricardo and Marx regularly used corn and cloth in their examples of market analysis, and in doing so they treated these goods as self-evident, unproblematic and uniform: classic homogenous, substitutable and therefore competing commodities. To some extent they did this as neo-classicals would, bracketing the object in order to treat markets as given structures within which they could analyse quantitative relationships. At the same time, this is odd for a perspective which was otherwise so sensitive to industrial histories of innovation. The additional factor is that corn and cloth were, in early modernity, stabilised by considerably more than methodological strategies. Even where there was already considerable innovation in these goods, or the ways in which they were processed, sold and understood, they were held in place by a range of regulatory structures. To be clear: they were fixed by regulation, not by the cruder materiality or physicality of a temporally earlier, less opulent or less 'cultural' epoch. The Edinburgh corn market down the street from Smith was not filled with generic 'corn', but rather with corn that was divided into varying grades of quality and price, differentiated into market sectors; moreover, it was customary to divide the market into different conventional periods – marked off by the sound of the market bell – during each of which sale was restricted to particular classes of consumers. These classifications were matters of custom and right – that is to say, they evolved over histories and were sanctified by time. Hence, for example, E. P. Thompson's 1971 classic account of eighteenth-century battles over the moral economy of grain markets is largely about the attempt to retain time-honoured anthropologies of things that were deemed legitimate and ethical by virtue of their historicity. Similarly, every known pre-modern market has a history of market law, market policing, and market punishments, much of which concerned questions of adulteration, weights and measures and other time-honoured ways of fixing standards, hence of stabilising goods (for example, Braudel, 1982). Establishing the legitimate comparability of things such that recognisable and legitimate market relationships can obtain is never guaranteed by the body of the object; rather, the body of object is produced by legitimate regulation (for a contemporary Internet-based example of the stabilisation of transactable things through social regulation, see Slater (2000 and in press)).

We need only look to the (super)market shelves down our own streets today to see that, if we are no longer able to speak unproblematically about corn or cloth, it is not because of a crisis of materiality but rather a crisis of regulation. More precisely, regulatory structures are themselves plural and problematical, no longer stabilised by time or custom and therefore are themselves unstable, provisional and contradictory. To take but one obvious set of examples: super-market shelves may contain organic foods, genetically modified foods, low-calorie and diet foods, frozen, dried or tinned foods, 'normal' foods from sources that are either unknown or (politically, nutritionally or otherwise) dubious. This fracturing of the object is obviously not just a matter of signs or brands: these categorisations are established and stabilised, or destabilised, disputed and redefined – as well as diversely understood – by a bewildering range of voices and institutions: legal and governmental regulators; scientific and expert voices with variable degrees of accredited legitimacy; consumerist associations; businesses and trade associations, consumer constituencies.

What differentiates today's supermarket from the corn market of Smith's day is a destabilisation that does not arise because goods are 'less material' but because the social materiality of the good has become a battleground under conditions of detraditionalisation and pluralisation. There is a wider range of alternative categorisations of goods; all categorisations appear provisional; and producers, retailers and consumers are all aware of both this diversity and its provisional character, and they see it as a legitimate object of their own interventions through which they stabilise or dispute categorisations of things.

Disembedded goods and system complexity

We could regard early modern corn and cloth as relatively embedded in a rel-atively enduring material culture. Although in the early modern corn market, corn could certainly be alienated as a commodity, its commodity status was considered subordinate to its status within material culture, which is precisely why, in Thompson's account, issues of moral economy and market regulation arose. By contrast, with the rise of modern market society, the spatial aggre-gation of dispersed local markets into regional, national and global markets means that objects have to be produced as disembedded and impersonal, non-local. Yet this is a highly contradictory process, and it accounts for much of the contemporary dynamic of object stability and instability. On the one hand, we might take the example of the rise of branded packaged goods (from the 1880s onwards, not the 1990s): here, we can see that the aggrega-tion of national markets was often associated with the packaging and brand-ing of traditional bulk commodities (for example, flour, or butter or bread). This allowed manufacturers' goods to be recognisable across localities but largely on the basis of traditional categorisations of things. And, indeed, as current debates about glocalisation indicate, it is a normal condition that goods sold across localities must nonetheless make sense within each locality, either because producers and retailers secure global understandings of their goods, or because they tailor their goods to particular localities, or because each locality is able to make its own sense of the goods.

At the same time, however, the disembedding of goods through long-distance trade means that fissures, conflicts and unevenness are opened up between the different levels and contexts in which goods are defined and categorised. Marketing discourses within producers and retailers must inevitably regard goods not as stable categories but as negotiable entities across highly diverse contexts. The material cultures from which these goods may originally have been drawn, or into which they are to be sold, become objects of instrumental calculation rather than sources of legitimate cultural authority. The point, again, is that this process cannot be understood in terms of a movement (or even a distinction) between the physical and the symbolic. An embedded good is held in place by both physical and symbolic structures, just as a disembedded one is. The issue is rather that the mechanisms by which goods are socially materialised – are given stable forms as objects and as categories – are distributed between processes, actors and interests operating at different spatial scales, and hence – yet again – the body of the commodity becomes both the site of contest as well as its prize.

Management and marketing organisation

The kinds of developments I have been examining are treated by economic and commercial actors both as problems and as opportunities, and, in devising strategies for managing them, those actors also intensify them. The potential destabilisation of social objects is both an inescapable condition of economic action and a way of reconceptualising business strategy. It has been a central axiom of management discourse since the mid-twentieth century (for example, the works of Peter Drucker) that businesses must not try to sell to consumers what they make, but rather to make what the consumer wants. We interpret this as reflecting a transition from a world of relatively stable material cultures and market relations (in which, despite innovation, manufacturers could think in terms of relatively self-evident object categories) to a world of increasingly unstable material cultures and market relations.

One symptomatic management and marketing term that responded to this situation is the 'product concept' or 'product definition', along with cognate terms such as differentiation, segmentation, positioning and market 'gaps' that related destabilised, problematic goods to equally unstable competitive relationships. The idea of a 'product concept' renders abstract the very idea of 'a good', making it a matter of definition and something that is produced through the employment of cultural calculation, information and communicative skills at the very centre of corporate strategy. But it is absolutely *not* contingent on the increasing abstraction, dematerialisation or cultural character of the goods themselves. Rather, 'product concepts' are modes of strategising, organising and integrating *everything* which has a bearing on the social materialisation of the object in any of its potential social forms. The product concept includes the material and symbolic properties of the objects as it emerges from design and production processes, from the understandings of retailers, sales forces and diverse consumer constituencies and from the full range of cultural intermediaries. It includes the competitive position of the good in respect of alternative goods and practices, and the financial, cultural and social parameters of (close and remote) competitive structures. And it includes the understandings of the good (as technology, sign, practice) within diverse material cultures. Strategising in terms of product concepts can mean trying out different definitions of the product to see which will be optimal in terms of particular consumer and competitive relations; and it can mean trying to assess which social and competitive relations are capable of being altered (through a range of marketing and other technologies) in order to optimally position a product that has been defined in a particular way. Finally, the product concept is a command discourse: it is a way of conceptualising and choosing the different things a given product could be; and it organises and integrates the corporate practices through which a firm attempts to materialise a given product in a given way by intervening in all the social processes through which things come to be given things. These corporate practices involve heterogenous technologies and objects of intervention (for example, design, packaging, perceptions, consumer practices, media environments, retail spaces) which have generally become the domains of functionally differentiated departments, firms and consultancies. These generally have to be co-ordinated – precisely what product concepts, as management tools, are meant to do.

This routine description of corporate practice – which can be fleshed out in terms of developments within firms, business schools and management discourses extending over at least a century – makes no reference to any shift in products from physicality to sign, however conceptual or abstract the process of defining these products may have become. Indeed, these developments build on potentialities in the nature of commodities which were as available in the eighteenth century as much as they are today (thus, Wedgewood's marketing operation, so often described as a proto-postmodern translation of objects into signs (e.g. by Wernick, 1991), could more easily be described in terms of product concepts as outlined here). The issue is rather that social ontology – seen from the firm's perspective of managing, in the interest of competitive advantage, the processes by which things are materialised as things – has become recognised as central to commercial practice, because it can no longer be taken for granted and because it has become acknowledged as the basis of more effective market behaviour. As a result, corporate intervention in these processes has become more reflexive, more rationalised and more institutionalised within corporate structures and divisions of labour.

The conclusion of this kind of analysis is quite simply that we do not live in a 'more cultural' economy, or a society of the sign, or an enculturated economy but that we do live in a world that has opened up the black box of the social object, institutionalising and rendering reflexive processes which were always incipient. Hence, we live in a world of increasing instability at the level of material culture, and one which is driven by strategies of stabilisation and destabilisation, by contests over the materiality of the social world itself.

An 'economy of qualities'?

Let me end with one final approach to these issues which is fruitful because it is both completely in tune with the analysis put forward here and yet retains some of the elements that I have been trying to critique. In a recent paper, Michel Callon (2002) offers the idea of an 'economy of qualities'. On the one hand, this refers to a process which is very like the process of social materialisation. Where this chapter talks of 'stability' and 'destabilisation', Callon talks of 'qualification' and 'requalification': Callon tracks the product through a gauntlet of institutional processes – within firms, regulatory bodies and consumer encounters with goods – over the course of which the object is endowed with different 'qualities', ever refined and contested between different parties. These qualities, moreover, are indiscriminate in respect of the physical or the symbolic; rather the focus is on the different technologies and metrics through which objects become determinate, and in terms of which they might eventually be regarded as more or less stable, though always provisionally (e.g., Callon distinguishes products – which denotes things in their relationship to the process of qualification–requalification – from 'goods', a term which connotes a sense of the object as more or less stable). Moreover, Callon is explicit about the implications of these processes for market structures: drawing on Chamberlin (1948), he argues that categorisations of goods are fundamental to market structures.

However, he does not delineate the full extent to which this has become operationalised as a competitive strategy within corporate practice; he is more concerned with the status of expert knowledges in the qualification–requalification process and hence with what he regards as the increasing reflexivity of markets as more explicit knowledges become involved. Callon (2002) regards reflexivity as the result (indeed the 'inevitable' result) of the usual move from a material or manufacturing economy to an economy of signs, or information, or services or – in this case – 'qualities':

> The key argument in this article is the suggestion that, in the economy of qualities, which can also be called the service economy, co-operation between scholars and economic agents and the constitution of hybrid forums [reflexive spaces of heterogenous debate over the structure of markets and goods] are inevitable, for the questions they raise are largely identical.

The bulk of Callon's analysis is concerned with the process of qualification (which could be treated, as in this chapter, in terms of a range of social conditions and practices), but Callon seems to wed this position to the conventional assumption that it is a historical change in the kinds of goods (services rather than manufactures) or in the composition of goods (more sign, less body) that produces increasing reflexivity and destabilised things. And yet this causal relationship is not substantiated. On what basis is it assumed that the greater importance of reflexivity and 'qualities' is the *result* of a move from manufacturing to services? Is it not just as plausible to argue in the other direction, that increasing reflexivity and qualification processes are the *cause* of changes in the kinds of goods or services that are offered over economic histories? Could it not be the case that increasing rationalisation of the possibilities inherent in all transacted 'things' (i.e. their potential destabilisation) – which arises from a vast range of contingent factors – has resulted in new processes of materialisation, or materialisation as a new and explicit battleground of market actors? Perhaps there appear to be more 'dematerialised' goods in the economy *because* the dynamics of stabilisation and destabilisation have become part of everyday social actions. And, finally, does not this form of explanation – reflexivity based on a move from goods to services – resurrect the distinction between objects and signs, or at least a division between the materiality and immateriality of objects, that Callon would everywhere else oppose? The problem is that Callon's account of historical change bypasses the central question (which the notion of an emerging 'economy of qualities' might otherwise partially answer): what are the diverse conditions under which processes of materialisation are carried out at different times?

The distinction between goods and services loomed very large in older accounts of cultural and economic transitions out of industrial systems into various formulations of a 'new economy'. It is obviously different from the object–sign distinction, but it equally obviously maps historical transitions on to a shift from material to 'immaterial' commodities, from the production and circulation of physical objects to the direct sale of commodified labour and social relationships. To be clear: the goods–services distinction is important and real in many respects. To use a standard textbook example, the different degrees of transportability of goods and services have a considerable bearing on foreign trade (although even here the distinction is not straightforward: not all goods are transportable – for example, buildings – and not all services are confined to a place – for example, insurance and financial services, particularly in the age of the Internet). However, from the perspective of materialisation processes there seems little reason to distinguish them. If, in the case of goods, we have to go beyond their physicality in order to consider how they become *socially* material, so in the case of services we have to go beyond their apparent intangibility to see how forms of labour and interaction (serving a meal, fixing a car) can be socially formed into discrete and transactable things.

Ironically, given that the movement from goods to services has grounded so many narratives of historical transition, we find that it is precisely movement in the reverse direction that was central to some of the earliest modern forms of commercialisation and marketisation, in the seventeenth and eighteenth centuries – the materialisation of services in the form of transactable goods. This is particularly clear in the commercialisation of leisure activities, which was crucial to early consumer culture. It was in this period that a range of sports (above all, horse-racing), entertainments (masquerades, pleasure gardens and local assembly halls) and spectacles (such as circuses and

theatres) were transformed from amorphous happenings into socially material things: they were re-located to purpose-built, materially bounded spaces
(for example, racetracks or assembly halls rather than streets or houses); they
were given temporal boundaries (fixed starting and stopping times, with
internal rhythms and event sequences that structured them as objects); and
they were rendered transactable through the sale of tickets or subscriptions
(which already presumed their materialisation as discrete social things). It is
hardly a giant step to thinking about modern tourism in the same terms.
These developments within services correspond closely to the dynamics of
singularisation and separation that Callon maps out in *Laws of the Market*
(1998) and 'The economy of qualities' (2002).

The idea that an event can be rendered a transactable thing is a prerequisite to its commoditisation and to the possibility of stable markets in these
goods. However, there is another and complementary possibility, and this
emerges from other aspects of Callon's analysis: that we need to think of
goods far more in the way we think of services, in terms of their service-like
properties. Callon, borrowing from Gadry, argues that in buying services we
are in effect leasing for a limited time the effective properties of a socio-technical network. In taking my car to be fixed at a garage, I am purchasing the
mobilisation of certain effects that I cannot or will not mobilise through my
own direct labour. From the perspective of materialisation, this relationship
depends on being able to 'cut out' (as in the semiotic *découpage*) or erect
boundaries around (and then to black box) a particular set of socio-technical
effects ('servicing my car'), so that it becomes a discrete and transactable
event/object, access to which is regulated through an act of purchase. This is
formally equivalent to buying a ticket to a sports event whose transactability
and utility both depend on its ability to mobilise quite specific capacities, but
not others (a recognisable football match, but not a riot, and hopefully not
an American-football-style extravaganza). And we could (and should) apply
the same analysis to objects (physical goods) which are supposed to be always
already discrete and bounded. I do not buy a car in the first place because of
its being-in-itself but because of its capacity to mobilise, by connecting with,
a complex amalgam of socio-technical systems with emergent properties.

The potentials for stability and instability are in principal the same in the
case both of goods and of services or events: as transport and communications systems change, as urban structures and regulations change, so does the
car (for example, certain trips are rendered unnecessary by the Internet, or
mobile phones change the way we co-ordinate urban movement). Conversely, the materialisation of the car in particular physical and meaningful
forms may stabilise or destabilise surrounding socio-technical systems (car
manufacturers, promoting their investments, buy and dismantle tram and
trolley systems).

The difference between a good and a service, from the point of view of
materialisation processes, is a very banal one. It is not materiality versus
immateriality, or thing versus action or event, but simply (as Gadrey, 2000,

argues) that purchasing a good normally means permanent transfer of ownership whereas buying a service is more like leasing or renting (I hire the restaurant chef to make me a meal; I do not actually buy him/her or the restaurant). They are different forms of alienating *things*, but the issue of thingness remains the same. The stability of goods and of services in terms of their perceived materiality does not arise from different properties of goods and services, any more than that of objects versus signs, but rather from precisely what concerns Callon (and this chapter): the contingent conditions under which social materialisation takes place, and the reflexivity and rationalisation through which economic and cultural actors avail themselves of the opportunities that arise from these conditions.

Finally, and perhaps ironically, it could be argued that far from it being the case that the goods–services distinction has *produced* increasing market reflexivity, the truth – to the contrary – is that reflexivity about stability and destabilisation in markets has been *eroding* the goods–services distinction. That distinction is possibly the first casualty, rather than the enduring cause, of contemporary economic change. Economic actors have become virtuosos in deconstructing and reconfiguring things, in giving any combination of social factors a form that is stable enough to allow transaction, at least for a limited period. This virtuosity is possible precisely because it does *not* discriminate between object and sign, between physical and cultural things – it is only concerned with materialising things as transactable entities.

As a final example, one might consider the most common exemplar of 'new economy' and dematerialisation: the brand. Without denying for a moment that a brand involves the production of a commanding and binding symbol, we also know that it is considerably more than that. The idea that Nike, for example, is exemplary of the 'new economy' because its property consists in cultural capital rather than ownership of factories is completely disingenuous. On the one hand, like any business of the last one hundred years or so, it is more than a brand: it is the organisation and co-ordination of a productive apparatus capable of delivering volumes of discrete material things (not just physical shoes but a stabilised social object: *Nike* trainers with all the design, physical materials, cultural processes and imagery which that involves). That is to say, Nike is a productive apparatus in precisely the same sense that Callon or Gadrey would define a service as the mobilisation of a socio-technical device (and which I would extend to all goods). And it is precisely the same deployment of product concepts as conceptual and practical organisations of production that I attributed to the emergence of management discourses over the twentieth century. Moreover, this form of organisation is not very different from the organising and re-branding role of retailers and mail-order firms either at the turn of the last century (which gave a considerable impetus to the whole development of branding) or in the 1980s, when they acted as pioneers of flexible production.

On the other hand, what has certainly changed, as I have argued, is both the increasing volatility of things – their shorter and more insecure social life –

and the extent to which corporate practices respond to this by institutionalising, intensifying and reflecting on this as a normal condition of business life
and competition. Early brands – along with the very idea of packaging goods
– were part of a process of stabilising goods (packaging, bearing a logo, divid-
ing bulk commodities into discrete objects with uniform quantities and qualities, underwritten by a nationally known and dependable manufacturer).
This is certainly still the case with brands like McDonalds and Coca-Cola
which promise a uniform experience anytime, anywhere. Yet that is hardly the
whole story, and certainly not for their managers: rather, the brand acts as a
container for the constant innovation necessary in today's markets. Brands
like Nike and McDonalds hold their objects stable at a level of abstraction
above the almost daily renovations and adjustments of their product lines.
Hence, some of the more interesting contradictions in the contemporary
economy are between the stability, even the stodginess, of the overall marque
(for example, Ford as a company) and the constant reconfiguration of products (individual Ford cars). To reiterate: the issue here is not that commodities have become dematerialised ('Nike is nothing but a logo') but rather that
their materiality is understood and managed in relation to a backdrop of pro-
found instability that constitutes the very premiss of business practice.

Conclusions

The argument presented here is not intended to conclude that nothing has
changed, that 'new economy' (or service economy, information economy or
any of the other labels with which I started) is a myth. It is rather an attempt
to put our search for 'what's new' on a firmer conceptual footing, one which
is not indebted to an untenable social and commercial ontology. This chapter is therefore offered as a reinterpretation of long-running themes within
social and economic analysis. We need not deny the evidently increasing
centrality – in both practice and perception – of conceptual processes in the
conduct of contemporary economic processes: the centrality of information
and communications, social skills, cultural knowledges and cultural intermediation, and all the other developments that have been noted in the many different formulations of 'new economy' over the post-war period. But we need
to understand these factors not in terms of an untenable social ontology but
rather in terms of the changing conditions under which social objects are
brought into being in the first place.

References

Barthes, R. (1986), *Mythologies*, London, Paladin.
Berry, C. J. (1994), *The Idea of Luxury: A Conceptual and Historical Investigation*,
    Cambridge, Cambridge University Press.
Bourdieu, P. (1984), *Distinction: A Social Critique of the Judgement of Taste*, Cam-
    bridge, MA, Harvard University Press.
Braudel, F. (1982), *The Wheels of Commerce*, New York, Harper & Row.

Callon, M. (ed.) (1998), *The Laws of the Market*, Oxford, Blackwell and The Sociological Review.

Callon, M. (1999), 'Actor–network theory – the market test', in Law, J. and Hassard, J. (eds), *Actor Network Theory and After*, Oxford, Blackwell, pp. 181–95.

Callon, M. (2002), 'The economy of qualities', *Economy and Society*, 31(2), pp. 194–217.

Chamberlin, E. H. (1948), *The Theory of Monopolistic Competition: A Re-orientation of the Theory of Value*, Cambridge, MA, Harvard University Press.

Douglas, M. and Isherwood, B. (1979), *The World of Goods: Towards an Anthropology of Consumption*, Harmondsworth, Penguin.

Fine, B. and Leopold, E. (1993), *The World of Consumption*, London, Routledge.

Gadrey, J. (2000), 'The characterization of goods and services: an alternative approach', *Review of Income and Wealth*, 46(3).

Giddens, A. (1991), *Modernity and Self-Identity: Self and Society in the Late Modern Age*, Cambridge, Polity.

Gronow, J. and Warde, A. (eds) (2001), *Ordinary Consumption*, London, Harwood Academic.

Klein, S. and Leiss, W. (1978), 'Advertising, needs and commodity fetishism', *Canadian Journal of Political and Social Theory*, 2.

Lancaster, K. (1971), *Consumer Demand: A New Approach*, New York, Columbia University Press.

Lash, S. (1999), *Another Modernity: A Different Rationality*, London, Blackwell.

Marcuse, H. (1964), *One-Dimensional Man*, London, Abacus.

Miller, D. (1987), *Material Culture and Mass Consumption*, Oxford, Blackwell.

Poster, M. (2001), *What's the Matter with the Internet?*, Minneapolis, University of Minnesota Press.

Sahlins, M. (1976), *Culture and Practical Reason*, Chicago, University of Chicago Press.

Sekora, J. (1977), *Luxury: The Concept in Western Thought, Eden to Smollet*, Baltimore, MD, Johns Hopkins University Press.

Slater, D. R. (1997), *Consumer Culture and Modernity*, Cambridge, Polity.

Slater, D. R. (2000), 'Consumption without scarcity: exchange and normativity in an internet setting', in Jackson, P., Lowe, M., Miller, D. and Mort, F. (eds), *Commercial Cultures: Economics, Practices, Spaces*, London, Berg, pp. 123–42.

Slater, D. R. (in press), 'Capturing markets from the economists', in Gay, P. D. and Pryke, M. (eds), *Cultural Economy: Cultural Analysis and Commercial Life*, London, Sage.

Slater, D. R. (in press), 'Making things real: ethics and order on the internet', *Theory, Culture and Society*, special issue: Sociality/Materiality.

Thompson, E. P. (1971), 'The moral economy of the English crowd in the eighteenth century', *Past and Present*, 50, pp. 78–98.

Veblen, T. (1898–99), 'The instinct of workmanship and the irksomeness of labor', *American Journal of Sociology*, 4.

Veblen, T. (1990 [1914]), *The Instinct of Workmanship and the State of the Industrial Arts*, New Brunswick, NJ, Transaction Publishers.

Warde, A. (1994), 'Consumption, identity-formation and uncertainty', *Sociology*, 28(4), pp. 877–98.

Warde, A. (1997), *Consumption, Food and Taste*, London, Sage.

Wernick, A. (1991), *Promotional Culture: Advertising, Ideology and Symbolic Expression*, London, Sage.

6
Between markets, firms and networks: constituting the cultural economy

Fran Tonkiss

Introduction

Cultural and creative sectors have come to represent key areas of growth within a number of regional and national economies, and figure prominently within arguments regarding the increasingly 'cultural' character of economic processes and the restructuring of market forms. An emergent cultural economy is also of critical interest for institutional analysis, and for a number of reasons. Firstly, such an analysis addresses very clearly the need to take culture seriously within the study of economic organisation – not simply in terms of seeing culture as a kind of 'padding' for economic activity, but as a sector of production, distribution and consumption involving distinctive organisational forms, market relations and competitive logics. Secondly, within the cultural field market actors, market segments and market commodities are constituted in innovative and often unstable ways. Thirdly, contemporary cultural industries are subject to a highly variable mix of markets, firms and networks as means of shaping economic processes and exchanges.

The discussion that follows traces key aspects of this governance mix for the constitution of a cultural economy, as the contingent nature of cultural products, cultural markets and cultural work puts into question certain established frames for analysing economic organisation.

Cultural industries make slippery analytic objects:[1] sectoral boundaries can be hard to define; 'firms' can be only loosely integrated, hidden, short-lived or very mobile (and often are all of these); product design, labour processes and work practices can change very rapidly, running ahead of the unwieldy analytic categories that lumber in their wake (see McRobbie, 2001). It is difficult to capture the range of products, the forms of knowledge and expertise, the business types and economic actors that constitute the cultural economy in different places and across different sub-sectors.[2] My concern here is to develop a number of conceptual and critical points relating to the analysis of cultural economies that may have extended relevance to the study of contemporary market relations, competitive processes and economic organisation.

The discussion begins with the problematic notion of 'cultural industries'. Such a category mimics the convention of defining industries on the basis of distinct outputs – indicating here a set of industries producing broadly 'cultural' products – in a context where more and more economic goods might be said to involve cultural or aesthetic content. In thinking about what is distinctly 'cultural' about the cultural economy, then, the discussion turns to the role of specialised knowledge in framing goods for cultural markets, and in constituting market segments themselves. The skilled deployment of technical expertise in tandem with economic nous and cultural knowledge appears as particularly crucial in a setting where demand for products and for labour can shift very rapidly. This has critical implications for the nature and the role of the firm. As the discussion goes on to suggest, the status of the firm as a site of organisational culture and collective knowledge is precarious in sectors where products, ideas and know-how quickly become dated, and as cultural workers adopt (by choice or necessity) a more 'detached' relation to employers. Increasing reliance on cultural–economic networks for the exchange of knowledge, for work, and for the promotion of shared work cultures can be seen as a kind of *hollowing-out* of the firm as an economic organisation, as its typical knowledge and cultural functions are taken up across an extended field of market or network 'non-organisations'.

Culture and economy – framing the cultural industries

The classification of distinct industrial sectors is an imperfect art, and the case of the cultural industries appears more problematical than many. In a context where the language of 'culture' has come to infect economic analysis, the notion of relatively coherent cultural industries can be seen as much as an effect of economic policy, academic discourses and market rhetoric as it is a reflection of institutional realities. Precisely what is to be considered 'cultural' in relation to economic activity is rather open to question. Since the 1980s, economic development strategies in a number of national contexts have placed increasing emphasis on the role of cultural goods and services in labour market growth, urban and regional regeneration, and foreign trade. Here, 'culture' is taken to refer to a specific domain of aesthetic and expressive production that is susceptible to commodification in economic terms[3] (see McAnany and Wilkinson, 1995; DCMS, 2001). Over the same period, theoretical accounts within economic sociology have focused not only on cultural production as an economic sector, but on the increasingly cultural content of wider production processes, of economic goods and services, and of economic life more generally (see Lash and Urry, 1994; du Gay, 1997; Ray and Sayer, 1999). Such arguments look to the symbolic and aesthetic practices, images and goods that enter processes of production, distribution and consumption in complex ways. In the most obvious sense, an enhanced role for design within manufacturing, product differentiation and marketing foregrounds the aesthetic content of goods that might not otherwise be seen as expressly *cultural* products. Consumption choices, meanwhile, are played out (within all the usual constraints of scarcity) via the informed calculation of cultural codes and symbolic associations. It follows that an enlarged field of cultural production and consumption gathers in an array of items – from foodstuffs or bedlinen to branded clothing and designer refrigerators – whose symbolic character is at least as important for market differentiation as are the functional claims that might be made for them.

On such an account, cultural industries are only a subset – if rather exemplary – of an extended range of economic processes that have an integrally cultural character. This complicates what it might mean to think about a discrete cultural economy, analytically separate both from a more general enculturation of economic life and from other sectors of economic activity. By convention, industrial sectors are defined on the basis of what they produce, or by the primary factors involved in production – such a convention renders different sectors quantifiable, comparable and, by extension, governable. Under that definition cultural industries are those engaged in the production or distribution of goods and services broadly deemed 'cultural', 'aesthetic' or 'expressive', further divisible into a number of sub-sectors based on different types of cultural output (see Pratt, 1997).[4] Of course such distinctions – within cultural industries as elsewhere – are artificial: there tends to be a significant degree of crossover between sub-sectors, and a high degree of diversity within them. A music venue, for instance, looks more like a theatre – in terms not only of its product, but also its organisational structure, labour process, skills' profile, market orientation and internal culture – than it does a musical instrument manufacturer's premises, even though both would be classed as members of a 'music' sub-sector. It depends on how you slice it. While the various outputs of art galleries, film production companies, graphics firms or costume designers may all be cultural products, the range of goods and services brought under the heading of 'the cultural industries' – from paintings to club nights to web-pages – and the kinds of labour processes involved – from craft production to performance to software programming – are extremely diverse.

The notion of coherent cultural industries in that sense sets a frame around an set of unstable processes, products and actors. As the art critic Adam Gopnik (1993, p. 166) has written:

> Only someone who has never actually seen an industry can imagine that the art world – with its small-scale, speculative, boom-and-bust economy, its discoveries and outrages – is one. An industry produces a standardised product for a more or less reliable mass market of consumers. The art world is not an industry. It isn't even a business. It is a carnival with a casino attached.

Gopnik was writing specifically (and ironically) against the notion of an 'art industry', but the remark resonates across the cultural industries more generally. If a 'carnival' air animates a great deal of political rhetoric and market boosterism about the creative economy, the latter's casino-like aspects have been only too evident in the variable fortunes of the first publicly floated Internet companies and the rapid burn-rates of others. But there is a further and more serious point to be taken here. Gopnik's conceit works by contrasting the volatile art market with *real* industries, defined in terms of standard outputs and the 'more or less reliable' markets for them. In these terms it is questionable, indeed, how far a set of distinct industries can be said to produce 'culture' in the same way that others produce automobiles or tobacco.

Markets and cultural knowledge

What are broadly grouped together within 'the cultural industries', then, consists of a range of institutions with a common orientation to a creative field of products and practices. However, different firms are involved in producing material and non-material outputs, operate in different markets, and take in a range of skills, services and corporate structures. One suggestive alternative to an output-based definition is to consider the knowledge capacities and organisational routines enfolded in different types of economic activity. 'Firms are in an industry', as Metcalfe (1998, p. 19) contends, 'by virtue of certain things that they know in common.' Such an approach places greater emphasis on labour processes and organisational cultures in constituting industrial sectors – and particularly on the forms of knowledge and skill that are reproduced therein – than it does on the nature of common outputs.

A process-based definition, foregrounding the role of economic actors and the knowledge exchanges between them, seems especially appropriate to the analysis of cultural industries. This has to do not only with questions of technical or creative expertise, but with a wider investment in forms of cultural knowledge. What brings multimedia companies, fashion wholesalers, record labels and set designers together under the umbrella of 'the cultural industries' is in part an orientation to cultural modes of knowledge, practice and distinction that shape the organisations themselves, that steer design and production, and that are closely linked to issues of marketing and consumption. While it may sound clumsy to say that certain industries 'produce' culture as others produce cars, the metaphor can be reworked to indicate how specific agents (individuals and firms) create or mediate cultural products and services for nascent markets. To think about culture as an economic product, here, is to consider how cultural goods, images and concepts are translated into marketable commodities by economic agents. The effect of such a 'production of culture', what is more, is not simply to re-frame certain ideas, expressive forms and aesthetic goods in commodity terms, but also to frame potential markets for them (cf. Callon, 1998). In the context of new media, Pratt (2000, p. 427) suggests that business start-ups are concerned not simply to find a niche in some broadly identifiable market, but simultaneously to 'imagine a market, a niche, and a product'. Supply and demand are 'co-constructed' (Callon, 2002) through the qualification and 'singularisation' of goods, and the positioning of potential consumers for them. Markets, market segments, and marketable products are mutually emergent within speculative processes of *market making*.

Knowledge has a critical role to play in these market processes. While the cultural economy is not unusual in placing a premium on knowledge, it is distinctive in drawing together forms of economic and cultural expertise in such an integrated manner. The competence of cultural workers as 'knowledge workers' bears not only on the conception and design of products and services, but also on the way these agents must work to anticipate trends, appraise tastes and inculcate preferences. Marketing and distributive functions therefore are not easily set apart, especially at the start-up stage, from technical or creative functions. These competences can be hard to distinguish not only because an emergent cultural economy includes numerous smaller businesses unable to support a pronounced division of labour, but because such a division of labour is meaningless in relation to the ways in which many goods and services are conceived, produced and marketed. A significant degree of crossover between technical, creative and marketing functions in new cultural sectors is given partly by the size of firms, but also by the unstable, short-lived or volatile nature of both the products and the markets for them. The tasks of designing cultural products and directing them to specific market niches form a process combining creative talent, technical skill, economic calculation and cultural knowledge. Knowledge and competences are deployed across processes of production and distribution, and are exchanged between actors and technical capital in a form of what Callon (2002) calls 'distributed cognition'.

Part of this knowledge work, furthermore, is done by consumers – as Metcalfe (1998, p. 29) points out, 'intelligent consumers are as much a part of the innovation process as intelligent suppliers'. Hodgson's call (1999b, p. 251) within institutional economics for a more serious engagement with culture focuses on the ways cultural factors shape economic preferences, as well as aiming to bring the culture of organisations into the purview of institutional analysis. In emergent cultural markets, these two dimensions are closely linked. The culture of the firm, as well as the content of its product, can help shape the preferences of its consumers. Organisational cultures – forms of representation and self-presentation, and values, language and symbolic codes – are not simply 'embedded' in the routines of organisations (especially of those which have not been around long enough to have developed any durable routines), but also are qualities to be strategically cultivated, marketed and de-coded by consumers.[5] In that respect new cultural sectors are exemplary of what has been termed an 'economy of qualities' – oriented towards the positioning and qualification of mutable products in highly protean consumer markets, and in which competition is driven by the hyper-differentiation of producers and of consumers, as well as of products (Callon, 2002; see also Metcalfe, 1998, p. 11; Scott, 1999, p. 808).

Firms and 'disentangled' labour

The labile character of cultural products and markets is reflected in the way that cultural enterprises do not necessarily or immediately constitute themselves as firms in a coherent or stable sense. It follows that a conventional business model is not always appropriate to the ways economic actors organise their activities in these sectors. It can be difficult, for example, to analyse business size in terms of employee numbers, or to capture the distinct functions of different workers, given the elastic employment practices of cultural enterprises, including the high degree of multi-tasking and doubling-up within smaller and newer businesses. Highly variable recruitment practices are dictated by specific labour processes as well as by the nature of products and markets, as businesses take on staff for given projects and events – for one night in certain music venues, for instance, to three- or six-month contracts in film and video production (Skills Observatory, 2000, pp. 5, 10). This is not exactly the same as freelance employment or 'consultancy' – at times it is closer to the seasonal work model typical of tourist or agricultural industries. In other contexts, workers are far more able to set their own employment terms, with contract and freelance work acting as a marker of labour market power rather than one of insecurity. That is most likely to be the case in fields such as multimedia and software programming where companies have difficulty in recruiting specialist staff, and confront high rates of turnover and dynamic, often international, labour markets (Skills Observatory, 2000, p. 5).

The labour market effects of this kind of skills' shortage are compounded by a strong freelance ethos in growth sectors where working outside a company's structure is seen as preferable – in both a financial and a cultural sense – to working inside one (see Pratt, 2000, p. 421). In certain fields of cultural production, at least, the language of flexibility does not appear simply to put a spin on processes of casualisation and insecurity. Rather, the market position of skilled workers in new media and related sectors is enhanced by the temporary nature of contracts and consultancies, in a field where products, ideas, technical solutions and forms of expertise can date very rapidly.[6] One should be wary, of course, of confusing adaptation with progress, of taking accommodation for innovation. As Richard Sennett (1998, p. 25) notes, when corporate wisdom cautions against becoming 'entangled' in long-term employment contracts, 'detachment and superficial co-operativeness are better armor for dealing with current realities than behavior based on values of loyalty and service'.

Such 'disentangled' labour sits at the top end of a labour market marked by varieties of casualisation. As such, it raises in high relief certain critical questions about the nature and role of the firm in emerging economic sectors. Ronald Coase's 1937 classic account turned on a contrast between the organised structure of the firm and a market of self-employed producers, each contracting freely with others under competitive conditions. One advantage of the firm over an ideal-type market lay in its ability to minimise the costs of transacting with any number of free agents, replacing the latter with employees whose productive activity was directed inside the firm itself. It is open to question how far cultural labour markets can be seen as markets of self-employed producers – as a real-world example, that is, of Coase's ideal-type. However, it is certainly the case that for a significant minority of skilled workers the contract for services has come to replace the employment contract *per se* (see Hodgson, 1999a). Such individuals contract with firms to provide given services, or enter into (more or less stable) relational contracts with other individuals via networks. Either way, the formal architecture of the firm is eroded or bypassed.

The cost to business of this kind of transacting is evident in the price some freelance workers are able to command for their services in cultural labour markets, and in the problems of uncertainty faced by firms lacking the in-house expertise to deliver on specific projects. What is less clear is how far working outside a firm structure allows 'disentangled' workers to retain control over the labour process. Both factors of course are relevant to the co-ordinating role of the firm: the ability to economise on transaction costs, and the ability to direct labour processes in line with its own ends. The contract for services in this way becomes a key instrument for regulating cultural work, but the degree of specification is problematical – as is the nature of ownership – when the 'products' involved are innovative, speculative or highly creative (see Lury, 1993). This adds something to Callon's notion of 'distributed cognition' across design, production and marketing functions, as concepts and goods are subject to forms of qualification and re-qualification that alter the terms under which contracts for services are entered. Here, an ethos of creativity can be a means of managing flexible labour processes, the open-ended nature of creative work and the unstable nature of creative products lending themselves to the 'reflexive' re-specification of original briefs. Long or erratic working hours, nail-biting deadlines, confused, poorly conceived and constantly changing briefs, all can be explained away as aspects of the mercurial nature of 'creativity' (see McRobbie, 2001). A creative ethos, in that sense, represents a cultural strategy for handling the social costs of transacting with workers who are expected to be flexible, if not exactly free, agents.

Other institutional economists (including Coase in his later work) expanded the social costs' account of the firm by emphasising the latter's role in capturing information and promoting knowledge. In its weakest version, such an argument points to firms' attempts to lock-in knowledge and information in the form of individual workers' expertise. A stronger version holds that the firm itself – *as an institution* – is the key locus of knowledge. It is firms, rather than the individuals within them, that really are knowledgeable – after all, 'it is firms, not the people who work for firms, that know how to make gasoline, automobiles and computers' (Sidney G. Winter, quoted in Hodgson, 1999a, at p. 199). This extended account sees the firm as more than a technical solution to transaction costs and problems of imperfect information. As a durable institution the firm is not merely constituted via contract, but reproduced via an organisational culture involving forms of knowledge and modes of learning. As Hodgson would have it: 'The advantage of the modern capitalist firm over market- or exchange-based alternatives may lie in its capacity to develop an integrated corporate culture to facilitate learning and the acquisition of specialist skills' (1999b, p. 246).

It follows that the shift to contracting in the cultural economy raises serious questions about the ability of firms to capture and promote knowledge. In a context where the increased complexity of production (especially in software and new media) places a premium on specialised skills, firms are at a disadvantage when forced to buy-in knowledge and expertise on a one-off or time-limited basis. The 'market problem', here, remains primarily 'an information problem' (Metcalfe, 1998, p. 12). Of course, this cuts in two ways: firms also can rapidly update knowledge by 'updating' knowledge workers in flexible labour markets. Either way, this kind of transacting for knowledge in markets has interesting implications for the nature of the firm. Long before the vogue for human capital in socioeconomic analysis, Veblen (1990) highlighted the value of institutions as sites of knowledge even over their value as sites of capital (see also the discussion in Hodgson 1999a, pp. 193–7). Technical, tacit and processual knowledge is reproduced within institutions as part of an organisational culture of rules, routines and norms. Institutions such as firms, moreover, are sites of collective knowledge as much as they serve to foster individual knowledge: the things that a firm knows are emergent from the individuals working within it over time, but ultimately are not reducible to them *as* individuals. It is this collective nature of institutional knowledge that a great deal of human capital theory downplays, emphasising the education and training of individuals over the role of corporate cultures. At the same time, the collective nature of institutional knowledge – the fact that it is firms rather than individuals that know how to make cars, or (to use Adam Smith's classic example) know how to make pins – comes under question in sectors where it is individuals rather than firms who know how to make new software applications.

Recent theories of the 'weightless economy' place heavy emphasis on intangible assets – knowledge, information, expertise and ideas that can be capitalised in various ways (see Quah, 1996; Cameron, 1998; Coyle, 1999; Leadbeater and Oakley, 1999; cf. Pratt, 2000). The value of such cognitive assets is especially salient for those 'weightless' firms that do not hold much in the way of the tangible – the spectre here is the failed dot.com, whose intangible assets turn out to be neither fungible nor exclusive (or, of course, are simply over-valued), and whose passing leaves nothing but a roomful of computers, a few potplants, and dizzying losses. Economic knowledge, however – if frequently more portable than some other economic assets – is rarely exactly 'weightless'. An institutional perspective, for one thing, points to the way that knowledge is embedded in organisations, often in highly material ways. Institutional knowledge is embodied in labour processes and practices, is reproduced through the organisation of spaces and facilities, and is distributed across technical components. Neither does the disentangling of workers from the institutional setting represent a decisive move towards weightlessness. The status of certain cultural workers as self-employed producers is given not only by their possession of intangible assets in the form of knowledge or skill, but often by ownership of their means of production (software, specialised equipment, etc.) – where in contracting for certain services, that is, firms are hiring-in both labour *and* capital. Labour processes in cultural growth sectors typically combine intensive human input with specialised technologies (Scott, 2000, p. 11). Indeed, it can be difficult in new media sectors to make a distinction between capital and labour, between technology and expertise, between tangible and intangible assets. In that context cultural workers might be thought of in terms of what Jean Gadrey (2000) calls 'socio-technical capacity' – a combination, as it were, of human with technical capital (see also Callon, 2002).

Network cultures

The contract for services, especially where this involves the purchase of 'socio-technical capacity', sits within a wider framework of network transactions that are characteristic of the cultural economy. Cultural economies tend to be organised around dense networks of small–medium enterprises, producing high degrees of interdependence, with larger firms networked in at certain points (see Lash and Urry, 1994, pp. 114–20; Scott, 2000, pp. 11–13). Contracts for services remain, it should be stressed, a form of market exchange, but one based on network relations that are both more and less formal than transacting in markets: more formal, in that relational contracts develop institutional and durable features that spill over the boundaries of the firm; less formal, in that social ties are an explicit and even necessary component of these arrangements. There is a pronounced overlap between labour markets and social networks within cultural economies; also between supplier markets and social ties (Pratt, 2000; Scott, 2000; Skills Observatory, 2000; McRobbie, 2001).[7] Of course, there are questions to be asked about the strength of these particular weak ties. The rather different and sometimes conflicting desires for 'disentanglement' on the part of cultural workers and employers means that social ties can be distinctly attenuated, provisional or instrumental in character.

How then to square these competing logics of economic culture? The disentangled knowledge worker cultivating 'detachment and superficial co-operativeness' in insecure labour markets (Sennett, 1998, p. 25), against the capacity of the firm to 'facilitate learning and the acquisition of specialist skills' through an organisational culture (Hodgson, 1999b, p. 246). There clearly is a case to be made that economic networks reproduce some of the innovative and informational virtues of markets. Given the rate of change in those cultural sectors most dependent on new communications technologies (film and new media, music and interactive software), networks can be more effective in the exchange and upgrade of information than firms, more subject to lock-in by contract, sunken capital investment and routine. In enhancing information and promoting innovation, relational ties between firms and individuals can be a critical part of the competitive process – 'collaboration', as Metcalfe

(1998, p. 14) has it, is a familiar 'corollary of competitive activity', but its effects are not simply or always anti-competitive.

It also can be argued that networks replicate the somewhat different informational and knowledge capacities typically attributed to the firm (see especially Scott, 1999, 2000). This argument works on the assumption that networks are capable of reproducing the kind of integrated knowledge culture that has been one of the firm's strong suits – even if neither networks nor firms are currently much given to promoting 'values of loyalty and service' as an economic good (Sennett, 1998, p. 25). For Scott, such an effect depends on particular kinds of economic agglomeration, based on the concentration of cultural industries in key sites. This is a version of the network as cluster, where cultural linkage is a function of spatial proximity (see also Pratt, 2000). Scott invokes Alfred Marshall's notion of an 'industrial atmosphere' to describe the shared forms of knowledge, skill and work practice generated and reproduced within cultural–economic districts. It is a perspective that has affinities with Veblen's even more expansive claims (1914) for the cultural nature of work, distinctive not only of different 'industrial arts' but of the industrial character of nations: 'a set of relevant habits, acquired over a long time, widely dispersed through the employable workforce, reflective of its culture and deeply embedded in its practices' (cited in Hodgson, 1993, at p. 133). Industrial atmosphere, it should be noted, is not simply a question of ambience, but finds its material expression in routines, in practices and in norms of social exchange. Highly spatialised network relations in this sense mirror the role of the firm as milieu, providing a context for the development of collective as well as individual knowledge, competences, routines and norms. This indicates how networks can evince certain organisational qualities while remaining relatively 'informal', but also gestures to the point at which economic networks 'harden' into more durable institutional forms. It is at this point that networks become objects of economic governance.

Questions of governance

In Scott's account, success in the cultural economy – given the role of networking, the degree of interdependence between firms, and the tendency towards agglomeration – is a collective rather than simply an individual matter. He therefore sees a key part for certain 'agents of collective order' (Scott, 2000, p. 27) in promoting economic efficiency and growth. The state, in other words – and in its various extended guises – encourages both competition and agglomeration on a number of levels. At the most basic, policy measures determine the competitive environment within which firms and individuals operate, most obviously in instituting a legal framework for competition. Moreover, governance agencies steer competitive processes in stewarding innovation in research and technology. Business support and start-up initiatives, meanwhile, foster the entry of new market competitors. In respect of agglomeration, on the other hand, the development of dedicated infra-structure, locational planning, training and labour market strategies, and the institutional support of industry networks all promote the clustering of cul-tural industries. If network relations between individuals and firms are par-ticularly salient for the organisation of cultural–economic activity, governance agents play a strategic role in brokering sector networks, and in providing institutional leverage such that informational, technical and financial resources can be mobilised via these networks. Public and quasi-public actors, it follows, possess various means for hardening and embedding cultural–economic networks into a fairly stable institutional landscape.

This array of measures offers something of a wish-list for the effective gov-ernance of cultural sectors as an economy of networks. As it stands, cultural industries – however enthusiastic the governmental designs upon them – are broken up by different logics of accumulation, co-ordination and regulation. Forms of cultural production cut across state, market and non-profit sectors in often complicated ways. Given the extent to which recent thinking about the creative economy has been bound up with images of entrepreneurial or risk-taking behaviour (see Leadbeater and Oakley, 1999) – from the mix of self-promotion and private sponsorship that produced the Young British Artists in the 1990s, to the virtual economic bubbles of an expanding Internet economy – it is worth noting how much cultural activity remains located in the public and non-profit sectors (see Boorsma *et al.*, 1998; Salamon *et al.*, 1998). This only compounds the difficulty of mapping the cultural economy – and of quantifying, for the purposes of national accounting, its overall con-tribution to national wealth. It is not always clear which (part of what) organ-isation should be counted, or the extent to which overlapping public subsidies and private contracts distort the measure of economic outputs (although see DCMS 2001 for an attempt to stabilise such a measure). The cultural econ-omy in this way represents a laboratory of mixed economic governance, with a dense cross-cutting of public subsidy, market activity, private contract, grant funding and volunteer labour – all of them liable to shrinkage and shift.[8]

Conclusion: beyond the firm?

It is not especially novel to suggest that the distinctions between markets, firms and networks, viewed as different technologies of economic co-ordi-nation, are breaking down (see, most notably, Williamson, 1985; Hodgson, 1999b). This is partly a reflection of the 'growing networks and increasing intermediate relations between firms' that extend across different economic sectors (Hodgson, 1999b, p. 242), and which characterise the cultural econ-omy in particular. On another level this blurring reflects the growth of net-work theory within socioeconomic analysis, such that firms and markets can come to look to the analytic eye simply like different versions of a network. There is a danger here of collapsing the categories of 'market' and 'firm' into a general theory of networks (see Thompson *et al.*, 1991, pp. 14, 18; Callon,

1998) – blunting the analytic edge of each term, that of 'networks' especially. However, in the context of the cultural economy it seems questionable, given the spread of relational contracts and the disentanglement of labour, how far a definition of the firm that understands this as 'an organised enclave, apart from the market' can be sustained (Hodgson, 1999b, p. 237).

In examining how cultural–economic activity is organised in broad terms, or in tracing more closely the path of a cultural product from conception to consumption (see Callon, 2002), one is continually *led out* of the firm via different networks and, at certain moments, into markets of various kinds. For Scott (1999, p. 808),

> modern cultural–economic systems almost always take the form of complex networks of workers *within* firms, linked together by tightly wrought networks of transactions *between* firms, in which many different hands are brought to bear on products as they go through the process of conception, fabrication and final embellishment.

There are particular implications here for how we might think about the nature and the role of the firm. Accounts of economic organisation within institutional analysis, suggests Hodgson (1999b, pp. 232–3), typically have centred on the classical form of the capitalist firm, based on private property and the wage relation. This model is put into question as the contract for services comes to replace the wage relation for a significant minority of workers, especially those who combine creative expertise with technical capital (whether we want to describe them as 'self-employed producers' or as a sort of 'socio-technical capacity'). Such a shift has highly variable implications for different cultural workers in respect of income, working conditions and employment security; these changes also have marked effects on the culture of organisations, particularly in respect of their ability to capture, hold and reproduce knowledge.[9]

As a laboratory of mixed economic governance, the cultural economy does not lend itself always or easily to the ordering categories of market, firm and network. Hodgson attempts to open out the conventional analysis of these three categories as distinct (and exhaustive) terms, by locating them within a more general model of 'organisations and "non-organisations"'. In this account economic activity is co-ordinated via more or less organised means, and the capitalist firm is just one – if rather dominant – mode of organisation among others (including the mutual or public enterprise, for example). Network relations, crucially, can be seen to cut across the boundaries of organisations and non-organisations, at certain times evincing the innovative capacities of markets, at others taking on more stable, durable and institutional features that replicate the capacities of the firm. Within the cultural economy this produces a kind of hollowing-out of the firm, as collective knowledge, conventions of work practice and cultural norms come to be mediated by relational ties. This is not to say that networks can or do simply displace firms as modes of economic co-ordination – the path of even the most freestyle cultural producer, as McRobbie (2001) puts it, tends to remain one from 'clubs to companies'. At the same time, where demand for labour as for products is insecure, networks can promote disentanglement as much as they secure economic embeddedness. Being both inside and outside a firm represents something of an each-way bet. The point is that there are exchanges at the margins between organisations and 'non-organisations', as actors and products move in and out of the market 'frame', as networks harden at certain points, and as the boundaries of firms become more porous, their internal organisation less orderly, what they 'know' more provisional, their lives shorter.

Notes

1 The arguments developed in this chapter have emerged from research into cultural industries in London – carried out as part of a larger project in partnership with colleagues at the University of East London and Greenwich University (see Skills Observatory, 2000). The project strand which informs the current discussion was based on interviews with seventy-five organisations, fifteen each in the cultural industries sub-sectors of audio-visual, design and publishing, music, performing arts and visual arts.

2 These analytic problems are in part the effect of an emergent cultural economy itself, and in part they reproduce the more general problems of researching the small and medium-sized enterprises that are typical of much of that sector. The focus of the London research was on the small–medium enterprises that characterise the cultural economy in east and south-east London. Firms interviewed ranged in size from micro-businesses with fewer than ten permanent employees to medium-sized firms employing up to 400 people. However, casual, contract and freelance employment meant that the 'size' of businesses varied widely on a project or an event basis – for example, one music venue had a handful of permanent employees, but could employ several hundred for particular events. The seventy-five firms were selected so as to ensure: a geographical spread across the study area; a spread of business type; and a spread of business size within the small–medium range. The single exception in the sample was a large newspaper publisher employing 6,100 people.

3 In Britain in 2001, the creative industries were calculated to account for 5 per cent of GDP (at £112.5 billion, including £10.3 billion in export earnings), and to provide over 1 million jobs. See DCMS (2001).

4 The definition of 'cultural industries' used in the London Skills Observatory study was conventional in focusing on outputs, based on five sub-sectors: audio-visual, design and publishing, music, performing arts and visual arts. Britain's Department of Culture, Media and Sport defines the creative industries in terms of the following sectors: advertising, architecture, art and antiques, crafts, design, designer fashion, film and video, interactive leisure software, music, performing arts, publishing, software and computer services, television and radio – although these categories at times are extended to take in the broader domains of sport and leisure, tourism, and facilities such as parks and libraries. Such categories are hardly exhaustive, and are given to extension and expansion as the cultural economy undergoes rapid change. McRobbie (2001) contrasts the usual suspects from

the policy field with a range of self-styled job titles among new cultural entrepreneurs, ranging from 'cultural strategist' to 'incubator' and 'music portal'.

5 The strategic or acquired nature of organisational 'culture' is evident in the comparison between different informants in the London study: people working in a printer's, using design software to produce fine art postcards and selling over the Internet, appeared less clearly identified with the 'cultural economy' – in spite of their creative and technical skills, in spite of the nature of the product, in spite of their use of new media – than did those doing clerical work in a medium-sized advertising agency. Believe, in other words, the hype.

6 In other fields displays of loyalty and commitment appear more evident as labour market strategies. The Skills Observatory 2000 study found that visual and performing arts organisations, in particular, tended to a greater use of volunteer and placement staff, especially but not exclusively in the public and non-profit sectors. Voluntary work or work for low pay in those contexts was a way of demonstrating commitment to an organisation and to a creative field, as well as a means of gaining relevant skills and knowledge. A comparison between firms within the design and publishing sector sheds further insight on the variable nature of cultural labour markets. One advertising agency reported being swamped by unsolicited applications from graduates, while a number of printers reported difficulty in recruiting graduate and female workers – in spite of salaries competitive for the sub-sector, the skilled nature of the work and the opportunities these firms provided for in-work training. One informant reflected that printing simply wasn't 'trendy' – it remained stubbornly 'old economy' in spite of its nominal categorisation within the cultural industries.

7 Indeed the London study suggested, somewhat contrary to conventional analysis of cultural industries, that social ties were of more immediate relevance to supplier markets than to labour markets (Skills Observatory, 2000). This may, however, be skewed by the interview study being based on employers rather than on employees. More generally, where a firm buys-in human and technical capital in the form of 'socio-technical capacity' – a freelance designer using her own equipment, say – the distinction between labour and supplier markets is a difficult one to sustain.

8 Moreover, different kinds of 'governance mix' characterise different cultural sub-sectors. The London study found that businesses in visual and performing arts tended to be more closely tied to forms of public and civic support than those in the audio-visual, software, design and publishing fields (see Skills Observatory, 2000).

9 See McRobbie (2001) for an account that considers the effects of such economic arrangements both for individual workers and for wider organisational and professional cultures, especially in terms of de-politicisation.

References

Boorsma, P. B., van Hennel, A. and van de Wielen, N. (eds) (1998), *Privatization and Culture: Experience in the Arts, Heritage and Cultural Industries in Europe*, Boston, MA, Kluwer.

Callon, M. (1998), 'Introduction: the embeddedness of economic markets in economics', in Callon, M. (ed.), *The Laws of the Market*, Oxford, Blackwell.

Callon, M. (forthcoming, 2002), 'The economy of qualities', *Economy and Society*.

Cameron, G. (1998), 'Economic growth in the information age: from physical capital to weightless economy', *The Journal of International Affairs*, 51(2), pp. 447–72.

Coase, R. (1937), 'The nature of the firm', *Economica*, 4 (November), pp. 386–405.

Coyle, D. (1999), *The Weightless World: Strategies for Managing the Digital Economy*, Boston, MA, MIT Press.

DCMS (2001), *Creative Industries Mapping Document 2001*, London, Department for Culture, Media and Sport.

du Gay, P. (ed.) (1997), *Production of Culture, Cultures of Production*, London, Sage.

Gadrey, J. (2000), 'The characterization of goods and services: an alternative approach', *Review of Income and Wealth*, 46(3), pp. 269–88.

Gopnik, A. (1993), 'Death in Venice', *The New Yorker*, 69(24), pp. 66–73.

Hodgson, G. M. (1993), *Economics and Evolution: Bringing Life Back into Economics*, Cambridge, Polity.

Hodgson, G. M. (1999a), *Economics and Utopia: Why the Learning Economy is Not the End of History*, London, Routledge.

Hodgson, G. M. (1999b), *Evolution and Institutions: On Evolutionary Economics and the Evolution of Economics*, Cheltenham, Edward Elgar.

Lash, S. and Urry, J. (1994), *Economies of Signs and Space*, London, Sage.

Leadbeater, C. (1999), *Living on Thin Air: The New Economy*, London, Viking.

Leadbeater, C. and Oakley, K. (1999), *The Independents: Britain's New Cultural Entrepreneurs*, London, Demos/ICA/Adam Smith Institute.

Lury, C. (1993), *Cultural Rights: Technology, Legality and Personality*, London, Routledge.

McAnany, E. G. and Wilkinson, K. T. (eds) (1995), *Mass Media and Free Trade: NAFTA and the Cultural Industries*, Austin, University of Texas Press.

McRobbie, A. (2001), 'Clubs to companies: notes on the decline of political culture in speeded up creative worlds', in Nixon, S. and du Gay, P. (eds), *Cultural Studies*, special issue on cultural intermediaries, London, Routledge.

Metcalfe, J. S. (1998), 'Evolutionary concepts in relation to evolutionary economics', *Working Paper*, No. 4, ESRC Centre for Research on Innovation and Competition, University of Manchester.

Pratt, A. C. (1997), 'The cultural industries sector: its definition and character from secondary sources on employment and trade, Britain 1984–91', *Research Papers in Environment and Spatial Analysis*, No. 41, London School of Economics, Department of Geography.

Pratt, A. C. (2000), 'New media, the new economy and new spaces', *Geoforum*, 31(4), pp. 425–36.

Quah, D. (1996), 'The invisible hand and the weightless economy', *Occasional Paper*, No. 12, Centre for Economic Performance, London School of Economics.

Ray, L. and Sayer, A. (eds) (1999), *Culture and Economy: After the Cultural Turn*, London, Sage.

Salamon, L. M., Anheier, H. K. and Associates (1998), *The Emerging Sector Revisited: A Summary*, Center for Civil Society Studies, Johns Hopkins University Press.

Scott, A. (1999), 'The cultural economy: geography and the creative field', *Media, Culture and Society*, 21, pp. 807–17.

Scott, A. (2000), *The Cultural Economy of Cities: Essays on the Geography of Image-Producing Industries*, London, Sage.

Sennett, R. (1998), *The Corrosion of Character: The Personal Consequences of Work in the New Capitalism*, New York, Norton.

Skills Observatory (2000), *Pilot Project on the Cultural Industries: Final Report*, Centre for Urban and Community Research, Goldsmiths College.

Thompson, G., Frances, J., Levacic, R. and Mitchell, J. (eds) (1991), *Markets, Hierarchies and Networks: The Co-ordination of Social Life*, London, Sage.

Veblen, T. (1914), *The Instinct of Workmanship and the State of the Industrial Arts*, New York, Macmillan.

Veblen, T. (1990 [1919]), *The Place of Science in Modern Civilization and Other Essays*, New Brunswick, Transaction.

Williamson, O. E. (1985), *The Economic Institutions of Capitalism*, New York, Free Press.

7

Regulatory issues and industrial policy in football[1]

Jonathan Michie and Christine Oughton

Introduction

The peculiar economics of professional sports leagues has long been recognised (see Neale, 1964). Traditionally, the essence of the problem was seen to lie in the fact that sports leagues and the individual clubs that make up the league provide a joint product that depends on effective co-operation between competing clubs. Clubs agree to join, and be regulated by, a league because co-operation in the supply of a joint product increases the economic value of the product supplied by each individual club. The output of the league and its constituent members is maximised when there is some degree of competitive balance in the league so that the outcomes of matches are uncertain. If leagues become unbalanced, lack of uncertainty over the outcomes of matches reduces demand by spectators/viewers. In the absence of regulation, leagues have a tendency to become unbalanced. Leading clubs attract more spectators and viewers, sell more merchandise and can command higher prices for tickets and for the rights to broadcast matches. Those revenues can be reinvested in players, which serves to maintain and enhance the dominance of the leading clubs. In the absence of measures to check those forces, leagues tend to become unbalanced, attract sub-optimal levels of spectators/viewers and face the dual threat of the bankruptcy that plagues lagging clubs and the possibility that breakaway groups of leading clubs will seek the competitive balance afforded by a rival league. For that reason most leagues play a regulatory role by redistributing income from stronger to weaker teams (Findlay, Holahan and Oughton, 1999).

More recently, two further peculiarities of professional football leagues have become apparent. The first concerns the nature and role of match-going supporters in the production of live football matches and issues in corporate governance, while the second concerns the vertical production relationship between football clubs and, on the one hand, the league and, on the other, television broadcasters.

In the UK, football, the largest professional league sport, has traditionally been regulated by the Football Association, the Football League and more recently the Premier League. In recent years the economic problems facing sports leagues have increased as the growth of pay-TV has opened up a new market for viewing sport that has significantly increased the revenue streams flowing into the game. As the commercialisation of professional sports leagues has increased, government has intervened with the Football Task Force, and there have been regulatory interventions from the Restrictive Practices Court and the Monopolies and Mergers Commission. At the same time, many football clubs have become plcs and in doing so have bypassed the key FA regulation against the commercial exploitation of clubs by gaining FA agreement that the newly created plc holding companies would be exempt from rule 34 which had, up until that time, prevented the owners of clubs from extracting profits. This change in the corporate governance of football clubs has heightened conflict between the various stakeholders – match-going supporters, TV viewers, shareholders and managers.[2]

The institutional arrangements around the creation and development of the market for professional football in Britain – and subsequently increasingly of the market for the broadcasting rights for professional football, including for pay-TV in the form of both subscription channels and pay-per-view on an individual match basis – have thus been purposively constructed. Over time, it has also been deliberately changed, significantly, under the influence of internal and external pressures on the game. This has taken the form of the richer clubs breaking away from the existing league structure to create their own 'Premier' league. It has seen media companies buying into football clubs, most dramatically with the attempted merger between Manchester United and BSkyB. And as discussed below, the Office of Fair Trading (OFT) tried and failed to break up the collective selling arrangements by the leagues to media companies.

This chapter analyses the economic and policy implications of three inter-related aspects of the corporate governance and regulation of professional league football that underlie these changing institutional arrangements: first, changes in ownership structures and corporate governance; second, vertical integration between broadcasting companies and football clubs; and third, the collectivity of football leagues and the sale of broadcasting rights. The next section deals with issues of corporate governance and argues that fan equity should be recognised as 'goodwill' in clubs' accounts and that supporter-shareholder trusts should be formed to solve the problem of misaligned incentives and the associated principal–agent problems between supporter shareholders and commercial investors. The third section deals with issues of vertical integration between football clubs and broadcasters, while the fourth looks at the welfare implications of league collectivity and the exclusivity of broadcasting rights. The final section draws some conclusions and argues that the three factors comprising the 'peculiar economics of football' require a dual system of regulation: regulation from below to resolve problems of corporate governance and misaligned incentives and regulation from above to prevent distortions of the competition in broadcasting and preserve the collectivity of the leagues.

Corporate governance

There is now a growing recognition that match-going fans are intrinsically involved in the joint production of football matches. Crowd involvement and support can add greatly to the entertainment value of matches, and a match played before a packed stadium is more enjoyable and provides more quality-adjusted units of output than one played in front of empty seats. This is particularly the case for matches that are screened live, where the crowd adds greatly to the audio-visual content of the programme. For that reason, together with the considerations that football supporters, unlike almost any other industry's customers, are unlikely to switch allegiances or brands no matter how sub-standard the product. Football supporters are clearly stake-holders in their clubs. This particular form of stakeholding has been termed 'fan equity', (see Hamil 1999 for a discussion of this notion). Of course, it is difficult to estimate the economic value of 'fan equity', but the problem of valuation here is no different from the standard problem facing companies which regularly put a value on 'goodwill' in their annual accounts. Moreover, there have been numerous cases where the extent of fan equity has had clear monetary dimensions. For example, many clubs faced with bankruptcy have turned to their fans for financial support to keep the clubs up and running. Plainly, there are few industries where the customers would organise a whip-round to prevent a company from closing. Recognising fans as stakeholders in this way means that issues of corporate governance take on particular dimensions (as discussed below) and regulatory implications.

The change in corporate governance structures that has occurred as clubs have been transformed into plcs raises particular issues in the case of profes-sional league sports. In particular, it is evident that institutional investors in football clubs may have very different objectives from those of supporter shareholders. Unlike the latter, institutional investors do not contribute directly to the joint production of the product. At the same time institutional shareholders are not subject to the kind of brand loyalty that makes them peculiarly vulnerable to exploitation of local monopoly power. This implies that there is an incentive for financial and institutional shareholders to exploit brand loyalty and local monopoly at the expense of supporter share-holders. Finally, the stockmarket flotation of football clubs has allowed sup-porters and media companies to acquire significant ownership stakes in leading clubs. However, the interests of these two groups of shareholders are often diametrically opposed. For example, media companies may have an interest in the formation of a European 'Super League' as a means of max-imising pay-TV (satellite and cable) subscribers in the European marketplace, while supporters have an interest in maintaining national leagues as the main competitive arenas.

The Government set up the Football Task Force to investigate these corpo-rate governance issues, and its unanimously approved third report (Football Task Force, 1999) supported the formation of supporter-shareholder trusts.

The resulting formation of Supporters Direct aims not only to assist the formation of such trusts, but also has the declared aim of encouraging the election of representatives of such trusts to the boards of directors of football clubs.[3]

Vertical integration

The arguments in this section are illustrated by reference to the issues raised by BSkyB's attempted take-over of Manchester United. In September 1998 British Sky Broadcasting Group made a formal offer to acquire Manchester United. The bid, which amounted to an attempt by Britain's dominant pay-TV sports broadcaster to control Britain's leading football club, rang warning bells among BSkyB's competitors and Manchester United's shareholders and fans. The former feared that the take-over would consolidate BSkyB's already dominant position in the market for live football broadcasting and make it even more difficult for others to make inroads into the industry. The latter felt that Manchester United's interests would become subservient to BSkyB's broadcasting interests, as the club would become a bargaining and marketing tool for a broadcasting company intent on enhancing its dominant position in the pay-TV market. The director general of Fair Trading agreed that both the fans and BSkyB's competitors were right to be worried, and on 29 October 1998 he referred BSkyB's proposed acquisition of Manchester United to the Monopolies and Mergers Commission (MMC) for investigation under the Fair Trading Act 1973.

The MMC was charged with the task of investigating the proposed acquisition and determining whether it might be expected to operate against the public interest. It is normal for the MMC to consider public interest concerns but unusual for the OFT to *require* this in the referral. This unusual step no doubt reflected the unprecedented number of submissions, received by the OFT, overwhelmingly opposed to the take-over. The MMC set up a panel of five experts drawn from the members of the Commission, chaired by Dr Derek Morris, the overall chairman of the MMC. During the next four-and-a-half months, the panel investigated the proposed acquisition, taking evidence from over 350 parties.

On 12 March 1999, the MMC delivered its findings in a report to the secretary of state for Trade and Industry (Monopolies and Mergers Commission, 1999). Four weeks later, on 9 April 1999, Stephen Byers, secretary of state for Trade and Industry announced his decision to block BSkyB's proposed acquisition of Manchester United based on the basis of a full acceptance of the findings of the MMC. In his announcement to the Stock Exchange Mr Byers said:

> Having considered the [MMC's] report, advice from the Director General of Fair Trading and also taking into account further representations which have been received, I have decided to accept in full the unanimous recommendations of the MMC. The MMC's findings are based mainly on competition grounds, where they concluded that the merger would adversely affect competition

between broadcasters. But they also examined wider public interest issues, concluding that the merger would damage the quality of British football. I accept these findings. (Department of Trade and Industry, 1999)

In this section we outline and assess the issues raised by the BSkyB–Manchester United case and discuss their implications for the future of British football. We start by considering the nature of the footballing industry. An appreciation of this, and of the peculiar 'brand loyalty' of the consumers (fans), is important to a proper understanding of the effect that the acquisition of football clubs by broadcasting companies would have on the public interest. We then analyse the anti-competitive effects that the attempted acquisition would have had on the broadcasting and media markets, before going on to consider broader public interest concerns relating to the quality of British football.[4]

The nature of the football industry

The nature of the British footballing industry, with its local and community involvement, and its fan loyalty, creates public interest concerns and also makes the industry peculiarly vulnerable to anti-competitive behaviour. Before detailing the grounds on which the attempted acquisition of Manchester United by BSkyB would have acted against the public interest it is important to appreciate, firstly, the unique nature of the industry; secondly, the rather different notion of the 'firm' that is appropriate to an analysis of this industry than is the case when analysing most other industries; and, thirdly, the peculiarities of this industry's customers – the football fans.

Firstly, regarding the nature of the football industry, while it has become fashionable to refer to the range of stakeholders that a firm or industry has beyond its shareholders, in the case of football the importance of those other stakeholders – and in particular of the local communities – is absolutely vital.[5] While anti-competitive practices should be opposed whatever the industry, the precise way in which such practices operate varies from industry to industry, and so an appreciation of the impact of these practices in the case of the acquisition of a football club by a media company is assisted when the nature of the footballing industry is understood.

Secondly, regarding the 'firms' involved in the industry, the importance of the football club to the local community – and conversely the importance of the local community as a key stakeholder in the football club – has been reflected in the fact that the firms which own and control football clubs have generally been dedicated to this task. There are of course football-related activities in addition to the operation of the actual football club, but this does not detract from the fact that the main line of business of the firm is not with the media or other interests but, rather, the football club. Also, while wealthy individuals have often bought football clubs, those individuals have tended to be supporters of that club, and have not used the club to promote their own business operations to the disadvantage of other firms competing in whatever markets their own business operates.

Thirdly, as Hamil (1999) argues, the relation of the customer – in this case, football fans – to the product and hence to the company, is rather different from that which obtains in other industries. In most industries, if a firm's product is not sufficiently competitive in terms of price and other factors, consumers will be lost to rival firms. In the case of football, the customers tend not to switch allegiances so easily (either between clubs or sports). This creates a situation analogous to one of local monopoly, discussed below. It is true that fans can continue to support the club and may be able to consume the product through pay-TV (currently, in the UK, by subscribing to BSkyB which holds the exclusive rights for broadcasting Premiership matches live), rather than paying through the turnstile at the ground. But that is a rather limited form of competition, since it does not involve the consumer switching from one team to another, and even this limited degree of competition between outlets would have been eliminated entirely in the case of Manchester United if the attempted acquisition had been allowed to proceed. The special nature of the footballing industry thus both creates particular public interest concerns and influences the way in which specific restrictions on competition operate in that market. The particular and peculiar nature of the footballing industry, and the concomitant necessity for regulatory intervention, have long been recognised. It led, for example, to the Football Association's rule 34 which aimed to prevent the commercial exploitation of clubs,[6] and more recently to the establishment by the Government of the Football Task Force.

The peculiar nature of the footballing industry can be illustrated, finally, by reference to one of the consequences which the attempted acquisition would have had – which has not, as far as we are aware, been commented on to date in public discussion – namely that several thousand shareholders who have a keen and passionate interest in the future success of the company in which they have a stake (as owners as well as supporters) would be forced by law, against their will, to part with their shares. This is a rather dramatic reversal of the whole impetus of governmental policy over several years now, across both Conservative and Labour Governments, to encourage wider share ownership. Indeed, one of the main arguments used in favour of floating Manchester United Football Club as a plc was precisely to encourage wider share ownership. BSkyB made clear that their aim was to acquire the 90 per cent of shares which would have allowed them, by force of law, to require all remaining shareholders – which in the case of Manchester United plc consists of several thousand fans – to then part with their shares in their club. As one shareholder put it at the November 1998 Manchester United plc AGM, his share certificate is displayed proudly on his wall at home; had the acquisition proceeded, he would not have replaced it with a share certificate in BSkyB.

Anti-competitive threats and restrictions on competition
BSkyB's bid raised three separate areas of concern regarding anti-competitive threats and restrictions on competition:

The market for watching Manchester United   There is a large market for watching Manchester United. This market is part of the wider market for watching football, which in turn is part of the general market for watching sport, itself a part of the broader market for entertainment. While there are therefore related and segmented markets, there is no doubt that there is a distinct market for watching Manchester United, for which a match between, say, Coventry and Wimbledon (two other Premiership clubs) is not a close substitute. There are two outlets for this market for watching Manchester United – either attending the ground or else watching games live on television. The sales *via* these two outlets are organised and priced by separate companies, namely Manchester United and BSkyB respectively. Had the attempted acquisition been successful it would have created a monopoly provider for the two outlets. This would have resulted in at least two anti-competitive threats.

Firstly, the monopoly provider would be able to decide on price rises for the two outlets simultaneously. And although as with any monopolist there would be a point beyond which price rises became unprofitable, the monopoly provider would no longer be as concerned as would a non-monopoly provider, at the prospect of a price rise shifting some customers to the other outlet, of watching on television. The welfare effects of vertical integration and vertical mergers are normally judged on a case-by-case basis. In contrast to horizontal mergers the impact of vertical mergers on economic welfare depends on the nature of the vertical relationship between the two companies. Vertical merger between two companies that are producing complementary goods is unlikely to be welfare decreasing, in the sense that raising the price in one part of the company will be offset by a fall in demand not only in that industry but also in the complementary industry. In substitute industries vertical mergers can have more serious adverse effects because an increase in price in one segment of the market will lead to an increase in demand in the firm's other market segments. In effect, the vertically integrated company is able to use price increases in one market as a means of raising demand in its related substitute market.

Secondly, there would have been a wider danger of this restriction on competition leading to an abuse of the resulting market power, with behaviour detrimental to the interests of attending fans, such as altering the day of the week and the time of day when matches are staged.[7] This is already done to some extent, in the interests of maximising viewing figures, but at least there is a strong countervailing force with the interests of the attending fans being represented by a company (Manchester United) separate from the broadcaster.

Anti-competitive practices and restrictions on competition   BSkyB has a huge financial interest in its televising of live Premiership football. The attempted acquisition would have weakened the competitive position of BSkyB's broadcasting rivals and would have strengthened BSkyB's already dominant position in pay-TV. The football club in question would have been owned by one of the broadcasting companies and would therefore inevitably have been used to distort the bargaining process, creating restrictions on competition.

If the attempted acquisition had proceeded, then, in any subsequent negotiations over the rights to televise football, there would have been a change in the balance between the TV company and the football clubs: BSkyB and its rival broadcasters would be on one side of the bargaining table, and on the other side would be the clubs, with BSkyB owning and representing the biggest and most powerful of those clubs.

It is the interest of all league football clubs to reach agreement with whichever broadcasting company offers the best deal. With the attempted acquisition, other broadcasting companies would have been put at a competitive disadvantage *vis à vis* BSkyB. Manchester United could have been used to push for an acceptance of the BSkyB offer. The club might have done this even if the deal had not been in the interests of the footballing industry taken as a whole, provided it was in the interests of its parent company, BSkyB.

Manchester United's vote – and more importantly, its power and influence – would have been used to favour a deal with BSkyB rather than with BSkyB's competitors. In addition to representing a distortion of the competitive process to the detriment of other broadcasting companies, such a situation could also have posed an anti-competitive threat to other football clubs in the Premiership (and might in addition have had a deleterious effect on clubs outside the Premiership). If the merger had gone ahead and the Restrictive Practices Court had ended the current bargaining arrangements, then other broadcasters would have been at a competitive disadvantage *vis à vis* BSkyB in attempting to secure television rights, since the biggest and most popular club would already be owned by one of the other broadcasting companies. This would no doubt have provoked those other broadcasters to buy up top football clubs themselves. Whether the BBC would have been permitted to defend itself in this way is, however, rather to be doubted. Nor would such a defense of the BBC's interests be something to be welcomed; on the contrary, it would replicate many of the anti-competitive dangers described in this section, and would further divide the Premiership between the few top clubs, on the one hand, and the rest of the league, on the other.

In addition, the position of other football clubs *vis à vis* BSkyB would have been affected by BSkyB's ownership of one of the clubs. Had the attempted acquisition been reported as Manchester United acquiring BSkyB, objections would no doubt have been raised by the other clubs that the main broadcaster was to be owned by a Premiership club. BSkyB ('owned' under this scenario by Manchester United) would even have the right to move the dates and times of crucial games to be played by Manchester United's rivals in the title race. This is just one of the more minor ways in which vertical integration between a broadcaster and a football club could be abused, to the more general implications of which we now turn.

Abuse of vertical integration   The attempted acquisition would have decreased competition through the vertical integration of the supplier (Manchester United) and broadcaster (BSkyB) of Manchester United football matches. In the event of Premier League clubs individually negotiating television rights, Manchester United would then find itself 'negotiating' with its owners – a most extreme case of exclusive trading. There is reason to be concerned that such vertical integration may even have operated against the interests of Manchester United itself. If BSkyB were to require the participation of Manchester United to launch a European Super League, or any other such venture, there would be a risk that the club would be forced by its parent company to break away from the Premiership, if that was what was required to accomplish the parent company's media goals.[8]

The vertical integration of BSkyB and Manchester United would have created three additional anti-competitive threats.

Firstly, in 2001 when the other broadcasters had to compete with BSkyB over the rights to televise live Premiership matches, BSkyB would have been in a position to offer more than its rivals, since a proportion of BSkyB's offer would have returned directly to the vertically integrated company. The proportion of the money that would have returned to BSkyB, *via* its ownership of Manchester United, would have been far greater than 5 per cent,[9] as matches involving Manchester United are shown more frequently and attract more viewers than matches involving many other Premiership clubs.

Secondly, such vertical integration would risk the natural competitive processes in both industries – broadcasting and football – being distorted through cross-subsidies. The likely direction would be for the broadcaster to cross-subsidise the football club, since the competitive advantage this would give the football club against the competitor clubs would be expected to produce a subsequent pay-off to the broadcaster, as success on the field led to increased viewing figures, including through pay-TV.[10] Such cross-subsidising would lead to a growing inequality and competitive imbalance; these effects would have been intensified had the BSkyB bid proceeded, and would subsequently have triggered other bids by broadcasters for Premier League clubs. There is also the possibility that the cross-subsidising danger would work the other way, with the broadcaster using profits from the football club to allow BSkyB to undercut its rival TV companies for a time.

Thirdly, the attempted acquisition would have represented a form of vertical foreclosure, thus impeding competition. The market for football broadcasting and packaging is increasingly a market for ideas in which diversity and creativity matter. Such a market is best served by being fragmented, allowing new entrants to innovate and compete. Vertical integration restricts such processes. Indeed, the attempted acquisition would have been a move against the trend, deliberately promoted by Government, to encourage outsourcing from broadcasters to other content providers.

Public interest concerns and the quality of football

The bid by BSkyB to acquire Manchester United represented a serious threat to the interests of British football both as a leisure activity and as a business sector. It is important to maintain – and indeed strengthen – the current links between the various sectors of the footballing industry. The majority of Premiership players start their careers in the lower divisions, including non-league clubs. The majority also finish their footballing careers outside of the Premiership, either as players, managers, or in some other football-related occupation. There are therefore strong bonds within the game. These links are vital to the continued health of the sector, and in the long term even to the success of individual Premiership clubs despite the fact that over the short and medium term their profitability could be boosted by neglecting such links.

It is important to stress two points here. Firstly, rich individuals have in the past bought clubs, and clubs have also been floated as plcs. The attempted acquisition of Manchester United was quite different from all previous takeovers or flotations, in that it would have left the football club as only a small part of the parent company's operations; in addition, the main interest of that parent company (BSkyB) – namely broadcasting – would be other than football, and yet at the same time there would have been a strong incentive to use the footballing part of the business in the interests of the parent company. The link between this football club and other clubs in England would have become, at best, less important in the eyes of the relevant–BSkyB–shareholders.

Secondly, the attempted acquisition should not be considered in isolation. Had this acquisition been allowed to proceed, it is likely that similar takeovers of other major Premiership clubs would have followed. Such a process would have been inimical to the long-term development of the game as a whole. It could even have led to a formal breakaway of such 'super clubs' from the rest.

There is also the local monopoly aspect of football clubs that needs to be taken into account. Football fans almost invariably support only one team, and this support is translated commercially through attendance at matches and watching or listening to them through TV and radio, and through purchasing associated goods and services. Such consumers (fans) do not readily switch their consumption to another football club. Support and loyalty creates a lock-in to one club. Thus, the owners of football clubs are, in effect, local monopoly suppliers of a unique product, and that raises major regulatory concerns. There have been various factors preventing the abuse of this monopoly power in the past, including the FA's rule 34, referred to below. The success of the attempted acquisition would have constituted a serious risk that this monopoly power would be exploited against the public interest.

A couple of additional comments are called for in relation to the claim that each club is to a large extent a local monopoly. As mentioned above, this is due to the nature of football support, with clubs relying on local support and this in turn resulting in fan loyalty to the local club. This monopoly power derives both from geographical locality and from the nature of fan loyalty.[11]

In other sectors of the economy (such as the water industry) such local monopoly would be seen as sufficient reason for direct regulation. In the case of the footballing industry this has not, to date, proved necessary as there has been a general recognition both of the above facts and also, therefore, of the importance of not over-exploiting this monopoly power. There is serious reason to doubt whether BSkyB would have exhibited the same degree of self-restraint.[12] There was thus good reason to suspect that an abuse of monopoly power would have resulted. As indicated above, the attempted acquisition would have diminished what restraining influences there are at present, such as the choice between attendance at the ground, on the one hand, and paying for a BSkyB subscription to watch Premiership games live on television, on the other.

The MMC's findings

The MMC broadly accepted the points made above, and recommended against the merger, a recommendation that the Government accepted. In announcing his decision, the secretary of state for Trade and Industry stated that

> the proposed merger may be expected to reduce competition for the broadcasting rights to Premier League matches. This would lead to less choice for the Premier League and less scope for innovation in the broadcasting of Premier League football. The MMC also concluded that enhancing BSkyB's ability to secure rights to Premier League matches in the future would reduce competition in the market for sports premium television channels. This would in turn feed through into reduced competition in the wider pay TV market.[13]

On the question of wider public interest concerns, the Commission concluded that the merger would adversely affect football:

> We have concluded that the merger would reinforce the existing trend towards greater inequality of wealth between clubs, weakening the smaller ones. We have also concluded that the merger would give BSkyB additional influence over Premier League decisions relating to the organisation of football. On both counts the merger may be expected to have the adverse effect that the quality of English football would be damaged. This adverse effect would be more pronounced if the merger precipitated other mergers between broadcasters and Premier League clubs. (Monopolies and Mergers Commission, 1999)

Summary

BSkyB's attempted take-over of Manchester United plc would have strengthened BSkyB's dominant position in broadcasting. (Matches involving Manchester United account for 25 per cent of all BSkyB's viewers of Premier League matches.) Vertical integration between broadcasters and football clubs raises a number of issues surrounding competition and vertical restraints. In particular, vertical integration may

- distort the bargaining process for the sale of TV rights;
- facilitate market foreclosure in broadcasting;

- lead to greater exploitation of the local monopoly that clubs enjoy; and
- widen the inequality between the leading clubs and the rest.

The secretary of state's decision to block the merger may have deterred other broadcasters from attempting to take over football clubs but it has not stopped a number of media companies (including BSkyB) from acquiring vertical shareholdings in leading Premier League clubs. This goes against the arguments set out in the MMC's report[14] and raises the question of whether such vertical linkages should be prohibited in the case of football clubs and broadcasting companies, as they have been in a number of other industries, such as rail, gas and electricity.

League collectivity and broadcasting rights

The emergence of football as the main programming 'software' used to attract viewers in the pay-TV market has led to regulatory concerns over vertical integration between football clubs and broadcasters, as well as over the role of leagues as collective suppliers of live broadcasting rights. These two concerns have been the subject of a case brought before the Restrictive Practices Court (RPC) by the OFT against the Premier League over the latter's collective sale of television rights, and of a Monopolies and Mergers Commission inquiry, which recommended the blocking of the proposed vertical merger between BSkyB and Manchester United plc. The central issues underlying these cases are closely linked. The OFT's case against the Premier League's collective sale of television rights rested on the argument that the League was behaving like a cartel, raising prices and restricting output. This failed to appreciate the importance of the collectivity of the League and the fact that it serves at least two functions. First, unlike a standard price-fixing cartel, which contributes nothing to the product sold, it is actively involved in the joint production of the output. Second, the League plays a functional role by regulating the inherent tendency for imbalance by the redistribution of television revenues from the more successful clubs downwards. This may be compared with a situation of individual selling by clubs where the leading clubs would be able to charge considerably more than the lagging clubs for the TV rights to their matches because they attract more viewers per match. It was largely on those grounds that the RPC judgement went against the OFT.[15]

Conclusions

This chapter has identified three peculiarities of the economics of professional football. This triad of peculiarities suggests the need for multiple forms of regulation. Incentive conflicts between clubs, and between clubs and their league (where leading clubs can credibly threaten to leave to form a rival league) undermine the capacity of leagues, particularly the Premier League, to be self-regulating and suggest the need for an independent regulator. Incentives for vertical integration between clubs and broadcasters serve to distort competition in broadcasting, threaten the collectivity of the league and may adversely affect the quality and organisation of football. There is a clear need to prevent such vertical integration, as is the case in industries, such as rail, electricity and gas. Finally, stakeholder conflicts brought about by the stock market flotation of clubs may be resolved, or at least alleviated, by the formation of shareholder/supporter trust holdings. What is required is a dual system of regulation with top-down regulation to preserve league collectivity and distortions of competition in broadcasting and bottom–up regulation to resolve corporate governance issues.

Notes

1 We are grateful to Jeanette Findlay, Sean Hamil and Bill Holahan for valuable comments and discussion. The usual disclaimer applies.
2 For a report on the state of corporate governance at football clubs, see Hamil, Michie, Oughton and Shailer (2001).
3 For a description of the origins and operation of Supporters Direct, see the various contributors to Hamil, Michie, Oughton and Warby (2001).
4 This section draws on our submission to the MMC made jointly with Keith Cowling, Simon Deakin, Laurence Harris, Michael Kitson, J. Stan Metcalfe, Malcolm Sawyer, Ajit Singh and Roger Sugden, to whom we are grateful. We are grateful to Gordon Borrie, Sean Hamil, Alan Hughes and Geoffrey Whittington for advising on the drafting of the submission.
5 In the 1992 Fulham FC v. Cabra Estates plc case the Court of Appeal expressed the view that the company (Fulham FC) was more than the sum of its 'members' (i.e. shareholders), and on that basis blocked the sale of the football club's ground.
6 Rule 34 is discussed below.
7 This would be particularly detrimental to travelling fans who might have already made travel arrangements, including the purchase of flight or rail tickets which may be wholly or in part non-refundable.
8 In 1998 the Premiership did threaten, Manchester United and the other clubs involved with expulsion from the Premiership over their discussions regarding a European Super League (discussions which Manchester United had denied they were involved in, although this denial turned out to be false).
9 Five per cent, since Manchester United is one of twenty clubs in the Premiership.
10 Such cross-subsidisation would have implications quite different from the case where money is put into a football club by, for example, a benefactor; in the case of the attempted acquisition of Manchester United by BSkyB a cross-subsidising of Manchester United might have been pursued not just to favour Manchester United against other football teams, but because this would have then given BSkyB an advantage over the other broadcasting companies.
11 Gerry Boon of accountants Deloitte and Touche has refered to the demand inelasticity from this brand loyalty: 'That means you can put the prices up but the demand doesn't change. They still buy the product.' (cited in Conn, 1997, p. 155). Manchester United could probably continue to sell all tickets – even on an advanced season ticket basis – for all home games even if they increased prices

substantially. Indeed, average admission price increases of over 30 per cent were introduced for the 1991–92 season (Manchester United plc Prospectus, 1991).

12 Price wars involving *The Times* and *The Sun*, and between Sky and BSB, were pursued aggressively.

13 Department of Trade and Industry (1999), p. 2.

14 As argued by Nicholas Finney, OBE, MMC panel member for the BSkyB–Manchester United inquiry; see Finney (2000).

15 The peculiarity of the economics of sports leagues is perhaps illustrated by the fact that this was the first time the Office of Fair Trading has ever lost a case in the Restrictive Practices Court.

References

Conn, D. (1997), *The Football Business*, Edinburgh, Mainstream Publishing.

Department of Trade and Industry (1999), Press Release: Stephen Byers Blocks BSkyB/Manchester United Merger, London, DTI.

Findlay, J., Holahan, W. and Oughton, C. (1999), 'Revenue sharing from broadcasting football', in Hamil, S., Michie, J. and Oughton, C. (eds), *A Game of Two Halves? The Business of Football*, Edinburgh, Mainstream Publishing, pp. 124–38.

Finney, N. (2000), 'MMC's inquiry into BSkyB's merger with Manchester United plc', in Hamil, S., Michie, J., Oughton, C. and Warby, S. (eds), *Football in the Digital Age: Whose Game is it Anyway?*, Edinburgh, Mainstream Publishing, pp. 79–80.

Hamil, S. (1999), 'A whole new ball game? Why football needs a regulator', in Hamil, S., Michie, J. and Oughton, C. (eds), *A Game of Two Halves? The Business of Football*, Edinburgh, Mainstream Publishing, pp. 23–39.

Hamil, S., Michie, J., Oughton, C. and Shailer, L. (2001), *The State of the Game: The Corporate Governance of Football Clubs 2001*, Research Paper, No. 2001/02, Football Governance Research Centre, Birkbeck, University of London.

Hamil, S., Michie, J., Oughton, C. and Warby, S. (eds) (2001), *The Changing Face of the Football Business: Supporters Direct*, London, Frank Cass.

Monopolies and Mergers Commission (1999), *British Sky Broadcasting Group plc and Manchester United PLC: A Report on the Proposed Merger*, Cm. 4305, London, Stationery Office.

Neale, W. (1964), 'The peculiar economics of professional sports', *Quarterly Journal of Economics*, 78(1), pp. 1–14.

8

The evolution of the UK software market: scale of demand and the role of competences

Suma S. Athreye

Introduction

This chapter studies the evolution of the software industry in the UK. Previous work on the evolution of the software industry in the UK by Grindley (1996) emphasised the constraints imposed on the newly emerging software sector due to the steady erosion of a domestic hardware capability. While hardware manufacturers were an important source of demand and often supplied the entrepreneurship required for software firms in the early stages, we show that independent vendors of software gradually dominated the supply of output in this sector. They also replaced in-house development of software in a process of vertical disintegration.

The global emergence of the software market took two forms: outsourcing by large firms to independent software consultancies; and the emergence of a package software sector comprising genuinely independent producers of 'commodity' software. In the UK, the demand side of the newly emerging software market was always scale constrained, though less so than for other European countries whose markets for software were linguistically fragmented. This slow growth of software demand delayed a full-fledged arm's-length market in package software from emerging in the UK despite considerable national strengths in computing and related sciences.

When a market started to emerge for traded software in the 1980s, niche market strategies, driven by heterogeneous demand, had an important impact both on the evolution of firm competences and on the nature of competition and competitive advantage in the UK software sector. While outsourcing of software has been an important stimulus to the emergence and growth of the UK software industry, this trajectory of growth has had its limits. Firms are constrained both by the growth of demand and by the lack of marketing skills that might re-invent market boundaries so necessary for the development of software products. The absence of a large commodity software market has meant a less radical impact of the software industry upon industrial growth in the UK economy.

Thus, in this chapter, we describe the evolution of an industry driven by the need for outsourcing and limited by the competences developed by outsourcing. The UK software sector is not alone in this trend – indeed the situation is far worse for the European software sector. The body of this chapter is organised in the following way: the next section describes the role of demand factors in the process of vertical disintegration and distinguishes between the product and service segments of the software market. Section three reviews the changing need for software in the growth of the global software industry. Section four highlights the role of a narrow demand base in the emergence of a market for traded software in the UK. The fifth section examines the supply side of the software market and details the nature of the firms that are entrants to the industry in the UK. Section six examines the impact of these demand- and supply-side factors on the nature of competition, competitive advantage and barriers to growth for firms in the UK software sector.

Vertical disintegration and the growth of the software market

Vertical disintegration and the emergence of intermediate markets

Adam Smith in *The Wealth of Nations* linked the growth of the inter-firm division of labour and the emergence of specialised industries to the growth in the demand for final goods. The idea of inter-firm division of labour had received less attention from the economists of the nineteenth century than did the notion of intra-firm division of labour. In 1928, Allyn Young drew attention to the important notion of inter-firm division of labour and the consequent 'production round-aboutness' in the economy. To him this was an important source of increasing returns in the economy. Among later economists, Stigler (1951) developed the importance of the division of labour for the vertical disintegration of production and Rosenberg (1963) drew attention to the emergence of intermediate technology markets due to the growth in demand and to the economies of specialisation that an economy as a whole derives due to the existence of specialised technology sectors.

Rosenberg's work on the machine tool industry drew attention to another important phenomenon that he associated with the rise of specialised technology sectors. This was the phenomenon of *technological convergence* whereby several industrial sectors begin to share a set of common techniques. Thus, he pointed out that industries as diverse as bicycles and sewing machines and firearms shared the same mechanical principles and in fact the manufacturers of sewing machines made the first bicycles. The cross-sectoral demand made possible by technological convergence created a large enough scale of demand for the specialised machine tool sector to emerge. Firms no longer needed to manufacture their own machines but could buy them from the independent firms in the machine tool sector. In turn, the capital goods sector that emerged was a technology market capable of serving diverse upstream sectors which benefited from the efficiency improvements in design and innovation simply by virtue of production round-aboutness.

The emergence of the software industry has many characteristics reminiscent of the growth of the capital goods sector. Firstly, the growth of the package 'product' software industry has been fuelled by the widespread computerisation of administrative and production activity. Thus, it is an intermediate demand based on the growth of computerisation in the economy. Secondly, the market for package software is often across sectors of use. Lastly, the package (or commodity) software industry today serves many upstream sectors, and embedded new software is rated an important source of innovation in several services sectors.

The 'product' and 'service' segments of the software market

In the software industry the distinction between *professional services* (including customised software) and the *software packages* and *products* segments of the market has always been recognised by industry analysts. The professional services component of the software demand depends upon the outsourcing of IT needs by other firms, while the software packages and products segment of the market resembles an arm's-length market. The key difference between the two types of market revolves around the degree of client/customer concentration for a typical firm operating in these markets.

Service markets are generally outsourced markets with a large element of customisation, and they tend to have small numbers of buyers. The average value of transaction for each buyer, however, can be high, making the scale of demand viable for market-based production even though customer numbers are often small – ranging from five to eight customers a year. In contrast, firms create software product markets by anticipating and bundling the software needs of users, whether in the area of operating systems or software applications. There are large fixed costs in the development of products: R&D expenditures, testing of prototypes, and marketing expenditures. Products are successful when there are many users willing to buy them. This spreads the fixed costs over many units and brings down the value of each transaction. A large number of customers also implies the relative anonymity of any individual customer. Client concentration is low, and in that sense product markets are like arm's-length markets.

The larger part of the aggregate revenues from software in every country comes from the professional services segment. Nevertheless the size of the package segment is indicative of the extent to which arm's-length markets have developed in software. The package software market is also the more rapid growth segment of the market. As Malerba and Torrisi (1996) show, Europe lags behind America in the relative size of this sector. The UK has a smaller package software market when compared to the USA, but is ahead of other countries of Europe.[1]

Hoch *et al.* (1999) observe that the product and services segments of the market operate to very different competitive logics. Product provision in software is akin to the commodification of software, and requires investment in anticipation of demand. Software product providers, however, have mostly fixed costs. The only variable cost they incur is the cost of additional units, which for software is the cost of reproduction. When there is the large dominance of fixed costs, standard economies of scale accrue to the producer. Total profits increase as market share grows.

Service providers in software, in contrast, have very few fixed costs. Typically their costs are incurred as they produce, and often with the client incurring those costs. Most of their costs are the costs of labour and they maximise their profits by utilising their labour resources fully. Their objective is to develop their human resources and to utilise the human capital created as fully as possible. Achieving large scales of output is not necessarily a goal.

In microeconomics' terminology, the balance of fixed and variable costs differs according to whether a firm is a product provider or a service provider. This affects both the way in which firms think and compete and also has consequences for the market structure that emerges. Throughout the remainder of this chapter the emphasis will be on the first rather than the second.

A final difference between the service and product segments of software concerns the way that marketing is actually done in the two segments. Service software is customised and its selling is closely tied to how well the software producer understands the business domain of the firm that she is selling to. Close and repeated interaction with the user are useful in expanding the credibility of the service producer, and a successful project with one user will create a market by establishing a reputation for the service producer.

Product segments rely on different modes of marketing, depending on the nature of the product they are selling. Information about the uses of the product is created initially through advertising, usually in trade magazines.[2] Trial promotions of software products have usually taken place through retailers of hardware who distribute some software free with the computers sold by them. More specialised software (for example, computational programs, specialised database products) are usually advertised through the educational press in a manner similar to the promotion of textbooks. Similarly, the marketing of games borrows the instituted selling arrangements that are often used for the selling of films for the screen. Thus, depending upon the nature of the product, the method of actually marketing the product borrows from the institutions that exist to market other similar products.

Demand factors and the changing need for software in the global economy

Computer software is the machine-readable stored code that instructs a microchip to carry out specific tasks. Over the thirty years of its evolution the software market has encompassed this basic functionality, across a range of differentiated uses. Based on the function of the software and the sorts of tasks it instructs the microchip to carry out, there are three broad categories of software: operating systems, tools and applications. Conceiving of the software sector in this way, in terms of the need for code, defines the importance of particular computer science skills that are required to write those kinds of software. A second classification is in terms of how software and its associated services are provided by producers. Thus there are 'product providers' or 'customised software/service providers'. Each of these two kinds of producers may provide operating systems, tools or applications. Such a classification is useful because it emphasises the associated differences in the nature of the markets and the competition between the two segments (Mowery, 1996; Hoch *et al.*, 1999). It is therefore that distinction which is emphasised in this chapter.

Hoch *et al.* (1999) argue that the software business unfolded in five stages. The first stage (1949–59) comprised the development of professional service firms in the USA, which developed tailor-made solutions for several big software projects underwritten by the US government and, later, by large corporations. The SAGE and the SABRE systems were products developed in this period. Nevertheless, in the 1960s the demand for software came from a few large firms, and the conventional wisdom was that software could not, by itself, make money.

The decade 1959–69 saw the emergence of the first two software product companies. *Mark IV* written by Informatics was one of the most successful software products. The other software product came about due to a failed contract. ADR produced the product *Autoflow* for another firm (RCA) which decided that the product was not what it wanted after all. ADR tried to recover its costs by selling the same product to other buyers. Eventually ADR rewrote the product slightly for the IBM 1401 and later for the IBM 360 series.

The 1970s started with the unbundling decision of IBM. The immediate consequence was that a number of software product companies emerged, providing database applications across a range of business operations, for finance and insurance companies. These companies, also called independent enterprise solution providers, included firms like SAP, BAAN and Oracle – all established during this period.

The 1980s saw the rapid spread of the personal computer and the associated need for a different kind of software – mass-packaged software that could be installed on small systems. The software market splintered into areas of application. Prior to the 1980s there were two competing platforms for operating systems on personal computers, viz. the DOS system and the Mackintosh. In the 1980s, Windows emerged as the standard operating system. Applications software for the personal computer were written based on the operating system on which it was to run, and this grew as a distinct area of software.

The spread of the PC created the possibility of replacing mainframe systems with networked PCs. From this there emerged a new kind of software market where PCs, whether running different operating systems or the same operating system, could 'talk' to each other. The Internet is an extension of that basic idea. The possibility of writing software that enables different microchips to communicate with each other also opens up whole new areas of application – in telecommunications, in media and in 'intelligent' consumer durables. These are also the important growth areas for the future of the software industry.

Demand for software in the UK economy

Demand for software was slow to develop in the UK despite the involvement of the universities of Cambridge and Manchester in the first attempt to build a modern computer at the University of Pennsylvania, and despite the uses for the computer envisaged by Maurice Wilkes at Cambridge, who foresaw that software would dominate the use of the computer. More than anything else this reveals that a capacity to develop computer science in the universities was necessary to but not sufficient for the development of a software market.

The emergence of independent vendors and the growth of the software market in the UK really took place only with the spread of microcomputers in the 1980s. Many companies were using in-house developed software and computerised systems in administration or for embedding in electronic capital goods such as telecommunications and defence systems. Such software was, however, produced internally for use within a large firm. Only a small proportion of software written by firms was 'traded' between firms. Thus, Grindley (1996, p. 208) shows that in 1984 only about a quarter of all software production was traded software: the total 'market' for software was only $1.4 billion, though the UK produced software worth $5.9 billion.

Though the emergence of a software market was delayed in the UK as compared to the USA, when it did emerge it mimicked the stages of evolution of the software industry described earlier (pp. 147–9). Figure 8.1, based on the *SDQ9 Business Monitor* series for computer services, shows the gradual process of vertical disintegration in the growth of the UK software sector. It charts the growth of billings for computer services (including software) between 1971–87. The share of billings from parents and associate firms declined over time, while that of private vendors increased. The government's demand for services was never very high and that of foreign billings shows a marginal increase overtime.

In the US, the initial demand for software came from government laboratories, followed by hobbyists and large firms. In the UK there was a notable absence of any large-scale governmental demand, and large firms were slow to adopt computerisation. It is very difficult to get a sense of which sectors of the UK economy drove the demand for software. Table 8.1, derived from data based on the CBR survey (see Appendix), indicates that those sectors were manufacturing, finance and financial services, followed by trade and other service sectors.

Table 8.1 Sector-wise distribution of computer software and services sales

Sector	% of all firms reporting any sales to the sector
Manufacturing	46.5
Financial and business services	44.2
Retail and wholesale trade	37.2
Other services	37.2
Health and education	21.9
Central and local government	32.6
Personal consumers	4.7

The newly emerging computer software firms were dependent on the spread of computerisation and the replacement demand for computers (across sectors of industry) to expand the demand side of the market. The big shift from mainframe to distributed computing produced this opportunity: small and medium-sized firms also could benefit from computerisation. This expanded the overall market for software rapidly, as is clear from Figure 8.1.

The generally slow spread of computerisation took place alongside development of a heterogeneity of hardware platforms for which software had to be written. This, in turn, was because of a lack of standardisation among the operating systems both across companies and across different vintages of computers from the same manufacturer. Furthermore, industrial sectors differed in the kinds of software they needed for computerising their administrative tasks: for example, payroll systems and inventory systems differed

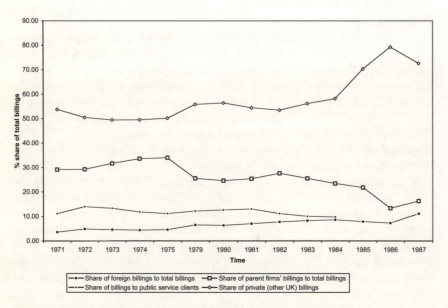

Figure 8.1 Breakdown of billings to clients in the UK software sector (1971–87)

across industrial sectors. All these factors meant that UK software producers (of operating systems, tools and applications) faced fairly heterogeneous demands for software. This heterogeneity created a further segmentation of the newly emerging software market, especially in application areas. Consequently, the emerging software market developed mostly due to the externalisation of software production by large firms, rather than because of a radical redefinition of market boundaries around the attributes of software, as had happened in the USA when the first product software packages emerged.

Some support for these arguments comes from the CBR survey of UK computer firms. The survey found very few software firms that did not earn revenue from services as well: 63 per cent of the software and services firms interviewed over 1995–96 felt that they were doing work which clients once did themselves. As table 8.2 shows that roughly two in three UK software firms sold half or more of their total output to large private firms.

Table 8.2 Rankings of sales (%) to large private sector firms

% of total sales	Number of firms	% of all firms
Less than 10	11	28
10–50	3	8
Over 50	25	64
Missing	4	
	43	100

Though independent vendors of software gradually replaced in-house departments of large firms as suppliers of software, there were parts of the software market that they did not manage to redefine in the way that the first producers of products had done in the USA. This is in part because in many of these areas UK firms still face the stiffest competition from US firms. A consequence of this inability to redefine software market boundaries, however, was that though a market for software supplied by independent vendors did emerge in the UK in the mid-1980s it was a market that was still tied to a narrow base of demand that emanated from a few large firms, with a large service component attached to it. In what follows I argue that this had important consequences for competition and competitive strategies.

Nature of firms and the supply side of the UK software market

As I have indicated the supply side of the UK software market showed the expected changes overtime. Initial entry into the newly emerging software market was by firms in adjacent sectors: hardware firms and education and training establishments. Grindley (1996) details the nature of firms that provided software in the period 1983–89, and this is reproduced in the second column of table 8.3. The table shows that independent providers of software were becoming important in the professional services category, dominating hardware manufacturers. The faster growing software packages market, for which no detailed figures are reported here, was still dominated by hardware manufacturers.

More recent data drawn from the CBR computer survey (see Appendix) for the period 1996–97, and reported in the fourth column of table 8.3 present a different picture. The randomly drawn sample of the survey revealed that only 2 per cent of software and services firms faced serious competitors who were hardware manufacturers. The serious competition for UK software and services firms in the mid-1990s came more from independent software houses and system houses/integrators.

Table 8.3 Sectors of origin of the main competitors

Share of market by provider (%)	1989	Share of firms reporting one or more competitor, by type (%)	1995–96
Hardware	5	Hardware manufacturers	12
Independent software vendors	24	Independent software vendors	55
Subtotal of all professional services	29	Suppliers of EDP	24
Training companies	7	System houses/integrators	38
Facilities management companies	5		
Processing services	22		
Subtotal package software	38		

Sources: Column 2 is from Grindley (1996): Table 8.2, p. 207; column 4 is derived from the CBR survey, which is described in the Appendix.

The late start of the software market has meant that UK software producers have always faced severe foreign competition. Over 40 per cent of firms face no overseas competition, but for others the consequence of the late UK start in the software has also meant that the stiffest competition they face is from US competitors. This is clear from table 8.4.

Table 8.4 Nationality of the main overseas competitors

No. of serious competitors	US firms	European firms	Other firms
1–2	12	7	3
3–5	6	2	1
Over 5	1	–	1

Competition, competitive strategies and barriers to growth of firms in the UK software sector

The discussion thus far has shown that, as a whole, the UK software industry has been constrained by an insufficiently large demand for homogenous software products, and thus professional services accounts for the greater part of software revenues. At the same time, on the supply side the nature of entrants has changed, with hardware manufacturers accounting for a diminishing portion of the competition and giving way to independent vendors. In this section I explore how the aggregate changes on the demand side have influenced the nature of competition and of competitive advantage in the software market. The barriers to growth reported by software firms are considered and are related to the nature of demand and competition facing firms in the UK software market.

Firms in the UK software market operate principally in small outsourced niche markets where they are insulated from competition and where they can develop specialised products for a few large firms. The CBR computer survey gives many indications of this tendency, as already reported. Table 8.5 reports the evidence on the nature of competition faced by firms. Less than a third of firms faced more than five competitors and most firms faced between three and five competitors. This is what one would expect in niche markets.

Table 8.5 Serious competitors faced by UK software and computer services firms

No. of serious competitors	No. of firms	% of firms
0–2	10	23.8
3–5	20	47.6
Over 5	12	28.6

Firms were asked to score the most important factors that contributed to their competitive advantage on a scale of 1 (not important) to 5 (crucial to the firm). The frequency of the extreme scores of 4 and 5 is reported in table 8.6 below. The factors that received the largest proportion of extreme scores across firms were niche market specialised expertise and an ability to deal effectively with particular clients. Generalised skills, like R&D expertise and marketing and sales expertise, in contrast ranked very low. The importance of established reputation to firms in securing competitive advantages is also clearly indicated.

The relatively low importance of domestic and foreign demand growth in imparting any advantages to the firm is also significant, and is indicative of the demand constraints faced by UK firms in this sector. However, from table 8.7 it is clear that demand is not the most important barrier to growth reported by UK software firms. The highest barriers reported by firms are those concerning the availability of finance and of marketing, management and technical skills.

Table 8.6 Factors contributing to the competitive advantage of firms

	Extreme scores	
Factors in competitive advantage	*N*	*%*
Specialised expertise	41	95
Long-term relations with clients	37	86
Responsiveness to client needs	36	84
Product quality or design	34	79
Established reputation	31	72
Technological leadership and innovation	24	56
Growth of market demand in the UK	22	51
R&D expertise	20	47
Marketing and sales expertise	16	37
Competitive prices	14	33
Diversification	12	28
Growth of market demand globally	11	26
Growth of market demand in Europe	10	23
Low production costs	10	23
Total firms	43	

Table 8.7 Barriers to the growth of UK software firms

Type of barrier	Extreme scores	
	Frequency	*% of firms*
Availability of finance	21	49
Marketing and sales skills	19	44
Availability of highly qualified staff	15	35
Management skills	14	33
Cost of finance	13	30
Growth of demand in principal product markets	10	23
Increasing competition globally	9	21
Increasing competition locally/nationally	9	21
Total firms	43	

Both the availability of finance and marketing ability are crucial factors if a firm is to successfully make the transition from service provider to product provider. The different costs in the product and service segments of the software market were discussed earlier (pp. 145–7). This different balance of fixed and variable costs is accompanied by a different balance of skills and competence among firms in the two segments, making the transition from one segment to another very difficult. Indeed, there is not a single example of a firm that has successfully made the transition from service firm to software product firm in the global economy.

In an earlier study of the West European software industry, Malerba and Torrisi (1996) found that reputation and knowledge of user needs, usually acquired through long-term relationships with the customer, were the important barriers to entry to the customised market. The package software market demonstrated barriers to entry on account of marketing and distribution networks as well. The balance of skills needed and their requisite variety is clearly evident in table 8.8.

Table 8.8 Entry barriers for different types of European software producer (average scores)

Firm type	Financial resources	Marketing and sales network	Knowledge of user's environment	Technological skill and capabilities	Image and reputation	Corporate culture
Software and services	2.83	3.25	3.64	3.20	3.86	2.69
System software and						
utilities	1.50	2.00	3.50	5.00	4.00	4.00
Packaged software	3.50	3.36	3.73	3.00	3.45	3.50
Services (EDP,						
Consulting/training)	2.23	3.36	3.73	3.14	4.36	2.50
Technical services						
(software development						
tool expert systems)	3.50	3.25	3.25	3.00	2.25	1.00

Note: Scores from 1 ('not relevant') to 5 ('very relevant').
Source: Malerba and Torrissi (1996), table 7.9, p. 178.

It is remarkable that the barriers to growth reported by UK firms are those which also constitute barriers to entry in the product segments of the software market. But perhaps this is not surprising. Niche markets along a narrow demand base could have predisposed firms to acquire specialised client-specific management skills over generic management skills of various types. The further growth of such firms, however, requires value addition to the product or a broadening of the demand base. A useful analogy here is that of tailors and readymade garment manufacturers in the clothing industry. The history of clothing tells us that the best tailors did not set up readymade garment shops. Yet many tailors went out of business because of the emergence of those shops. A similar outcome is likely in the product and services segments of the software industry.

Conclusion

This chapter has examined the emergence of the UK software and computer services sector using the available empirical evidence on the industry. The analysis shows that independent software vendors came to replace in-house development of software as the market for software services grew. The growth of the traded software market was, however, slow to take off, despite a strong science base, and even as late as 1984 only 25 per cent of the total software produced was traded. Entry to the newly emerging software sector was effected by firms from many other sectors, and in the 1980s the existence of different platforms meant that hardware producers were also the dominant software producers. This situation changed in the 1990s, when independent software houses became the primary source of competition for other software firms.

Externalisation of their software demand by large firms remains the dominant process underlying the growth of this sector. For UK software firms this has meant a narrow base of demand and the pursuit of niche market strategies in segmented markets that are relatively insulated from competition. But such a strategy has its limits. Niche markets do not develop the skills required for larger-scale product development and marketing. Breaking into the more lucrative and higher growth software product market is hampered by the lack of marketing and management skills and the availability of finance for investment.

I have suggested that a story of cumulative causation underlies the pattern of growth of the UK software market. The emergence of demand and the formation of markets in the UK software sector have predisposed firms to the acquisition of skills that are suitable for niche markets. Crossing over to a commodity or product market is difficult, because to do so requires a more balanced distribution of technical, financial, management and marketing abilities. However, the lack of an arm's-length 'product' market also reduces the scope for externalities of the sort described earlier (pp. 145–7). Thus, the way that software markets have formed in the UK has probably lessened the potential impact of software on the economy.

Notes

1 Grindley (1996), table 8.1, shows that in 1994 package software (including applications solutions and applications tools) accounted for 37 per cent of all software revenues in the UK, compared to 32 per cent for all of Europe.
2 In the UK these are magazines such as *PC World*.

References

Athreye, S. S. (2001) 'Competition, rivalry and innovative behaviour', *Economics of Innovation and New Technology*, 10(1), pp. 1–22.

Grindley, P. (1996), 'The future of the software industry in the United Kingdom: the limitations of independent production', in Mowery, D. C. (ed.), *The International Software Industry: A Comparative Study of Industry Evolution and Structure*, New York and Oxford, Oxford University Press.

Hoch, D. J., Roeding, C. R., Purkert, G. and Lindner, S. K. (1999), *Secrets of Software Success*, Boston, MA, Harvard Business School Press.

Malerba, F. and Torrisi, S. (1996), 'The dynamics of market structure and innovation in the Western European software industry', in Mowery, D. C (1996) (ed.), *The International Software Industry: A Comparative Study of Industry Evolution and Structure*, New York and Oxford, Oxford University Press.

Mowery, D. C. (1996) (ed.), *The International Software Industry: A Comparative Study of Industry Evolution and Structure*, New York and Oxford, Oxford University Press.

Rosenberg, N. (1963), 'Capital goods, technology and economic growth', reprinted in Rosenberg, N. (ed.) (1976) *Perspectives on Technology*, Cambridge, Cambridge University Press.

Stigler, G. J. (1951), 'The division of labour is limited by the extent of the market', *Journal of Political Economy*, 59(3), pp. 185–93.

Young, A. (1928), 'Increasing returns and economic progress', *Economic Journal*, 38, pp. 527–42.

Appendix note on the data sources

Tables 1–7: The main source of data for tables 1–7 is the CBR computer survey of 83 firms in the UK computer sector (hardware and software/services), conducted by the author and directed by Dr David Keeble, in 1995–96. The averages reported here are based on data on the randomly selected software and computer services firms, which were forty-three in number. Very few of those firms provided products only, and about one-third of revenues for most firms came from the customisation services offered around the software products they provided, hence the term 'software and services' For more details on the survey, see Athreye (2001, pp. 21–2).

The survey of firms was conducted in two stages. The first stage was the sending out of a pre-interview questionnaire which asked the firms to report on factual details such as year of establishment, years of experience in the computer industry, sales, employment details, exports and R&D expenditures. In the second stage these questionnaires were followed up by detailed interviews with firms. The interview was based on a semi-structured questionnaire and addressed questions relating to innovation, competition and competitive strategies. The sampling frame used was a random sampling frame drawn from Dun and Bradstreet data on computer sector firms.

Figure 8.1 is based on figures obtained from *SDQ9 Business Monitor* series for computer services; various volumes, 1974–92.

9

Open systems and regional innovation: the resurgence of Route 128 in Massachusetts[1]

Michael H. Best

Introduction

The Boston area has the highest concentration of colleges and universities, research institutes and hospitals of any place in the world. The plethora of graduate research programmes suggested that the industrial future of Massachusetts was secure in the emerging knowledge economy of the late twentieth century.

However, the research intensity of the region has not insulated the state from the vicissitudes of the business cycle. For example, after enjoying a ninety-month expansion labelled the 'Massachusetts' Miracle', the Commonwealth lost one-third of its manufacturing jobs between 1985 and 1992. The country's first high-tech region had seemingly lost industrial leadership much more quickly in the new industries of the late twentieth century than in industries first established in Massachusetts in the nineteenth century.

The simultaneous collapse of the minicomputer and defence industry, with the end of the Cold War, touched off a downturn which, added to the long-term contraction of traditional industries, suggested that industry in Massachusetts was in terminal decline. Combined with the setbacks in these major markets was the emerging prominence of Silicon Valley, which was fostering and commercialising innovations much faster than was Route 128, and often in the same technologies. Clearly, few were willing to bet on the resurgence of Route 128.

Nevertheless, the predictions of industrial gloom turned out to be wrong, or at least premature. A return to growth beginning in 1992 long surpassed the 'Massachusetts' Miracle'.[2] Why the rise, the crash, and the rise again? Certainly the decline of the mini-computer industry and cutbacks in defence expenditures are part of the story, but not, in themselves, an explanation.

In this chapter I seek to explain the resurgence of Route 128. It was not widely predicted and the explanation is not obvious. In fact many were so convinced of the terminal decline of New England as a site of industrial production that articles continue to be written on the decline of the region years after its resurgence. Something about the region has given it the resilience to bounce back from 'structural' decline.

If the resurgence and the basis of the region's competitive advantage had to be accounted for in a two-word summary, my candidate would be 'technology management'. Industries have come and gone but, fortuitously, Massachusetts has sustained a regional technology management capability. But my candidate is not an obvious one. The notion of technology management is rarely invoked in discussions of competitive advantage and industrial growth. It seems to be lost within the white spaces of business organisation charts, and in the hallways of higher education it is to be located somewhere between the departments of engineering, management and economics.[3]

This chapter seeks to bring 'technology management' into the discussion of the reasons for regional growth and decline. My treatment of the notion bridges three institutional domains: business model, production system and skill formation. I use the idea of a 'productivity triad', shown in figure 9.1, to focus attention on the interrelationships among the three domains and the mediating link of technology management capability between the inputs and outputs of an enterprise or a region's production system. My hope is that the productivity triad will also sharpen our understanding of innovation dynamics in regional growth.

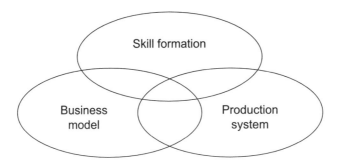

Figure 9.1 The productivity triad

I argue that the severe decline of 1985–92 in Massachusetts can be explained in terms of the emergence in Silicon Valley of a new model of technology management that undermined Route 128's competitive advantage in a range of industries. But, fortunately, the economic contraction did not destroy the region's production or skill formation capabilities. It put them under pressure, but the severity of the decline involved the 'creative destruction' of a business model that was no longer capable of driving regional growth. In its place a new business model emerged more suited to exploit the region's technological heritage and unique production capabilities. The decline played a critical role in the resurgence.

The business model was the weak link in Route 128's 'productivity triad'. The hierarchical, vertically integrated, organisational structure inherited from past successes had turned into a disadvantage. Its weakness was only exposed with the emergence of a new model in Silicon Valley. In head-to-head competition with the new, the old business model disarmed the region's inherited technological and production capabilities and choked the region's growth potential. I argue that the return to regional competitiveness can be explained in terms of the emergence of a new 'focus and network' business model that fostered a range of 'cluster dynamics' and thereby established the institutional foundations for a regional 'open systems' model of innovation. Fortunately, the new business model revitalised the region's unique heritage of technological and production capabilities and skill base, and thereby replaced the forces of decline with new regional growth dynamics.

That something new has happened is beyond dispute. But without a deeper understanding of the processes involved it gives policy makers little guidance with regard to sustaining regional growth. The idea of the productivity triad suggests that advancing or sustaining regional growth depends upon the ability to keep all three elements of the productivity triad 'in sync' in a world of interregional competitiveness. These are the enabling conditions that support a region's technology management capability.

Furthermore, the productivity triad offers a framework for exploring the sources of a region's competitive advantage and of regional growth and decline. While the productivity triad points to relationships among the constituent elements, each can be examined in terms of links to the others. I start with the business model.

The open systems business model

The entrepreneurial firm[4] was the driver of growth during both the Massachusetts' miracle and the resurgence periods. As a business model, the entrepreneurial firm is driven by a *technology–market dynamic*, a mutual adjustment process that advances a firm's technology capability as it refines its product concept in the market. Firms pursue emerging market opportunities by developing unique production capabilities, often of a technological form, but the process of developing such capabilities creates new product concept possibilities and thereby the opportunity to redefine the 'market'. A redesigned product that better meets customer needs sets the technology–market dynamic in motion again.

In the course of the Massachusetts' miracle a series of firms led by techno-entrepreneurs (often benefiting from government orders and research sponsorship) invested heavily in emerging computer-related technologies and established new markets. They joined others that were specialising in defence industry products and systems. The rapidly growing new firms organised according to the business model of vertical integration. This had a series of consequences.

Both the business model and the technology architecture of the leading enterprises were of the closed-system type.[5] DEC's components, for example, were hardwired to one another. The microprocessor, the motherboard, the memory chips, the disk drive, the operating system, the display screen, the software programmes, the printer, the printer microprocessor, the printer engine software, all of the computer peripherals were designed according to a proprietary (and closed) architecture.[6] Sub-contractors made peripheral parts but were not encouraged to develop independent design capabilities. This is not surprising: it was the business model that had served the nation well for roughly a century (Chandler, 1977).

What was inconceivable was that these highly successful high-tech companies, leaders in the rapidly growing markets, could stumble on the technological side. They were first movers in rapidly growing markets and they were integrated with the innovative milieu centered on Boston's universities and research institutes. But they did stumble, collectively. Ironically, their weakness was technology management, individually and collectively.

The miracle years in Massachusetts (late 1970s to 1985) were also a time during which new business models, with superior new product development and innovation performance standards, were being developed in other regions. The Japanese extended the Toyota production system to the Canon model that set new standards for rapid new product development and incremental innovation (see table 9.1).[7] This model established a technology management capability that integrated applied research and production in the service of product-led competition. The Canon model established new performance standards in time to market for new product development. A new technology-pull model of industrial innovation accompanied the new business model (Best, 2001). The Canon production system, however, did not pose the biggest threat to Route 128.

Route 128 companies rarely competed head-to-head with the Canon model. Industrial enterprises in Massachusetts had never developed high-volume manufacturing capabilities. Consequently, they were not vulnerable in industries like consumer electronics, automobiles, and electrical products in which the Japan enterprises were rapidly gaining market share. The vulnerability of Route 128 was to a third business model, one that emerged first in Silicon Valley. This 'open-systems' model established new performance standards for disruptive, as distinct from incremental, innovation. It was this vertically disintegrated but systems-integrated business model that exposed the weaknesses of Route 128's business enterprises and undermined the engines of growth in New England.

The 'open-systems' or focus and network business model is one in which firms specialise in unique capabilities, usually involving a technological dimension, and join networks to partner for complementary capabilities. Success at capability specialisation in high-tech usually involves the development of technology teams that span a range of scientific and technological disciplines.

The open-systems business model can be described in terms of the principle of systems integration, much as vertical integration historically fits the principle of *flow*.[8] The new business model unleashed the internal technology–market dynamic from containment within vertically integrated enterprises to

Table 9.1 Production systems model

1 Production systems	2 Exemplar breakthrough	3 Performance principle	4 Production capability	5 Application management	6 Production organisation advance vehicle	7 Technology	8 Industrial
PS1	Armoury	Standard- isation	Interchange- ability	Product parts	Product engineering	Specialist machine	Open
PS2	Ford	Cost (economies of time)	Flow	Single product	Throughput efficiency (synchron- isation)	Exogenous (R&D lab) pipeline)	Vertical integration
PS3	Toyota	Flexibility and quality (inventory turnover	Flow	Multiple products	Incremental innovation (cellular manufacture)	Process innovation (shopfloor incremental AR)	Closed
PS4	Canon	New product cycle-time	Flow	New products technology	New product development	Applied R&D (design and manufacture) DR+AR	Closed
PS5	Intel	New technology cycle-time	Systems integration	Technology innovation (multiple technologies)	New technology development	Technology integration teams (R&D and manufacture) BR+DR	Open

Notes: AR = applied research; DR = developmental research; BR = basic research.

drive a whole range of specialty component suppliers (not only those along the 'value chain' but across 'value networks'). Sun workstations, for example, were designed with common interface rules and operating system source code to plug in microprocessors from Intel, IBM, AMD, or Motorola; display screens from Sony or NEC; disk drives from Seagate or Quantum; memory chips from Hitachi or Samsung; printers from HP or Epson. In leading companies like Intel, HP and Sun it combined a leadership–ideas dynamic with the technology–market dynamic.[9]

These internal dynamics, in turn, set in motion the processes identified in 'cluster dynamic' or regional growth dynamics model shown in figure 9.2.[10] The new business model, enjoying increasingly far-flung applications, has proven highly competitive against both the Canon (closed system) and the Big Business (vertical integration) models. It is the organisational cornerstone of a new competitive advantage based on a regional model of innovation.[11] Three innovation dynamics can be distinguished.

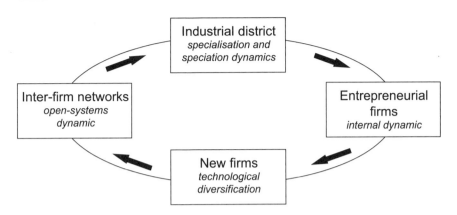

Figure 9.2 Cluster growth dynamics

Techno-diversification

The cluster dynamics of figure 9.2 is constituted by a virtuous circle of entrepreneurial firms driven by an internal technology–market dynamic generating both growth and new technological opportunities which, in turn, foster firm creation in emerging sub-sectors followed by new patterns of inter-firm networking. In the process regional innovations dynamics are fostered as the techno-diversity of the region increases and with it the probability of new technological combinations and the emergence of new entrepreneurial firms.

Examples of the repetition of the virtuous circle of regional dynamics leading to enterprises specialising in new technological 'species' in different technological domains are commonplace in the Massachusetts of the 1990s. One example is that of data storage systems, the 'filing cabinets of the electronics age'.

EMC is an entrepreneurial firm that simultaneously has developed a unique capability and spawned a new industrial sub-sector. The company began as a supplier of add-on memory boards for the minicomputer market in 1979, moved into mainframe storage a decade later, and 'added software to help manage its boxes as it made the switch to open systems in the middle of this decade' (Degman, 1998, p. 1). EMC has achieved the leading edge in storage technology with an engineering staff which, in 1998, totalled 1,200 and an annual research budget of $0.333 billion. In the same year the company opened a 682,000 square foot facility in central Massachusetts to test, qualify and assemble computer storage systems.

EMC has 'spawned a new generation of software and service companies providing ways for corporations to monitor and manage data, back up and protect it, find and fix disk-storage bottlenecks, and warn desktop computer users to clean out their hard drives before they run out of space' (Rosenberg, 1999). For example, a co-founder of EMC and a ten-year employee have formed StorageNetworks, a company that offers businesses data-storage services on the networking model of telephone switches or electrical power generators. Other nearby companies that are driving and redefining the data-storage business, each with a unique specialty are Astrum Software (monitors disk-storage usage at each PC and server within a department), HighGround Systems (storage research management), Connected Corp. and Network Integrity, Inc. (backup systems) (Rosenberg, 1999).

The eleven firms that have spun out of Cascade Communications in the internet switching equipment sector are another example. All are located north of the Massachusetts Turnpike on I-495, a Boston ring-road outside but paralleling Route 128.[12] The emerging firms specialise in a range of products and services unified by the integration of hardware and software required to move data, voice and video over networks. While the region has historically been a centre for communication switching equipment (ex-AT&T's Lucent Technology's 2 million-square foot manufacturing site is in nearby North Andover), many of the new firms can be traced to the technological capability and skill base created at Cascade Communications. Cascade specialises in frame relay technology for 'efficiently directing the congested streams of data flowing across phone lines'. Sycamore, likewise, combines networking and optical technologies. Each of the companies, however, specialises in a distinctive technological capability and uses open-system architecture. Principals in nine of eleven of the startups had been employed at Cascade (Zizza, Pelczar and Eisenmann, 1999). Several principals had worked at the Advanced Network Group of MIT's Lincoln Laboratory, at Motorola/Codex, and at DEC.

The examples of data-storage equipment and telecommunications switching equipment are leading cases. But they represent a large class of business enterprise genealogies in which the emergence of regionally networked groups of firms can be traced to the technology and market dynamic of an entrepreneurial firm. Other examples in the Route 128 region include semiconductor equipment manufacturers (Eaton Semiconductor, Varion Ion Implant, Teradyne, Micrion); electronic test equipment suppliers; digital signal processing semiconductors (Analog Devices, Mercury Computer Systems, Alpha, BKC Semiconductor, C. P. Clare); electro-medical products (over twenty companies led by HP, now Agilent); biotechnology; genome industry (nearly 200 Massachusetts's companies in 1998); enviro-technology; pump laser equipment (MIT Lincoln Labs, Lasertron); infrared imaging systems ('Lab 16' Raytheon, Honeywell Radiation Center, Lockheed Martin Infrared Imaging Systems, Telic Precision Optics, Inframetrics, Inc.); and industrial automation (Foxboro Instruments, Groupe Schneider's Amicon Division).

CorpTech, a data-processing company, categorises America's small and medium-sized (under 1,000 employees) 'technology manufacturers' (most of which are privately held) in seventeen industries as shown in table 9.2. The dispersion is indicative of the diversity of industries associated with Route 128. The mix of high-technology manufacturing in Massachusetts, with approximately 2 per cent of the nation's population, is remarkably similar to that of the nation as a whole. CorpTech estimates that over 8 per cent of America's

Table 9.2 Techno-diversification of Massachusetts' (MA) manufacturers (January 1999)

Companies	MA	%	US %
Factory automation	337	10.5	12.1
Biotechnology	151	4.7	3.5
Chemicals	95	3.0	4.1
Computer hardware	35	13.6	13.8
Defence	56	1.7	2.1
Energy	105	3.3	4.5
Environmental equipment	203	6.3	7.1
High-tech manufacturing equipment	421	13.1	12.6
Advanced materials	159	5.0	6.6
Medical	248	7.7	6.3
Pharmaceuticals	95	3.0	2.5
Photonics	240	7.5	5.0
Computer software	993	30.9	24.8
Sub assemblies/comp	530	16.5	17.2
Test and measurement	378	11.8	11.2
Telecom and Internet	415	12.9	15.5
Transportation	92	2.9	3.6
US holding companies	245	7.6	8.4

Source: CorpTech Directory of High Tech Manufacturers. CorpTech tracks America's 45,000 plus technology manufacturers with under 1,000 employees (90 per cent are 'hidden' private companies and the operating units of larger corporations). Of 42,342 US entities, 3,242 or 7.7 per cent are located in Massachusetts. These are independent companies, subsidiaries of major US corporations, and American operating units of foreign companies. Data extracted with permission from CorpTech website: www.corptech.com

small and medium-sized high-tech companies are based in Massachusetts, with a total of over 200,000 employees.[13]

These data support the theme that a process of techno-diversification has driven the resurgence of the Massachusetts' economy. Technology management in the Massachusetts' miracle growth industries of minicomputers and defence was locked up in vertically integrated enterprises. The downturn was critical to the upturn, as the demise of these enterprises facilitated the transition to an open-system multi-enterprise model of industrial organisation. The accompanying decentralisation and diffusion of design combined with a heritage of technological skills and capabilities to fuel the internal growth dynamic of entrepreneurial firms, which, in turn, fostered techno-diversification and regional innovation dynamics.

Open-systems networking

The box at the left of figure 9.2 represents inter-firm networking. Three types of inter-firm relation can be distinguished: market, closed-system, or *keiretsu*, and open-systems networking. Inter-firm relations are structurally linked to intra-firm organisation: Big Business and arm's-length market-driven supplier relations, the *kaisha* business model and *keiretsu* long-term supplier relations, and entrepreneurial firm and open-systems networking. The *kaisha* business model fostered the principle of multi-product flow and achieved performance standards (cheaper, better, faster) which established the 'new competition' of the 1970s and 1980s.

The third type is open-system networking, commonly referred to as 'horizontal integration', multi-enterprise integration, co-operation, networking or affiliated groups of specialist enterprises. Open-systems networking is the inter-firm counterpart to the increasing specialisation of the entrepreneurial firm. It has proven effective at both rapid new product development and innovation and, consequently, became the new competition of the 1990s. The open-systems model depends upon inter-firm networking capabilities.

Inter-firm networking has evolved with the shift from price-led to product-led competition. This entails integration of manufacturing and new product development processes. But rapid new product development is not simply adding a product (multi-divisional diversification): increasingly it involves a whole group of specialist companies operating at different links along the product chain or at different nodes in the value networks.

Open-system networks convert the inescapable dilemma of the individual entrepreneurial firm into a growth opportunity for a region's collective enterprises.[14] Abandoned possibilities are simultaneously opportunities for new divisions within subsidiaries or spin-offs or for new firm creation. The pursuit of new capabilities also opens new inter-firm partnering possibilities for complementary capabilities. Ease of entry, as well, enhances the regional capability for firms, existing and new, to respond to new market and technological opportunities.[15]

Open-systems networking is a model of industrial organisation that fosters specialisation and innovation. Historically, open systems prevailed in the design-led industrial districts of the Third Italy. More recently, the emergence of systems integration capabilities in technology has both fostered open-system networks and developed because of them. In both cases the business model of specialisation and inter-firm networking form an internal–external dynamic that fosters innovation and growth.

The starting point remains the technology capability/market opportunity dynamic that drives the entrepreneurial firm, the source not only of the growth of the firm but of a derivative set of regional growth dynamics. But the internal dynamic of entrepreneurial firms simultaneously enhances *regional* growth potential. Whether or not the potential is realised depends, in part, upon strategic choices made within the entrepreneurial firm and the extent of inter-firm networking capabilities.

The firm's dilemma is either a cluster's constraint or opportunity. The firm's dilemma is a *cluster constraint* in a region populated by enterprises that are vertically integrated.[16] But the firm's technology choice dilemma is a *cluster opportunity* in a region with 'open-system' networks.

The goal of the entrepreneurial firm is to develop the organisational capabilities to differentiate the firm's product in the market place and establish a market niche and an ongoing relationship with customers. Success requires product redesign and development capability. To the extent that firms are successful, the mode of competition shifts from price-led to product-led. The rebounding pressures of product-led competition in the market on the internal organisation of the firm reinforce the drive to develop unique products and production capabilities. A new dynamic between internal organisation and inter-firm competition is established. Regions that make the transition to product-led competition can enjoy a competitive advantage over regions in which the dominant mode of competition is price. Product-led competition engenders the entrepreneurial firm. The entrepreneurial firm, in turn drives the new internal/external dynamic. Success in the marketplace increasingly depends upon product development, technology management and innovation capabilities.

Inter-firm networking offers greater flexibility for new product development and innovation than does vertical integration.[17] Ironically, networking can foster the social relations necessary for effective co-location of specialist but complementary activities more easily than can vertical integration. While a vertically integrated company operates under a single hierarchy which can direct departments to co-locate, it does so within a bureaucracy and a set of technologies that were originally designed for different purposes. They become embedded in social systems and individual career paths within the firm that can offer resistance to organisational change. Open-systems-networking offers a range of co-design possibilities without locking an enterprise into any single design.

The Internet is a great facilitator of open systems networking. In fact, the Internet is an archetypal open-systems technology. It establishes interface rules that enable design modularisation. The Internet makes it possible to manage supplier relations by seamlessly integrating information across different computer systems, parts lists and even design programmes. All-but seamless integration across businesses enhances the simultaneous increase in specialisation and integration that Adam Smith identified as the principle of increasing specialisation.

As an easy plug-in system for specialist companies, the Internet lubricates the internal–external dynamics that spawn entrepreneurial firms. But it can also be seen as a metaphor for networking in general, and is thereby a target for policy makers seeking to increase entrepreneurial firms. In this, the Internet is the new invisible hand, but one that assists the creation of entrepreneurial firms and regional innovation.

The *new firm creation process* is itself an aspect of mutual adjustment. Just as the dynamics associated with new product development involve a continuous redefinition of product concept, carrying out the process can foster a proliferation of firm concepts. Diversity and the principle of variation, or increased speciation, mean the creation of new firm concepts. This process is enhanced in open-system networks in which specialist new firms can readily plug in to existing product chains. This process suggests that the strategies of firms are themselves shaped in the ongoing practice of refining a firm's concept or specific characteristic by which it distinguishes itself from other firms and thereby derives its market power.

The entrepreneurial firm startup system is particularly strong in the Silicon Valley and Route 128/495 high-tech regions in the USA and in the design-led and the fashion industries of the 'Third Italy'. Taiwan, Ireland and Israel have all established variants, if on a smaller scale. The greatest attention has been focused on financial markets as the enablers of entrepreneurial firm emergence and development. Venture capital and 'initial public offering' capabilities are certainly contributors to the high rates of new firm creation in both Silicon Valley and Route 128/495. As important as financial commitment is, the driving force must be the technological and market opportunities for establishing a firm with the profitability to make an attractive return to suppliers of finance.

The resulting open-systems business model is a business system that expands opportunities for yet more entrepreneurial firms. Collectively the open-systems business model sets higher performance standards in rapid new product development and disruptive innovation (as distinct from continuous improvement or incremental innovation). It is a driver of growth. Wealth creation involving technological advance and techno-diversification is a process analogous to Adam Smith's principle of increasing specialisation as applied to technological capability.

Techno-diversification and networking enhance both new product development and industrial speciation, or the creation of new industrial subsectors. The protean character of technological capability, particularly evident in high-tech sectors, is a feature of industrial change even in the oldest sectors. The electronics industry morphs into, for example, an information and communications sector. Furniture becomes interior design and furnishing. The process of industrial speciation cannot be done within a single firm. In fact, the very success of a firm's pursuit of one technology's trajectory can create obstacles to technological transition; hence the role of networks by which new entrants can focus on a technological capability and partner for the complementary capabilities. Regions with open-system networks have low barriers to entry for new specialist firms. This process drives down the time for technological change and the process of new sub-sector formation.

Regional specialisation and innovation processes

The upper box in figure 9.2 signifies the extent of capability specialisation and technological diversity within a regional population of industrial enterprises. Specialisation has regional and inter-regional dimensions. Greater specialisation internally is a measure of the technological diversity within a region. Greater specialisation externally is a measure of uniqueness of the regional capability and thereby of regional competitive advantage.

Greater diversity is particularly relevant to innovation. An industrial district, unlike any single firm, offers the potential for new and unplanned technology combinations that tap a variety and range of research- and production-related activities. Open systems offer wider opportunities to foster creativity, fill gaps, replenish the knowledge pool and match needs to research.[18]

Regional innovation capabilities lie behind the competitive advantage of 'low-tech' high-income industrial districts common to the 'third Italy'. Such districts have developed a competitive advantage in design capabilities that have fostered industrial leadership in a range of design-led or 'fashion industries'.

Recently, high-tech regions have developed similar capabilities for rapid design change and industrial innovation. In fact, regions such as Silicon Valley and Route 128 have developed regional innovation capabilities embedded in virtual laboratories in the form of broad and deep networks of operational, technological and scientific researchers which cut across companies and universities. Silicon Valley project teams are continual combining and re-combining across a population of 6,000 high-tech firms, making it an unparalleled information and communication technology industrial district.[19]

The core of the innovation process in this model is the fillip given to new product development (NPD) by the differentiation and integration process (see figure 9.1). Firms under strong competitive pressure and in demanding markets are seeking to push ahead with product improvements and new products as fast as possible. In doing so they encounter technical problems that they do not know how to solve, and they search for solutions, dipping into the specialist technological and scientific bodies of knowledge that are available in other firms, in universities and elsewhere. The companies best at effective and fast NPD have developed the capability to integrate technologies, starting with software and hardware. They know where particular kinds of knowledge and expertise can be located and how to dip into the pool of technological and scientific knowledge and expertise to solve particular problems. It is likely that this knowledge will be in identifiable 'chunks' related to the needs of the particular firms and industries and to the characteristics of the science and technology.

Models of innovation are associated with different business models. The *kaisha* variant of the entrepreneurial firm decentralises design and continual change into the operating units. The rapid gain in Japanese market share in many industries in the 1970s and 1980s was achieved, in part, by designing a complementary incremental innovation capability into production. It fostered a technology-pull model of innovation.

The regional model of innovation derives from the open-system regional growth dynamics (the diffusion and development of a range of growth dynamics issuing from the entrepreneurial firm). An American variant is the leadership and design dynamic which combines top–down and bottom–up actions captured by Andrew Grove's leadership–design dynamic. Technodiversification, technology integration, new technology combinations and industry speciation are all elements in processes that advance the technology capabilities of a region.

The regional growth dynamics model fosters combined development and diffusion of innovation. Regional innovation refers to processes that not only trigger the regional growth dynamics but which reshape it via the process of industrial speciation. Thus the regional growth dynamics from an infrastructure for new industry incubation and formation.

The idea of regional innovation dynamics suggests a *collective entrepreneurial capability* as a basis for regional competitive advantage which, like its enterprise-level counterpart, can be conceptualised as a technology market dynamic, but at the regional level.[20] Industrial districts compete against one another. Given different paces of technological development or a shift by one region to a higher model of technology management or a new technology platform, the losing region risks losing a whole swathe of enterprises.

As the networking capabilities of a region become more robust, the more that region takes on the semblance of a virtual collective entrepreneur. The virtual collective entrepreneurial firm is a self-organising change agent composed of networked groups of mutually adjusting enterprises.[21] The collective entrepreneurial firm is a composite of networking firms that collectively administers the regional growth dynamic processes of figure 9.2.

High-tech industrial districts such as the one found in Massachusetts:[22]

- Drive the new firm creation process. Intel's R&D strategy is based on 'the acknowledged role of the spin-off or startup', not in creating but in exploiting new ideas.
- Create a collective experimental laboratory. Networked groups of firms are, in effect, engaged in continual experimentation as the networks form, disband and reform. Both the ease of entry of new firms and the infrastructure for networking facilitate the formation of technology integration teams in real time.
- Expand the number of simultaneous experiments that are conducted. A vertically integrated company may carry out several experiments at each stage in the production chain, but a district can well exploit dozens simultaneously.
- Foster design modularisation and, with it, the decentralisation and diffusion of design capabilities. In computers, IBM got the process underway with the modularisation of the 360 computer which created an open system. This was greatly enhanced when the design modules for the operating system and the microprocessor were developed by Microsoft and Intel.[23] The resulting standards have created enormous market opportunities for specific applications software.
- Counter the inherent uncertainty of technological change with the potential for new technological combinations. This feature of the regional networking model of innovation is captured by a recent review of retrospective surveys of the conditions critical to successful innovation.

A survey by Ronald Kostoff (1994) finds that the first and most important factor is a *broad pool of advanced knowledge*. Kostoff's review indicates that 'an advanced pool of knowledge must be developed in many fields before synthesis leading to innovation can occur'. This advanced pool of knowledge, not the entrepreneur is the critical factor. In the words of Kostoff (1994, p. 61):

> The entrepreneur can be viewed as an individual or group with the ability to assimilate this diverse information and exploit it for further development. However, once this pool of knowledge exists, there are many persons or groups with capability to exploit the information, and thus the real critical path to innovation is more likely to be the knowledge pool than any particular entrepreneur.

The knowledge pool is developed through non-mission-oriented research in a range of fields 'by many different organisations'. Successful innovations tend to be preceded by *'unplanned confluences* of technology from different fields' (Kostoff; 1994, p. 61). In fact, the unplanned is combined with the planned: 'mission-oriented research or development stimulates non-mission research to *fill gaps* preceding the innovation'.

The second critical condition is *recognition of technical opportunity and need*. 'In many cases, knowledge of the systems applications inspires the sciences and technology that lead to advanced systems.' The second factor suggests that there is feedback on problems between of application engineers and scientific investigators. Radar, for example, was 'invented' in response to a clear need.

The third, fourth and fifth critical factors are a technical entrepreneur who champions the innovation; financial input; and management support. The sixth and final factor is *continuing innovation and development across many fields*. In the words of Kostoff: 'additional supporting inventions are required during the development phase preceding the innovation'.

Three of the six critical factors for success point to networking capabilities. From that perspective, an industrial district, unlike any single firm, offers the potential of a technological full-house with a variety and range of research- and production-related activities which can foster creativity, fill gaps, replenish the knowledge pool, link needs to research and incite unplanned confluences of technologies.

Complex system products

To contribute to economic growth, technologies must be embedded in production systems. The process by which technological capabilities are embedded in a company and a region's production system is an extension of the ongoing operations of entrepreneurial firms. The technology capability and market opportunity dynamic that drives the entrepreneurial firm is, simultaneously, a single step in a *cumulative* sequence by which a region's technological capability is extended.

The notion of the collective entrepreneurial firm extends to the region the technology capability and market opportunity dynamic that drives the growth of the firm. Regions can be thought of as developing specialised and distinctive technology capabilities which give them unique global market opportunities. The successful pursuit of these market opportunities, in turn, reinforces and advances their unique regional technological capabilities. Regional specialisation results from cumulative technological capability development and the unique combinations and patterns of intra- and inter-firm dynamics that underlie enterprise and regional specialisation.

Thus, a region's technological capabilities are an outcome of a cumulative history of technological advances embedded in entrepreneurial firms. But the historical process is also *collective*. Just as individual entrepreneurial firms develop unique technological capabilities, a virtual collective entrepreneurial firm advances a region's unique technological capabilities. The regional process of technology capability advance will likely involve a succession of firms, with new firms building on advances made by previous innovators.

A region's technological capabilities are like a seabed, or an industrial ecology, in which entrepreneurial firms are spawned, grow, flourish and die. At the same time, however, entrepreneurial firms, driven by a technology capability and market opportunity dynamic, are forever advancing their own capabilities. In the process, the region's technological capability seabed is revitalised by the ongoing self-organising activities of its inhabitants. It is a virtuous circle. Regional technological capabilities spawn entrepreneurial firms, which upgrade regional technological capabilities, which spawn more entrepreneurial firms.

Specialised and cumulative regional technological capabilities lie behind the competitive advantage of 'low-tech' high-income industrial districts common to the 'third Italy'. Such districts have developed a competitive advantage in design capabilities that have fostered industrial leadership in a range of design-led or 'fashion industries'. But beneath such design capabilities is a unique mastery of a range of technologies derived from a craft heritage combined with specialist engineering skills.

Massachusetts is remarkable for its extraordinary depth and continuity of technological innovation capabilities. It is part of a region that has been on the cutting edge of new technology development since industry began in America. The processes of technological capability development and diffusion, however, are obscured by the conventional linear conception of technology diffusion from university research to company R&D to NPD. This is doubly so in Massachusetts because of the region's renowned research universities. The region's university research laboratories have an unrivalled record as a generator of techno-entrepreneurs and business spin-offs. But the headlines generated by individual success stories obscure the region's unique technological capabilities cumulatively and collectively embedded in its production system. The success of New England in jet engine production, for example, has a technological genealogy that goes back to water turbine innovations in the 1850s to power the region's textile mills.[24] The continuity of technological capability is deeply intertwined with the region's extraordinary innovation record and is crucial to an understanding of the region's economic growth and productivity level.

If the production system that defines the regional competitive advantage of the American mid-west is mass production, the production system that defines the competitive advantage of New England could be called complex system products. I look next at its technological heritage in the region.

Technological Heritage

New England's competitive advantage does not lie in mass production of consumer goods. New England has a regional competitive advantage in the manufacture of *industrial* machines, equipment and instruments.[25] Industrial and commercial machinery (including computers), and electronic and electrical equipment (including telecommunication exchanges and switches, electricity transformers, chip-making machines, air traffic control systems, electro-medical devices) account for close on half of the region's exports. That share goes up to 75 per cent by adding in instruments, engineering chemicals and transportation equipment (primarily aircraft engines and parts) (Little, 1993, p. 9). Some refer to these as the high-tech industries. They are equally representative of the precision equipment industry, which utilises the region's production capabilities in precision machining and technology integration. The manufacture of precision equipment, including instruments, machines, and tools, is a critical input to *complex system products.*

Complex system products tend to stay in New England. New England's competitive advantage in complex products springs from several factors. First, Massachusetts has long enjoyed a world-class precision equipment-making capability made up by hundreds if not thousands of firms collectively making a range of products from turbines to jet engines to printing machines to telecommunication switching equipment to semiconductor-making equipment. The heritage of specialist machine shops, tooling companies, instrument makers, equipment manufacturers and injection moulders collectively constitute a flexible open-system supplier base.[26] After a slow start, this supplier base has embraced information technology in the form of computer-aided design to compress the time to market for NPD (Forrant, 1998). The Internet has been a similar tool hastening the transition to process integration of the supply chain (the *kanban* system).

Second, the region has a long heritage in core industrial technologies. For example, innovation in turbine technology dates back to the early days of the Lowell textile mills, in the mid-1800s.[27] As in the cases of many complex products, aircraft engine making represents a product concept that had been initiated elsewhere but was turned into a production capability in New England.[28] Pratt & Whitney and GE often capture an 80 per cent market share of new orders for large commercial jet engines world-wide (Almeida, 1999, p. 3).[29]

A leading post-war example is microwave technology, associated with the early development of radar in England. A team of scientists brought a single small magnetron (the microwave generating tube at the core of the machine) to the USA in 1940. Within five years a new industry had sprung up around

Route 128, creating the region's largest defence contractor, Raytheon, whose employment increased from 1,400 to 16,000 (Rosegrant and Lampe, 1992, p. 85). Raytheon developed lock step with MIT's Radiation Laboratory, set up in 1940 to co-ordinate microwave research. The Rad Lab, according to Rosegrant and Lampe (p. 84), developed over 150 systems 'that applied the versatile microwave technology to a dizzying array of applications'. The Greater Boston area may have been the only place where the capabilities and skills existed to ramp up a new industry so rapidly.[30]

Third, the region has a heritage of links between instrument making, scientific research and new industry creation. The region's extraordinary instrument-making capability has been an important contributor to the region's strength in scientific research, and Rosenberg (1999) cites numerous examples of technological innovations precipitating such research. Sometimes, this feeds back to foster new industries.

The world's biggest scientific instrument is the Hale Telescope installed on Mount Palomar. Russell Porter, the principal designer, worked at the Jones and Lamson machine shop in Springfield, Vermont, in the 1920s, together with a journeyman machinist in optics and instrument design (Wicks, 1999). The owner, James Hartness, drew on Porter's knowledge of optics to devise more precise measures of screw threads, but saw the opportunities in lens grinding for instrument making. Sixteen machinists in the shop were members of the Springfield Telescope Makers in 1921. Most built their own telescopes, which required accuracy to one-millionth of an inch. These capabilities and skills contributed to the emergence of an optical cluster in Sturbridge, Massachusetts, led by companies such as American Optical Company. They also contributed to advances in the science of astronomy and, eventually, the marriage of optics and electronics and the development of electron microscopes.

Fourth, the region has an industrial heritage not only in precision machining technologies but in combining and recombining technologies to improve old or develop new products. The technology map of the jet engine, for example, is based on patent statistics involving twenty-four technical fields. These include aeronautics, ramjets and rockets, airfoils, optic systems, electro-chemical machinery, metallurgical apparatus and processes, measuring and testing technologies, fluid-handling systems, control systems, fuel systems, exhaust nozzles, coating and chemical processes and apparatus, and materials and materials manufacturing (Prencipe, 1998, table 1, p. 8).[31]

But even with all of these advantages, the severe downturn of the 1980s need not have been reversed. Critical to the resurgence in growth was the re-invention of many industrial sub-sectors and the creation of new sub-sectors in terms of systems integration.

Systems Integration

The application of design modularisation methodologies complemented the region's technological heritage. The combination of systems integration and the region's unique production capability heritage in precision equipment may not have been planned, but it has been fortuitous. Systems integration is the great facilitator of the integration and re-integration of diverse technologies for the purposes of rapid NPD and innovation. The development of a regional capability to integrate information technology into the design, production and constitution of the product has been a source of competitive advantage. It has given leverage to the region's precision equipment and machine-shop heritage, forging a regional capability to combine and re-combine technologies in pursuit of new product applications.

The origin of systems integration in Massachusetts is the defence connection. Since the early 1950s, the Electronics Systems Centre of Hanscom Air Force Base in Massachusetts has co-ordinated a plethora of projects involving the integration of radar, communication, and computer and software technologies. Those projects were the foundation for America's air defence systems and air traffic control systems. Its digital computer sponsored project, known as Whirlwind, became the basis for the modern minicomputer, or business computer, which spawned Route 128's minicomputer giants such as DEC and Data General. The MIT Lincoln Laboratory, co-located with Hanscom, continues to specialise in radar, communications, digital processing, optics research and advanced electronics. In 1958 the non-profit MITRE Corporation was founded to focus on the 'systems engineering' requirements of air defense systems. The software challenges of systems integration are considerable, and Route 128 became a leader in developing computer-aided software engineering tools, user-interface design tools, advanced software design methodologies, and software testing tools (NCTP 1991, p. 55). This huge pool of software engineering talent fed back into the manufacturing base of the region to establish a unique capability for integrating hardware and software.

Integration of design and manufacturing

The defence connection and Massachusetts' industrial heritage, however, were not enough; systems integration as a driver of growth depends on the transition of a critical mass of industrial firms from sub-contractors to problem-solving enterprises with independent design and development capabilities. Rapid NPD depends upon a work organisation in which design and manufacturing are integrated. The hierarchical, functionally departmentalised, vertically integrated business model of New England that dominated during the Massachusetts' miracle years did not involve the decentralisation of design. The spread of the open-system business model was simultaneously about the development of high-performance work systems (HPWSs).

According to a recent report, the proportion of employees in firms that 'made some use of self-managed teams increased from 28 per cent in 1987 to 68 per cent in 1995'. 'A plant that has adopted a cluster of practices that provides workers with the incentives, the skills, and, above all, the opportunity to participate in decisions and improve the plant's performance has an

HPWS' (Appelbaum *et al.*, 2000, p. 9). The authors continue: 'Workers in an HPWS experience greater autonomy over their job tasks and methods of work and have higher levels of communication about work matters with other workers, managers, experts (for example, engineers, accountants, maintenance and repair personnel), and, in some instances, with vendors or customers' (2000, p. 7). New England was a leader in this transition.[32]

It was a critical change in the organisation of New England business that facilitated the development of the new regional model of innovation. I turn next to skill formation, the third element in the productivity triad.

Technology skill formation

The open-system model of industrial innovation as pioneered in Silicon Valley and Route 128 in the USA involves tapping into basic research conducted at the region's universities. In fact, the co-existence of MIT and Route 128, and of the University of California at Stanford and Silicon Valley, has led many to identify research activities conducted in prestigious universities as the driver of knowledge-intensive industries. There is good reason. But it is not the whole story.

MIT set the standard. No other institution has played a more central role in producing techno-entrepreneurs and shaping new industries over a span of more than a century.[33] According to a BankBoston study,[34] MIT graduates have started 4,000 companies nationwide and 1,065 in Massachusetts; the latter account for 25 per cent of sales of all manufacturing firms and 33 per cent of all software sales in the state.[35]

The close links between MIT's and Stanford's research capabilities and the high-tech enterprises around them are widely recognised. They have become models for policy makers the world over. Too often, however, the links between R&D conducted at research universities and industrial innovation and growth are defined in terms of a linear sequence model that obscures the underlying relationships. Dozens of prestigious universities located elsewhere are not associated with regional growth dynamics, just as most high-growth success stories do not involve a technology transfer role for prestigious universities.

The productivity triad and the capabilities and innovation perspective suggest a more complex set of relationships between basic research conducted at universities and industrial growth than the flow of technology and techno-entrepreneurs, important as they can be. Put differently, successful technology transfer, in terms of the growth process, is a consequence of three underlying and enabling relationships that are obscured by the linear sequence view:

- university research activities to assist the *technology–market dynamic* that drives regional growth dynamics;
- *manpower planning* processes to address the scale requirements of the growth process; and

- characterising and diffusing *engineering methodologies* to target technology transitions.

Enterprise capability–university research dynamic

Regional growth dynamic processes depend upon business models driven by the technology capability and market opportunity dynamic. The links between industrial innovation and productivity growth go beyond the transfer of new technologies from university labs, as important as that can be in special cases. Even in cases of successful technology transfer, the transfer is often a consequence of a mutual adjustment process driven by entrepreneurial firms with networking capabilities.

The rapid growth of entrepreneurial firms is simultaneously an advance in technological capabilities. The research capabilities and knowledge specialisation of universities may or may not be shaped by the unfolding process of unique technology capabilities of entrepreneurial firms, but the regional growth impact can be substantial (Best, 2001).

Such a mutual adjustment process between growing firms and university research capability development is critical to an understanding of both Silicon Valley and Route 128. Silicon Valley and Stanford, in the words of Leslie and Kargon (1996, p. 470):

> had grown up together, gradually adjusting to each other and to their common competitive environment. Each helped the other discover and exploit new niches in science and technology . . . In the proliferation of new technical fields and new companies that characterised the early evolutionary stages of these industries, the right kind of university could make a real difference in fostering horizontal integration and collective learning throughout the region.

A failure to understand that dynamic is responsible for the nearly universal lack of success in transplanting the Silicon Valley model, even by Frederick Terman himself. Terman emphasised the crucial role of prestigious universities and their capacity to attract leading scholars, not the mutual adjustment processes identified here. Entrepreneurial firms in Silicon Valley, such as Intel, have benefited considerably from research activities at Stanford University, but these have been the outcome of the nurturing of networking capabilities over a period of time.

Thus, the impact of university research on growth will depend in important ways on whether regional innovation processes are underway. University research, alone, will not drive a region's business model or shape the level of technology management capabilities. As shown in figure 9.2, an open-system regional growth dynamic is also an enterprise startup system that multiplies the number of entrepreneurial firms and drives a set of innovation dynamics. A responsive tertiary education system is critical to fuelling those growth processes with the requisite skills.

Manpower development planning

Entrepreneurial firms are successful because they advance technology capabilities to develop emerging market opportunities in an ongoing interactive process. But sustained regional productivity growth depends upon more than technology transfer and absorption.

In fact, even the combination of right business model and specific technology capability development will not sustain growth. The growth of firms will not translate into regional economic growth without the expansion of the requisite engineering–technological skill base. The regional growth dynamics depend as well upon a labour pool of engineers and technologists to convert the innovative ideas into production capabilities. As shown in figure 9.3 the role of tertiary education is critical for producing a pool of engineers and technologists to convert innovative ideas sparked by the internal growth dynamic of entrepreneurial firms into viable products on the *scale* and in the form required for regional growth.

An inelastic skill base will translate into skill shortages and wage pressures thereby choking growth and eroding regional competitiveness. Industrial development depends upon this process of labour supply development. Without a complementary growth in a labour force with the requisite skills, the innovation capabilities even of MIT would not have been translated into sustained regional growth dynamics.[36]

Figure 9.4 reveals an extraordinary supply response to the technology capabilities being developed during the Massachusetts' miracle. The number of batchelor's degrees in electrical engineering conferred by Massachusetts' universities and colleges increased from 718 in 1982 to 1,648 in 1988. The costs of this transition were heavily borne by the public education system. An expansion in graduates by 1,000 requires an increased intake of 4,000 students

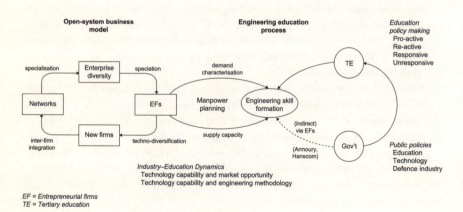

Figure 9.3 Regional growth and skill formation dynamics

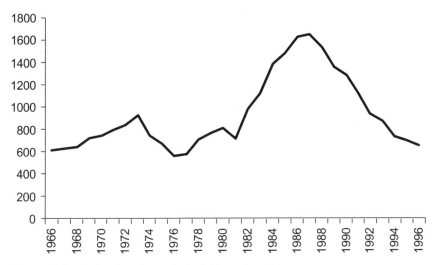

Figure 9.4 Electrical engineering graduates in Massachusetts

in electrical engineering degree programmes which, in turn, requires an expansion in faculty positions of nearly 300 (given a 15:1 student to faculty ratio) in electrical engineering, plus a corresponding investment in facilities.

The sharp drop-off that accompanied the crash of 1986–92 has not turned around. The resurgence relied heavily on skill formation investments by the educational system and human resource programmes of companies enacted during and preceding the miracle years. It has also relied on immigration. This is not always available.

The Massachusetts labour force benefits from roughly 15,000 immigrants per year. The proportion of the recent foreign immigrant population to Massachusetts in 'highly skilled management, professional, and technical occupations' is estimated to be 33 per cent. (According to the 1990 census, 28 per cent of the immigrant workforce in the state had a bachelor's degree or higher (MTC, 1998).) In-migration has taken up much of the slack from the shortfall of engineering graduates of colleges and universities in the state. The number of foreign-born and, in most cases, foreign-educated technical workforce has accumulated to a sizeable fraction of the total pool.

Furthermore, the figure suggests another source of increased technical labour supply in Massachusetts: graduates who remain in Massachusetts. Of the 6,000 graduates produced per year, a higher percentage stays in the state. The trend in net migration over the 'resurgence' has shifted from minus 60,000 to plus a few thousand. If this trend line continues and the international in-migration stays constant at roughly 5,000 per year, Massachusetts goes some distance to responding to the needs.[37] Here, again, the Massachusetts education system is supplying benefits that impact on growth.

Engineering methodologies and curriculum development

Integral to the notion of the productivity triad is the process of mutual adjustment between technology advancing, rapidly growing firms which, in fact, are driving a new technological trajectory, and engineering methodologies which make it possible to ramp-up an engineer–technologist skill base. These form a mutually interactive process in which technology capabilities in companies and engineering methodologies in the education system march forward together. This is particularly so with the application of the principle of systems integration and the development of the open-system business model that has opened up the terrain of knowledge-intensive industries.

This regional dynamic did not begin with MIT. Engineering disciplines are not static. As we have seen, precision engineering has been re-invented in each major technological era beginning with the mechanical age and extending into photonics and genome technologies. Each technological age has been accompanied by the development of a new engineering discipline that, in turn, became a vehicle for the diffusion of the new technology across the industrial spectrum. In the early days the agents of diffusion were machinists trained in interchangeability or, 'armory practices' – a term denoting the organisational capabilities that accompany and institutionalise the technical aspects of interchangeability (Best, 2001, pp. 25–8). Today they are likely to be engineering and science graduates who have specialised in disciplines such as information technology, opto-electronics (photonics) or life sciences. Here, too, New England has a rich heritage that fits both the continuity and change dimensions of technology.

MIT has been closely involved with industry-leading entrepreneurial firms.[38] But those linkages play a role in the development of an engineering curriculum that makes it possible to ramp-up skill bases to supply the needs of regional concentrations of industry and rapid growth. Examples include chemical engineering, and the chemical and then petro-chemical industries; electrical engineering followed by the electrical power and electric engineering firms such as GE; microwave technologies and the development of Raytheon. In all of these cases, the development of the technology and the industry-shaping and market-creating and expanding firms was not university technology spin-offs but partnerships in the co-shaping of emerging and unfolding technologies and engineering methodologies.

Systems engineering does not fit neatly into the educational curriculum, but is nevertheless critical to Route 128's competitive advantage. The region's heritage in complex system products is important here. Systems integration activities demand an ability to communicate across technological domains.[39] Complex system products are training grounds for systems integrators, individuals who can speak in several technological languages.[40] New England has a high share of cross-technology communicators. With each historic development of new engineering methodology the earlier ones were redefined to make them interoperable. Mechanical became electro-mechanical followed by integration with electronics and, later, information technology. Information technology plays a double role as independent technology domain and enabler of technology integration. Each revolution fostered a regional ability to communicate across technological domains. Most techno-entrepreneurs are cross-walkers – problem-oriented people who learn to read and converse in diverse technological languages. These are the vaunted communication skills that are often considered missing in engineering education.

The formal education system was of vital importances, but so too was the codified and tacit knowledge that was created in the process of pursuing the technology capability–market opportunity dynamic that defines the entrepreneurial (learning) firm. While the vertical integration business model became a drag on the region's innovation potential, it contributed to the development of a deep and broad skill base in systems integration. Together the enterprise and educational system dynamic bequeathed to the region a skill base in systems integration activity highly appropriate to the requirements of the new industries following upon the information technology revolution. If those skills had not been bequeathed from an earlier period, the region would have had to create them anew.

Conclusion

The development of competitive advantage in high technology in Massachusetts is as much about technological continuity as it is about change. The region's traditional technological capabilities in precision machining, complex system products, and science–engineering education positioned it well for the minicomputer and defence industries that grew rapidly during the period of the Massachusetts' miracle. Furthermore, there was a logic to the vertical integration business model that drove growth during these years. In both product areas, the business model reinforced integral or closed-system architecture. Design modularisation was not the challenge. It was only with the development of design modularisation elsewhere that the combination of a vertically integrated business model and an integral product architecture common to Massachusetts' was no longer viable.

The application elsewhere of the open-system business model of focus and network-fostered regional innovation and regional growth dynamics opened up a new regional competitive advantage. In the new model, business and industrial organisation were redefined to capture more fully the innovation and growth potential of systems integration and the associated decentralisation and diffusion of design.

But New England enjoyed two of the three elements of the productivity triad for systems integration.[41] From that perspective, the secret to the success of the resurgence was the transition from a vertically integrated closed-system business model to a focus and network model based on open systems at the technological and organisational levels. The challenge of design modularisation was met with the development of open-system architecture and standard interface rules.

Silicon Valley was the first to apply the principle of systems integration at both the technological and business model levels, thereby to institutionalise a new model of technology management. The irony is that systems integration has long existed in New England but as an engineering skill and technological capability, not as a unifying principle of production and business organisation. But systems engineering and systems integration as technological capabilities were confined largely to a closed-system architecture.

Silicon Valley demonstrated that a focus and network business model could drive the new innovation forces and convert them into a new competitive advantage. The development of the Internet as an open-system information highway was itself a paradigm example of the advantage of standardised interface rules and an enabler of specialist companies to plug into value networks.

Silicon Valley, as 'new competition', forced a wave of Schumpeterian 'creative destruction' across New England businesses. The region's sharp economic decline played a major role in explaining the timing and wide diffusion of the transition from the closed-system to the open-system business model. The severity of the industrial decline that ended the miracle years had two effects: widespread business failure involving companies organised according to the dictates of vertical integration and the release of a huge labour pool of those educated and trained in systems integration skills. The new business model depended on a supply of skilled labour. Without this pool the regional growth dynamics illustrated in figure 9.1 could not have driven sustained economic growth. Such growth would have been choked by technical skill shortages.

The skills in the labour pool and the technological capabilities that Massachusetts' enterprises had built over generations did not go away. They resurfaced in new firms, new products and new applications. But, most importantly, they eased the transition to a new open-system business model, a model more appropriate to exploit the opportunities offered by systems integration at the technological level.

The new open-systems business model advances two performance standards which are crucial to competitive advantage in New England, rapid NPD and disruptive innovation (as distinct from incremental innovation). The region's machine shops facilitated the rapid diffusion of systems integration. The job-shop heritage complemented a major dimension of systems integration, namely the capability to redesign the whole to take advantage of design changes in component parts, or modules. The region's custom design heritage in machines and tooling was re-invigorated. Design was again important. But it was now integral to the region's business model.

The open-systems business model made possible the full set of regional growth dynamics captured in figure 9.3. Now firm and inter-firm technology development teams could be formed and reformed in pursuit of the new opportunities emerging as a by-product of the techno-diversification process. It was an ideal fit for Massachusetts.[42] It has re-invented manufacturing in the region.[43]

The techno-diversification of Route 128 is itself a consequence of the conversion of systems integration from a technological to a business and industrial organisational capability. The conversion can be understood in terms of the diffusion of the new model of technology management, the establishing of a complementary business model capable of driving the new principle, and an advanced, diverse, flexible and targeted skill base. Industrial policy also played a key role, if inadvertently.

In fact, this specific industrial heritage turned out to be an ideal infrastructure for information technology. New England's heritage of complex systems product turned from a disadvantage in the age of consumer electronics and incremental innovation to an advantage in the age of information technology and disruptive innovation. Consequently, the region has been a major beneficiary of the information technology revolution.

In a sense the resurgence has been about the reinvention of a regional industrial system to fully exploit the opportunities inherent in the emergence of a new technology. As Ford had used electricity to redesign the manufacturing plant to apply the principle of flow, New England has, in effect, used information technology to redesign the region's industrial capability to apply the principle of systems integration. But, ironically, complex system products are in many ways a better production platform for the technological management of disruptive innovation than is that of mass production.

In conclusion, both the decline and the resurgence of Route 128 can be explained in terms of the emergence of a new competitive advantage based on the principle of systems integration which has both fostered and been driven by a comprehensive re-organisation of the business system. An open-system model of specialist and networked firms has transcended the old closed-system vertically integrated business model. The principle of systems integration, like all principles of production, is expressed technologically, organisationally (business model) and in engineering methodology (technical skill requirements and educational capability). The new business model involves a strategy of focus and networking, and an organisational structure of decentralised, diffused and complementary design capabilities across a wide range of business enterprises. The result has been a regional capability to rapidly create, develop and commercialise new product concepts, to re-invent products, diversify technologies, create new market niches and invent new industrial sub-sectors. These processes are part of a new regional decentralised–distributed model of innovation. An understanding of these processes holds the key to understanding the resurgence of growth in Massachusetts.

Notes

1 This chapter draws on material published in Michael H. Best, *The New Competitive Advantage: The Renewal of American Industry* (2001).

2 Symbolic of the decline was the sale of the Wang Towers in Lowell, Massachusetts, for $500,000 in 1992, a building complex that had cost $80 million to construct during the period known as the 'Massachusetts' Miracle'. In April 1998 Wang Towers, then home to thirty-five companies, sold for $120 million.

3 Deming (1982) and others use the term 'white spaces' to denote the space between the boxes in the organisational charts of functionally departmental enterprises.

4 The term 'technology–market dynamic' is a version of Penrose's productive capability/market opportunity dynamic (Penrose, 1995). The idea of the entrepreneurial firm as an extension of the entrepreneurial function from an individual attribute to a collective or organisational capability is developed in Best (1990).

5 A closed architecture is one that cannot accommodate components with independent design rules. It means, for example, a computer that will perform wordprocessing only with a software programme that is co-designed with the computer. Wang wordprocessors did not run *Word* or *WordPerfect*.

6 See Morris and Ferguson (1993) and Garud and Kumaraswamy (1993) for detailed examples.

7 For an elaboration of table 9.1 see Best (1998).

8 Chandler (1977) describes the devlopment of the central office–functionally departmentalised business model as an organisational structure established to pursue the business strategy of vertical integration. The vertical integration organisational structure was particularly appropriate to achieving high rates of 'throughput' or 'economies of speed', both measures of flow. But it was more effective under conditions of technological stability.

9 A leading example is Intel. Intel's 'dynamic dialectic', as described by co-founder Andrew Grove (1996), is designed to combine recurrent phases of bottom–up experimentation and top–down direction. Phases of experimentation, which stimulate new ideas and innovation, are fostered by decentralisation of decision making. The challenge of leadership is to allow enough time for free rein to stimulate the development of new ideas before managing a new phase during which the most promising ideas are pursued and the weaker ideas are abandoned. The challenge of leadership is to balance the phases of experimentation and direction so that the enterprise can benefit from the advantages of both bottom–up initiatives and top–down decision making. Too much experimentation can result in chaos; too much direction can stultify innovation. Built into the challenge of leadership is a requisite ability to manage organizational change; leaders must gain personal commitments to new directions, technologies, processes and products. Without personal commitments from top to bottom, human energies will not be mobilised to drive the redirection of organisational resources. While experimentation requires everyone to act as designers, direction demands that everyone enthusiastically accept the winning designs. This is no small organisational challenge.

10 The cluster dynamics model and its genealogy in the history of economic thought can be found in Best (1999).

11 Different models of innovation are explored in Best (2001).

12 The companies are ArrowPoint Communications, Inc., of Westford, Astral Point Communications of Westford, Cadia Networks, Inc., of Andover, Castle Networks, Inc., Convergent Networks of Lowell, Equipe Communications of Acton, Ignitus Communications of Acton, Omnia Communications, Inc., of Marlborough, Redstone Communications of Westford, Sonus Networks of Westford, and Sycamore Networks, Inc., of Chelmsford.

13 Massachusetts had 6.2 million people in 1999, 2.3 per cent of the USA's total.

14 The firm faces a dilemma: unique capabilities are both the source of competitive advantage and a constraint on future development. Firms that experiment and develop unique and/or new capabilities simultaneously must choose which of the

new possibilities to pursue as the basis of their competitive advantage. Given the inherent uncertainty regarding technological change, firms are required to place bets on which technological possibilities should be pursued and which abandoned. No firm, no matter how big, can pursue all technological possibilities. New opportunities, which require activities that are not consistent with reinforcing the firm's basic position, risk devaluing the firm's unique capabilities. Those not pursued internally become 'market' opportunities for other firms to advance their productive capabilities.

15 Each of these processes contribute to *potential* regional techno-diversification which, if activated, can trigger industrial 'speciation' or the emergence of new industrial sub-sectors (more on this in the next section).

16 Externally integrated enterprises are defined as productive units co-ordinated within 'closed-system' inter-regional networks or value chains directed by global enterprises.

17 Horizontal integration, the term used by Andrew Grove (1996) to describe open-system networking, can be considered an inter-firm consequence of Intel's production concept of integrated manufacturing (see Best, 1998).

18 The regional model of innovation offers a decentralised, self-organising explanation of the success of high-tech regions as an alternative to the linear science-push model of innovation. In the science-push model, technology is thought of as applied science; in the regional model, technology is part of the industrial process. It is built into the process by which firms establish unique capabilities and network with other firms. The science-push model, in contrast, fails to capture the extent to which research is woven into the production, technology and networking fabric of a region's industrial system as distinct from being an external autonomous sphere of activity.

19 Intel is not the only driver of new products. Approximately one in five of the Silicon Valley (and Route 128 in Massachusetts) publicly traded companies were 'gazelles' in 1997, which means they have grown at least 20 per cent in each of the last four years (the number for the USA is one in thirty-five). See Massachusetts' Technology Collaborative (1998).

20 The technology capability and market opportunity dynamic which drives the entrepreneurial firm has an analogous technology and market dynamic that operates at the regional level. This is a *collective* entrepreneurial capability. It underlies and explains a region's clusters.

21 See Best (1990, pp. 207–8).

22 The regional innovation processes can be be referred to as the 5Ds: disruptive (internal–internal dynamic), dip-down (fast new product development), design diffusion (leveraging creativity), dispersed (laboratories for experimentation) and diversity (new technological combinations).

23 See Katz (1996, p. 15). Katz also describes network economies and increasing returns.

24 James Francis's early experiments in turbine technology were conducted at the Wannalancit Mill.

25 In contrast, the American mid-west developed a regional technological capability and competitive advantage in mass production. In both cases the regional technological capability can be expressed in a wide range of final product areas. But, at the same time, regional technology capability is itself an expression of the cumulative dynamics of a region's production system.

26 The largest manufacturing sectors in Greater Boston in the mid-1990s in employment were instruments (35,000), industrial machinery (23,000), printing and publishing (22,000), electrical equipment (21,000) and fabricated metals (11,000) (Terkla, 1998, p. 15).

27 Turbine technology was originally developed in New England as part of the system of canals and locks built to power the Lowell textile mills. James B. Francis, designer of the system of locks and canals that powered the Lowell textile mills, was an innovator in water turbine technology.

28 Precision machining is equally encoded in the aircraft engine industry's technology. The Pratt & Whitney Machine Tool Company was established as an armaments' maker in 1860. Both Pratt and Whitney had been employees of the Samuel Colt Armoury which itself had links with Eli Whitney, a controversial figure in the development of interchangeability. Frederick Rentschler, former president of Wright Aero, was looking for a site to develop air-cooled radial engines for the US Navy. He went to Hartford and leased the rights to use the Pratt & Whitney name and located in empty space in Pratt and Whitney's machine shops. His design concepts were translated into a functioning engine and within three years the Pratt & Whitney Aircraft Company was an enormous success. Pratt & Whitney went on to produce close to half the total aircraft engine horsepower produced in America during the Second World War. GE developed the jet engine in Lynn, Massachusetts (see Almeida, 1999).

29 Jet engine production is not in principle different from car engine production but it inevitably requires more stringent testing of technological modification in any part on the performance of the whole, including the aircraft, under all types of conditions. In this respect, jet engine production is not intrinsically different from microprocessor production. But if jet engines were produced to the yield rates of the best chip-making fabs in the world, the airline industry would not be feasible. The combination of rigorous performance standards and interactive feedback effects presents stern engineering challenges of an order of magnitude higher than those of both car and microprocessor production.

30 The innovation potential which attracts firms from around the world into Massachusetts is based on the skill base, the diversity of technologies which are potential inputs to systems integrators, and the time compression facilitated by the wide and deep supply base for engaging in NPD . For example, Michel Habib, Israel's economic consul in Boston, estimates that the number of Israeli technology firms in the Boston area grew from thirty in 1997 to at least sixty-five in early 1999. The companies span a range of technologies, including optical inspection machines, medical lasers, digital printing equipment, scanning technology and bio-tech. In the words of one Israeli manager, 'There are a lot of technological resources and knowledge in the area we can take advantage of' (Bray, 1999).

31 An aircraft engine involves extremely precise tolerances, and this has in turn, fostered sustained technological advances in lightweight materials, super alloys and parts' fabrication. These all belong to the collective entrepreneurial firm and market opportunity dynamic which underlies the development of regional competitive advantage.

32 In early 1990, seven Boston-area companies formed the Center for Quality Management to work together in TQM (total quality management). It became a model for rapid application and diffusion of continuous improvement work organisation. The Center identified 135 kinds of diffusion channels (Shiba, Graham and

Walden, 1993). See Forrant and Flynn (1998) for a case study of making the transition to a high performance work system.

33 MIT's role in America's first high-tech industrial district inspired Frederick Terman, a dean of engineering at Stanford, to plant the seeds for a west coast high-tech version. He persuaded administrators to establish the Stanford Industrial Park and two of his students, William Hewlett and David Packard, to set up shop there. Another early occupant was Xerox's Palo Alto Research Center the site of a series of innovations that came to constitute the personal computer (Cringely, 1992). Sun Microsystems, Silicon Graphics and Cisco Systems are but three other examples whose origins can all be traced to Stanford's classrooms.

34 See MIT's: The Impact of Innovation website at http://web.mit.edu/newsoffice/founders

35 According to *Mass High Tech* (17(38). 1999. p. 23), the software industry of Massachusetts is driven by '. . . small firms founded by former executives who have cashed out before, or by recent graduates of the area's top engineering schools'.

36 Cambridge University researchers have developed many innovations, often in partnership with industrial labs and emerging companies. Rarely have these developments been translated into regional industrial growth. The development of engineering methodologies must involve methods for ramp-up in technical labour supply and the institutional capability to drive it. It is as if Cambridge, Massachusetts, has had manpower planning capability and Cambridge, UK, has not.

37 The figures on international and domestic migration for Massachusetts, 1991–98, are given in Massachusetts Technology Collaborative (1999, p. 41).

38 No other institution has played a more central role in the process of growing techno-entrepreneurs and shaping entire new industries over a span of more than a century. According to a study by the BankBoston economics department, MIT graduates have started 4,000 companies nation-wide. In Massachusetts, the 1,065 MIT-related companies account for 25 per cent of sales of all manufacturing firms and 33 per cent of all software sales in the state. See MIT's The Impact of Innovation website at http://web.mit.edu/newsoffice/founders

39 In Richard Adams's *A Hitchhiker's Guide to the Galaxy*, a 'Babelfish' device is placed in the ear to enable communication across inter-galactic languages. Technology integration requires a capacity to communicate across technology language fields (see Adams, 1989).

40 Machine shops require language capabilities in software, and mechanical and electrical engineering.

41 As noted above, the productivity triad is a form of systems integration. All three elements (business model, technology management capability, and specialist engineering skills) must be in sync for a region to benefit in the form of regional growth from technological advances. This observation goes some way towards explaining the 'productivity paradox', Robert Solow's observation that computers have shown up everywhere except in the productivity figures. Ditto the case (examined above) of electricity: advances in the application of electricity showed up years after its discovery when Ford used distributed power to redesign the production process according to the logic of flow (Best, 2001).

42 A company engaged in the manufacture of complex system products enjoyed the advantage of the flexibility of a job shop but lacked the efficiency of flow systems. But the mass-production systems are not designed to pursue the technology capability–market opportunity dynamic with the same degree of flexibility for

incorporating disruptive technological change as the 'open-systems' business model. In this sense, New England perhaps has gone further than Silicon Valley in establishing a complex system products business model as distinct from flexible mass production (lean production). By the integration of software and hardware, job shops that were organized hopelessly according to the dictates of world-class manufacturing found a new business model by which they could pursue a strategy of rapid NPD on technological systems integration.

43 The new business model, one of regional innovation, is simultaneously a technology management capability for rapid NPD. It is driven by competition over the rapid development of new product concepts which, in turn, thrives on the dip-down model of innovation. This business system pulls in, and integrates, basic research with the manufacturing processes.

References

Adams, D. (1989), *The More than Complete Hitchhiker's Guide*, New York, Wings Books.

Almeida, B. (1999), 'Jet engine manufacturing in New England: regional roots and recent restructuring', *Working Paper*, Center for Industrial Competitiveness, University of Massachusetts, Lowell.

Appelbaum, E., Bailey, T., Berg, P. and Kalleberg, A. (2000), *Manufacturing Advantage: Why High Performance Work Systems Pay Off*, Ithaca, NY, Cornell University Press.

Best, M. (1990), *The New Competition*, Cambridge, MA, Harvard University Press.

Best, M. (1998), 'Production principles, organizational capabilities and technology management', in Michie, J. and Grieve-Smith, J. (eds), *Globalization, Growth, and Governance*, Oxford, Oxford University Press, pp. 3–29.

Best, M. (1999), 'Regional growth dynamics: a capabilities perspective', *Contributions to Political Economy*, Vol. 18, pp. 125–40.

Best, M. (2001), *The New Competitive Advantage: The Renewal of American Industry*, Oxford, Oxford University Press.

Bray, H. (1999), 'Hub's high-tech allure drawing Israeli firms', *Boston Globe*, 7 April.

Chandler, A. (1977), *The Visible Hand*, Cambridge, MA, Harvard University Press.

Cringely, R. (1992), *Accidental Empires*, New York, Addison-Wesley.

Degman, C. (1998), 'EMC breaks a billion', *Mass High Tech*, 9–15 November.

Deming, W. (1982), *Quality, Productivity, and Competitive Position*, Cambridge, MA, Massachusetts Institute of Technology, Center for Advanced Engineering Study.

Forrant, R. (1998), *Restructuring for Flexibility and Survival: A Comparison of Two Metal Engineering Plants in Massachusetts*, Geneva, International Labour Organization.

Forrant, R. and Flynn, E. (1998), 'Seizing agglomeration's potential: the Greater Springfield Massachusetts metalworking sector in transition, 1986–1996', *Regional Studies*, 32(3), pp. 209–22.

Garud, R. and Kumaraswamy, A. (1993), 'Changing competitive dynamics in network industries: an exploration of Sun Microsystems' open systems strategy', *Strategic Management Journal*, 14, pp. 351–69.

Grove, A. (1996), *Only the Paranoid Survive*, New York, Doubleday.

Katz, J. (1996), 'To market, to market: strategy in high-tech business', *Regional*

Review, 6(4), Federal Reserve Bank of Boston, pp. 12–17.

Kostoff, R. N. (1994), 'Successful innovation: lessons from the literature', *Research – Technology Management*, March–April, pp. 60–1.

Leslie, S. and Kargon, R. (1996), 'Selling Silicon Valley: Frederick Terman's model for regional advantage', *Business History Review*, 70, pp. 435–72.

Little, J. (1993), 'Necessity and invention: trade in high-tech New England', *Federal Reserve Bank of Boston Regional Review*, 3(1).

Massachusetts' Technology Collaborative (1998, 1999) *Index of the Massachusetts' Innovation Economy*, Westborough, MA, MTC.

Morris, C. and Ferguson, C. (1993), 'How architecture wins technology wars', *Harvard Business Review*, March–April, pp. 86–96.

NCTP (1991), *Report of the National Critical Technologies Panel*, US Government, March.

Penrose, E. (1959[1959]), *The Theory of the Growth of the Firm*, rev. edn, Oxford, Oxford University Press.

Prencipe, A. (1998), 'Modular design and complex product systems: Facts, promises, and questions', *Working Paper*, Complex System Products Innovation Centre, University of Sussex, May.

Rosegrant, S. and Lampe, D. (1992), *Route 128: Lessons from Boston's High-Tech Community*, New York, Basic Books.

Rosenberg, R. (1999), 'Growing with the flow: endless stream of data spawns computer-storage firms', *Boston Globe*, 14 April.

Shiba, S., Graham, A. and Walden, D. (1993), *A New American TQM: Four Practical Revolutions in Management*, Portland, OR, Productivity Press.

Terkla, D. (1998), 'Greater Boston – hub of the Commonwealth's economy', *Massachusetts Benchmarks*, 1(4), pp. 9–11.

Wicks, F. (1999), 'Renaissance tool man', *Mechanical Engineering*, November, pp. 74–7.

Zizza, R., Pelczar, S. and Eisenmann, N. (1999), 'Cascade Communications and its offspring', unpublished paper, College of Management, University of Massachusetts at Lowell.

Conclusion

Stan Metcalfe and Alan Warde

In conclusion we draw together and evaluate a number of the themes raised in this volume and begin to sketch an agenda for future research about markets and the competitive process. Happily, this book resides within a now-flourishing broader stream of ideas at the interface between economics and sociology. Some of this new work signals the resurrection of economic sociology, while other aspects of it emanate from within the literature on innovation processes and, more generally, from evolutionary economics.

There has been a very significant revival of interest in economic sociology in the last decade (for reviews see Lie, 1997; Krier, 1999; Heilbron, 2001). The most visible version, promoted particularly effectively by Swedberg (1987, 1990, 1998; and, with Smelser, 1994), and currently influential in the USA, is referred to as 'the new economic sociology'. One of its key characteristics has been its concern to retain a serious dialogue with neo-classical economists and to engage in critique on its own grounds. However, the notion and practice of economic sociology has been revitalised also in France where the Regulation School, conventions' theory, the Bourdieusian school and the anthropology of science (for example, Callon, 1998), often drawing on the Durkheimian tradition, have provided new theoretical approaches to understanding the economy. The revived economic sociology has begun to pay attention to topics like capital, money and markets in a way that was previously absent. Its contributions include emphasis on the role of social interaction and interpersonal relationships in economic life and especially the making of markets, its pursuit of alternatives to rational action and rational choice theory and its insistence upon the embeddedness of economic activity in social and societal context.

There has been a parallel revival of interest in evolutionary processes in economics, stimulated largely by Nelson and Winter (1982), but drawing on a much deeper tradition of economic thinking about dynamics associated with Schumpeter and to a lesser extent Marx and Veblen. Its roots lie in a concern with the dynamics of capitalism, since all evolutionary theories are at root theories of why a particular kind of world changes in the way it does. As with the new economic sociology, evolutionary economists are wedded to a more sophisticated notion of individual behaviour than that embedded in the idea of Olympian rationality. In this view, there is nothing wrong with the argument that individuals seek to do the best they can in the prevailing circumstances, but neither what is best, nor what are considered to be the prevailing circumstances, will be the same across individuals. The point therefore is not that individuals optimise, for that does not amount to very much, but rather that their optimisations are locally contingent and are certainly not independent of the network of social interactions and the institutional frames within which any individual is located. Evolutionary economics depends crucially on the idea of the mutual determining of actions through the functioning of market processes and thus the instituted aspects of these processes. As such, markets as instituted relations between producers and consumers become the context in which evolution is possible. There is a natural complementarity between a concern to understand processes of evolution in modern capitalism and the mutual penetration of economic and social processes, for neither markets nor competition are givens, as we explore below; as instituted relationships, they also evolve.

Several chapters in this collection pick up themes and theses from the regenerated economic sociology, but generally not in a systematic fashion and largely without an overt attempt to develop theoretical positions. Other chapters display firmer attachment to the perspectives of evolutionary economics. Yet others pursue insights about instituted economic processes deriving from the work of Polanyi. There remains, in our opinion, a need for dialogue and debate between the different approaches within economic sociology, and indeed between economic sociology and evolutionary economics. There should be more comparative testing of such theories in the future, promising more ambitious development of theory. Meanwhile, the most important lessons emerging from this collection can be organised under four headings, which we treat in turn: markets as social and socially constructed institutions; the role of information and knowledge in the dynamics of the market process; social consequences of market relations; and, finally, the relationship between markets and competition.

Markets as institutions

The idea of markets as institutions, as habits, rules of social behaviour, is of course not new. Yet, implications of this point await their full development in terms of distinguishing between the market framework in general and markets in particular, and in distinguishing between the rules of the game at a point in time and the generative processes through which those rules evolve. The chapters in this book contribute more to a sophisticated understanding of particular markets than they do to the theory of the general market system. By general market system we refer to the ensemble of interdependent particular markets which exist within a particular monetary system. The important economic feature of the market system is that its particular markets are ultimately interdependent, indirectly if not directly, and that the processes of co-ordination within and between them depend upon every exchange being an exchange against money. Insofar as co-ordination depends upon interaction and the exchange of information between buyers and sellers, it is impossible to separate market activity from its social context – either generally in terms of the rules and norms of economic behaviour, or specifically in terms of the conventions which define each specific transaction. It is for this reason that markets have an affinity with the idea of social networks more generally.

Every particular market has specific rules of operation, which may be codified, as in the Liverpool Rules governing trading in raw cotton, or which may be informally and tacitly prescribed, as with the moral economy of pre-industrial capitalism as described by E. P. Thompson (1971) or Polanyi (1944) in his discussion of the emergence of a market in waged labour. Moreover, operative rules in particular markets are themselves subject to a process of development. They can be expected to change as the volume of exchange increases and as a market develops from narrow niches to serve wider groups of consumers. They can be expected to change when innovations shift the balances of competitive advantage between different sources of supply, as may be happening with the development of Internet trading. Among the major sources of change are ethical concerns and disputes concerning the interactions between agents involved in the market and their distributional consequences. Rules will often be informal and under-specified, such that they may be constituted solely in purely reciprocal expectations of behaviour. In that regard the norms of market behaviour are not much different from those of everyday conduct in other, non-economic, fields, where compliance depends as much on convention and trust as on sanctions. A striking feature of the history of capitalist development is the gradual spread of trust in market exchange. Helped by stabilising political institutions, trust increases confidence in money as a medium of exchange and a store of value, and improves generalised guarantees against malfeasance and opportunistic behaviour. This is the longer term outcome of an iterative process of wider and innovative forms of engagement in social and market processes, necessitating modification of the rules that govern exchange. Consequently, the institutions enveloping market exchange alter to meet new problems and to facilitate extended exchange within that market. This, in turn, allows the market to develop, requiring yet more amendments to the institutional rules. The scope of the market and the rules by which it operates co-evolve. Through such an evolution, market processes have come to cover more realms of economic activity and the acceptance of markets has increased commensurately, if fitfully.

All markets are regulated in general and in particular. The state, at several spatial levels, provides preconditions or circumstances for market exchange and competition, and it intervenes to counteract some of the propensities of the market to produce untenable and intolerable inequalities, or environmental hazards, or trade in unethical products. The interesting question is how the incidence and form of regulation vary over time and across specific markets. There are some cases – for example, in the provision of public goods such as law and order and military services – where the market's logic is deemed not to apply and state provision and regulation of those activities is normal. In others, self-regulation of the market process is combined with heavy external regulation, as in the case of food and drink provision, privatised utilities and drugs. In yet others, the regulatory hand of the state is lightly applied as in the case of markets for financial, legal and medical services, which are subject to strong professional regulation. Of course, in each of these cases the boundary between internal self-regulation and external regulation by the state is contested and, as Nelson points out, varies over time.

A strong position on embeddedness would maintain that there are different types of market transaction, but no autonomous market logic independent of a specific social integument. All markets depend on institutional framing which is historically constituted. Specific markets are not natural: they are not given and they have no automatic outcomes. All markets have a history, and the rules that might govern those particular markets are built up over time through adaptive practices of production, consumption and exchange.

Economic theory has made considerable advances by reducing market relations to the mutual interaction of demand and supply correspondences to represent the two sides of any transaction; but what lies behind demand and supply, as theoretical constructs, cannot be reduced to questions of the independent behaviour of autonomous individuals. Yet almost all approaches to economic behaviour presuppose the existence and primacy of independent individual agents (mostly persons and firms) who engage in purposive action in the light of their resources, knowledge and interests. Those are, as it were, self-contained and self-possessed agents whose economic behaviour is subject to control by themselves and themselves alone. The ontological reality is at least as much one of interdependence within and beyond the economic field. The social behaviours of each agent condition, to differing degrees, the social and economic behaviour of all others. Yet, the majority of economists, and a substantial proportion of scholars in most of the other social sciences, use an isolated independent rational individual as the rudimentary building-block of explanations of the most complex net of interdependences known in human history. One of the key features of an approach centred on social embeddedness is that it grasps rather better than most this texture of both economic and social interdependence. It insists on the interconnectedness of social and economic institutions and the inseparability of economic and social behaviours.

The implication of a 'strong' account of embeddedness is that there are no universal features of 'the market'. However, this seems to us a step too far. Swedberg (1998) observes a danger with accounts of embeddedness and social construction, namely that the specificity and logic of economic action get obscured. The emergence of 'the economy', recognised as a separate sphere of existence, a separate field in Bourdieu's terms, is itself a historical process. We understand economic phenomena as having specific characteristics precisely because there was some autonomisation of economic behaviour. This became obvious when market exchange came to predominate over gift relations, household production and simple barter. The efficiency norm, an emergent feature that developed in parallel with the spread of markets, without which it could scarcely have been recognised or implemented, is probably the defining feature of the modern capitalist economy, and few economic organisations or actors are impervious to its imperatives. Markets discipline behaviour not just because of the effects of our vocabularies and discourses of economic activity. Indeed a central consequence of market activity is the evaluation of competing ways of using resources in terms of costs, revenues and profits, and in so doing to provide tests of viability and the basis for differential growth of the rival courses of action. For that reason the rules by which activities are eliminated through the concept of insolvency are key aspects of the idea of a general market framework.

Talking of particular markets implies that they have common features, which permit their identification as instances. We would argue, after Sayer (Chapter 2; see also Ray and Sayer, 1999), that there are some distinctive and prevalent characteristics of economic action in modern economies which are precisely responses to the fact that transactions are exchanges against money in a competitive space. This involves observing that both the tenets of a code of strategic calculation in relation to the rivalry of sellers and the accords between sellers and buyers are essential to the operation and survival of individuals and the system. The capitalist economy is a field wherein instrumental, optimising, competitive, self-regarding action is not only legitimate but is positively encouraged and reinforced. Though modulated in different types of market, these features of conduct and procedure set limits to effective economic action, and they are sufficiently binding to allow us to talk of the imperatives, or the logic, of market behaviour. These codes have ramifications extending beyond the economic sphere as they diffuse and become incorporated into other spheres of life.

The economic logic of the market is based essentially around two propositions. The first is that markets are means of co-ordinating production and consumption, via the transmission of information and the exchange of goods and services against money. How that is accomplished for particular products will vary across space and time. The analysis of markets thus depends more on identifying their many types, specifying configurations of buyers, sellers and forms of bargaining, specifying forms of intermediation and charting their variations in time and space, than upon isolating the defining essential features of 'the market'. The second we might call the principle of competition, that markets are open to the rival behaviours of producers and consumers so that the outcome might be claimed to be that consumer needs are met in the most effective way possible. The logic of both is contingent upon the instituted context in which co-ordination and competition can take place. The means by which competition can be said to benefit consumers more effectively are many and varied. They may depend upon the introduction of new and improved kinds of products, on new methods of production which permit prices to be lower than they would otherwise be, or on the introduction of new externally imposed regulations.

As Sayer argues, an appreciation of the social aspects of markets and competition must not lure us into a belief that they are cosy affairs. Restless capitalism is often uncomfortable capitalism, and the consequence of competition is frequently deep uncertainty about the future of economic and social arrangements and any individual's position therein. Nevertheless, as the bulk of the contributions to this book suggest, further exploration of the socially embedded, or instituted, nature of markets and competition is the most promising avenue for future study. Despite Swedberg's warning (1998, p. 165) that 'embeddedness' is mostly used vaguely, the idea that economic behaviour occurs within institutional contexts and networks of interpersonal relations seems essential to understanding how markets emerge and operate. In undertaking such exploration it will be essential to develop a satisfactory taxonomy of markets and the processes of exchange which they define. Consider for example the following:

- Strongly *integrated markets* for *homogeneous commodities and assets*. In these markets, specialised intermediaries, market makers, set prices and hold speculative stocks to stabilise prices. These markets correspond to Marshall's organised markets in which there is a wide diffusion of information in relation to current and expected conditions of demand and supply. The preconditions for this kind of market include established metrics to determine quality, large numbers of buyers and sellers, over and above the market makers, and substantial fluctuations in the conditions of production or demand to make it worthwhile for professional dealers to hold stocks and attempt to stabilise the market. The markets for wheat or cotton, for foreign currencies or equities, are classic cases of what economists call 'flex-price' markets. The technical sophistication of the trading arrangements in these markets can be considerable and can cover trades in relation to future as well as current transactions; indeed, recent years have witnessed a considerable degree of innovation in relation to the kinds of instruments traded on, in particular, financial markets.
- Consider next markets for *highly variegated products*, in which firms set prices and producers and consumers bear the consequences of discrepancies in supply or demand by varying the stocks of money or goods that they hold. These cases correspond to many industrial markets. They can be distinguished according to whether production is to order or whether production is 'speculative'. In these cases independent market makers are absent and it is the supplier who typically bears the cost of forming the market relationship. Ships and aircraft are built to order, as are many arts' products (paintings, musical recordings and commercial photography, for

example). In mass markets, the speculative risk facing the producer is lower because many different categories of demand are consolidated and the risk of variation in demand is thereby reduced.

- Finally, consider the case of *retail markets* where manufacturers of differentiated goods and services quote the prices at which they agree to sell directly or indirectly through accredited agencies. These are markets where specialised intermediaries play an important role, not so much in setting prices but in providing and consolidating knowledge of the range and needs of customers and in holding stocks of manufactures.

These examples are sufficient to make the point that a detailed taxonomy of market forms is an important element in the research agenda of an economic sociology programme. They also hint that one differentiating dimension of such a taxonomy will be in relation to the way that market arrangements gather, collate and disseminate information on what is to be exchanged and on what terms and conditions.

Markets and information

Market activity implies that buyers and sellers are 'brought together' across time and space and that transactions are consummated and recorded. In this regard, one way to look at markets is through their role as providers and disseminators of information. Thus, what is available in the market, on what terms, in relation to price, delivery, post-purchase support and rights of redress are the principal items of information that market processes make available. What, then, are the instituted arrangements that underpin this flow of information? Broadly speaking the answer is that this flow of information is provided by market intermediaries who, as it were, form a bridge between the 'questions' and the 'answers' of buyers and sellers. Traditionally, intermediation has been provided by 'market traders', specialists in the provision of particular classes of good and service. That is still the case in many markets today, especially where the specification of the relevant goods or services is complicated. Traders accumulate the requisite knowledge and reap the economies of scale and scope that follow from turning that knowledge into flows of information valuable to consumers and producers. However, the relevant information involves more than the details of what is available and on what terms. As Casson (1982) usefully identifies, the intermediation function often extends to establishing the broader terms of contractual arrangements, the resolution of disputes, and the transport and storage of goods to meet the requirements of exchange. In other cases, the role of intermediation is played by the suppliers of the goods who provide the details of what it is they are selling and the terms on which they will do business. This form of market arrangement is typically found where the buyer has particular contractual needs that draw upon the skills of the seller. The form of intermediation is the answer to a particular economic problem, namely how the information and related market-making services can be most effectively provided. The provision of these services requires that real resources are committed by one or either side of the market and these costs have to be covered by the agreed terms of trade. The creation and circulation of knowledge and information are crucial to an understanding of the process of competition within markets. Moreover, the manner in which information flows will depend upon the specific institutional form of the market. Although much economic literature assumes that price is the pre-eminent type of information conveyed by markets, the reality is that price is only one element in the complex package of information which is necessary before exchanges can take place. Except for in a very narrow range of cases, it is not the market intermediaries who set prices; rather this function is typically established by the manufacturers or proprietors of the goods and services in question. Markets usually only condition the freedom that suppliers have so to do. Every firm has to answer the question 'Who are our potential customers?', and that information cannot be assumed to be readily available. To acquire it may involve considerable outlay, so that the market will only be made if there is sufficient scale and stability in the customer base to generate a required return on that investment. As the market grows, the costs of market making can be spread over a larger volume of transactions, and the opportunity will arise for the emergence of the specialised intermediaries, the suppliers of marketing, transport, storage, advertising and publicity services and trade publications. Thus the way in which the intermediation function is performed varies with the costs and returns associated with each different product and service. Markets do not come for free because neither knowledge nor information is free, and so the larger the scale of the market the more refined can be its operation. As markets grow, their mode of organisation is expected to change (Stigler, 1951).

We have suggested that patterns of interaction between individuals on either side of the market reflect the distribution of knowledge and purpose between the participants and that this interaction has to be organised. To the extent that social interaction is a mechanism for the transfer of information about market opportunities, the functioning of markets is socially contingent. Market activities are information generating and communication based. They are therefore kinds of networks that are regenerated through the process of exchange. Market activities codify and make publicly available the relevant information to facilitate transactions, but much information remains uncodified and is transmitted outside of formal market arrangements. Tacit understanding of the attributes of different products or services, for example, is often transmitted through processes of individual communication in social networks. How markets work then depends on the associated social structure.

Burt's 1992 contribution was to explore the role of information networks as factors shaping the outcome of the (market) competitive process. He argued that access to superior information depends on an agent having a large number of non-redundant contacts each of whom provides different kinds of information. Dense networks are not efficient because it is assumed that all of their members possess the same information and are in that respect substitutable for each other. His central hypothesis is that profitability increases with a firm's access to non-redundant network nodes, what he rather idiosyncratically calls 'structural holes'. Agents who bridge these holes, interpreted as gaps in linkages within the social network of market relations, have strategic capacity and significance in the transfer of information. Burt does not deal with the dynamic question of how such networks are to be created and sustained in the face of competitive actions of rivals. However, from our perspective, the process through which market arrangements are formed should be at the centre of a dynamic account of the embeddedness of economic relations. An immediate implication of this argument is, for example, the idea that firms compete by building non-redundant networks of customers and suppliers – their own particular networks of market relations. Here we find a close connection with Marshall's (1919) emphasis on the external organisation of the firm and with the idea of the social capital of the firm.

We hinted above that the traditional appraisal of markets is normally carried out in terms of the efficiency of the exchange process that they support. The maximisation of the efficiency of the use of given resources to meet given needs is the usual benchmark. This is too limited a perspective, for two reasons. First, it loses sight of the sources of increased efficiency in innovative behaviour and the role of markets in promoting and adapting to innovation. In a market economy, every economic position is, in principle, open to challenge by rival business conjectures, and that implies continued structural change in economy and society. Indeed that is the creative destruction aspect of capitalism. Second, it fails to account for the economising nature of market institutions themselves and for the fact that these instituted frames are not given but are created as part of the market process. These twin aspects of a dynamic perspective capture the central feature of modern capitalism, namely its capacity for internally generated transformation.

Social consequences of market relations

During the 1990s, sociological investigation of markets has tended to abandon earlier concerns with the social effects of the operation of markets and to concentrate instead on the social processes by which markets are made. In the resuscitation of interest in the work of Karl Polanyi, for example, it is the emphasis on the social embeddedness of markets and the social conditions of existence of market societies, rather than his critique of the malign effects of markets, that is pre-eminent. Not that the first is unsatisfactory – far from it. The demonstration that markets are dependent on frameworks of law and co-operation among agents in market relationships, and that they are subject to communal and collectively recognised norms and values, is enormously important both in understanding economic transactions and in challenging the empirical applicability of the axioms of economic theory. But it is noticeable, nevertheless, that much less attention is paid to the outcomes of market arrangements now than in the 1980s, when there were intense political debates about the effects of markets, as indeed there were to an even greater extent at the outset of the Keynesian era.

Possibly there is now some consensus that previous accounts of the effects of markets were over-generalised, unproven and empirically underresearched, such that the less beneficial aspects of market mechanisms were exaggerated. Indeed, for sociologists at least, the tendency was probably to consider markets in the more general context of a critique of capitalism which conflated markets with the system of private property ownership, thereby attributing effects to markets which were not necessarily generic (Zelizer, 1988). A more nuanced understanding might entail that there are no general outcomes characteristic of all markets, only *tendencies* for certain effects which might also vary between different types of market. Nevertheless there is a need to restate, in order to review, key claims about the social consequences of market relations.

First, market exchange alters the tenor of social relationships by fostering impersonal, neutral and impermanent interaction between agents. Even though many particular markets are home to networks of sustained interpersonal interaction, tendentially market relations increasingly weaken social ties within the economic realm.

Second, the proliferation of products and the manner of their promotion alter what people want, affecting their endogenous preferences (Knight, 1934; Bowles, 1998). One does not have to postulate that consumers are dupes to acknowledge that market strategies may be effective in stimulating desires for gratifications unattainable through the purchase of commodities. That overall realignments of wants contribute to greater general happiness or satisfaction is not a foregone conclusion.

Third, many would argue that intensification of market experience erodes civic association and faith in the effectiveness of democratic politics (for example, O'Neill, 1998; Kuttner, 1999). To the extent that one can buy what was previously co-produced voluntarily with other members of a community – for example, voluntary associations for recreation or mobilisations for improved social provision – then purposive communal ties within the public sphere are reduced. To the extent that the market is pronounced as superior to collective provision, then democratic determinations and collective solutions are disparaged. Also, the melding of notions of 'citizenship' with the status of 'a consumer', which Burgess (2001) shows is increasingly a feature within the European Union, individuates people, inviting them to weigh their personal interests rather than those of any collectivity.

Fourth, and associated, the free running of competitive markets tends to create inequalities which undermine principles of equality, particularly social equality which Marshall (1950) saw as the foundation of citizenship in the twentieth century. That political dominance by parties, ideologies and policies of New Right provenance coincided with increasing inequalities in income within the nation states of the Western world, strikingly so in the USA and Britain, should come as no surprise. Indeed, for Marshall (1950), it was precisely the tendencies of markets to generate material inequalities that called forth welfare provision which might give each citizen sufficient resources to participate fully in social life. Parallel inequalities conceived on a global scale compound the indictment.

Fifth, the dominance of markets appears to imply that employment is the only useful and valuable form of work that requires compensation and that only that which can be sold is worthy of being produced. National accounting systems consider only that work and that wealth which circulates in the formal economy. Economic services which are exchanged within families or communities and work undertaken in the home are not counted. The effect is a peculiar devaluation of domestic and communal activity which systematically materially disadvantages one half of the population, women, and devalues caring in relation to earning.

Sixth, justifications for outcomes as consequences of market logic generally allow economic decisions to be taken without reference to moral, political and social considerations. The efficiency norm, central to processes of rationalisation in modern economies, spills over into realms of human life where it is inappropriate or destructive. The application of rational action schemas to arenas other than the economic, as for instance in applications of the 'household economics approach' associated with Becker (1975), suggest that codes of conduct increasingly mimic economic motivations in fields like marriage, parenting, education and the like.

Indeed, and seventh, one effect of the prevalence of markets and their discourse is a tendency to legitimise and propagate the influence of economics as a mode of knowledge. Recently some scholars have come to argue that economics, in its neo-classical dominant form, is coming to act less as an explanation of economic activity and more as a prescriptive theory for the design of social institutions (Callon, 1998; Slater and Tonkiss, 2001; Miller, 2002; Slater, this volume, chapter 5). Through the offices of the World Trade Organisation and the like, institutional arrangements are forced upon supplicant states which are nothing other than the imposition of the doctrine of the free market as conceived by the academic discipline of economics. The best defence of the assumptions of neo-classical microeconomics, and of rational choice theory more generally, is that they are heuristic abstractions. They do not describe the world, but provide ideal–typical or schematic reductions, radically simplifying reality for purposes of measurement, modelling and prediction. To move from that to prescription of economic arrangements which institute the axioms of a highly simplified model – in the form of advocacy of 'free' markets, 'perfect' competition, etc. – is palpably misguided. Since the empirical study of markets indicates that the existence of a range of social and regulatory processes has hitherto been essential to the effective operation of actual markets, there is much scope for perverse policy recommendations.

Finally, appeal to the inexorable logic of the market provides a means of legitimisation for the rich and powerful by denying human responsibility for the distribution of valued resources. The winners in the competitions involved in markets typically legitimise their good fortune by re-expressing it as the natural and inevitable result of the operation of the market. This naturalises the distribution of resources in society and, by justifying success, allows the successful to attribute the blame for failure to those who fail.

Whatever the ultimate merits of these arguments, they provide compelling reasons to reflect on the social consequences of the spread of markets in the process of economic integration. A pertinent and concise summary of the negative social effects of the operation of intense competition through the market is offered by Lane (1991, p. 13) who describes the consequences of the efficiency norm thus:

> When the efficiency norm overrides other considerations in a consumer-driven economy, it sacrifices designing work to meet the needs and desires of workers; it lends credibility to government reluctance to redistribute income; it limits the force of ethical considerations; it uproots community life; it undermines ecological reparations.

The extent to which any of the effects listed is *singularly* the effect of the market is arguable. However, it is noticeable just how comparatively rarely these considerations are currently aired and debated. Some immediate reasons for this might include the prevalence of identity politics, a decline of scholarly interest in power and the powerful, and continued widespread acceptance of economic growth as the primary goal of political management. It is also partly an effect of the hegemony of the doctrine of consumer sovereignty and the discourse of the market: it is difficult to mount an overt intellectual challenge to the necessity and irreversibility of the continuing spread of market mechanisms. Old socialist objections are viewed as anachronistic, associated with nationalised enterprises and ineffective management within the public sector. More generally, the power of states has been subject to liberal critiques which equate markets with freedom and states with authoritarian control. Nevertheless, there exists substantial, *de facto*, practical and popular mistrust of markets among the population at large. Organisations for parents opposed to consumerism, public opinion polls indicating the extent of support for state welfare provision as in defence of the British NHS, the general hostility towards high salaries and salary increases for directors of private corporations, the constant demand for monitoring and regulation of private organisations from consumers' groups and associations, not to mention the resurgence of global anti-capitalist protest, suggest that not everyone has faith in the market system. However, these suspicions lack a coherent intellectual expression, not to mention a viable political vehicle, for their implementation.

Markets and competition

Markets are necessarily, but not solely, and to quite different degrees, competitive. In the absence of thorough reflection it is easy to overlook the collaborative aspects of market behaviour. The Latin root of the term competition is *competere*, to strive together. The nature of that striving together deserves more attention. Not only are markets orderly and organised, characteristics in the absence of which they can scarcely be said to be in existence, but it is also the case that something more than simply competing in accordance with the rules of a particular game is required.

Kuttner (1999) makes the ironic comment that in the USA, whenever there is any sign of the economy or any of its component organisations faltering, policy makers prescribe more competition. But competition is not necessarily good, or at least it is only so for economists. Lane (1991) comments that while economists think along a continuum from competition to monopoly, psychologists use one of competition and co-operation – the value judgements of the two disciplines are diametrically opposed. As the reflections of Harvey (chapter 4) suggest, co-operation and competition are neither wholly good nor wholly bad.

It can be argued that economic competition is generally beneficial when it has the following effects:

- if it is an impulse to creativity and innovation in products and the organisation of production and market arrangements;
- if it increases allocative efficiency;
- if it sustains an efficiency norm powerful enough to generate sustained economic development;
- if it increases the circulation of accurate information about products and practices, and enhances stimulation and cognitive engagement;
- if it gives consumers 'choice' by allowing them to exercise discretion about what to select;
- if it delivers diversity of products of differing quality and price to match the preferences of the consuming population; and
- when it protects the public good.

By contrast it can be argued that the negative effects of economic competition are found when:

- it exacerbates negative externalities of markets;
- it is indifferent to conditions of labour;
- it incites fraud and opportunism;
- consumers are forced constantly to take seriously the imperative of *caveat emptor*;
- it creates social failure in the absence of adequate means to handle fairly and constructively, or to offer adequate compensation to, those who fail in the competitive process;

- the efficiency norm generates hyper-competition leading to poor quality and defective products, ineffective guarantees for consumers, perversely short-term calculation, high levels of bankruptcy and bad debt, insufficient funds for future investment and inadequate training of workforces.

Such considerations clearly question the universality of the mantra that competition is always beneficial within particular markets and that unrestrained competition is good for the market system as a whole. It thus behoves us to explore more critically, and in greater detail, the different modes, modalities, levels, constraints and bounds to competitiveness in different types of market. This might be done partly by examining the role of competition in the emergence, stabilisation and disintegration of particular markets. But as consumer associations, more frequently in the past than the present, sometimes recognise, the consumer is also the worker and the citizen in other contexts. The costs of the efficiency norm and of negative externalities are exploited intensive labour and degradation of public provision.

The potentiality of competition says nothing about actual levels of competition; as Weber observed, even when there is only one incumbent the fact of it being a market means that some other firm, some challenger, may enter freely to offer similar, substitute or different quality items. Nor is the way in which competition is instituted preordained. For example, the product markets that Harrison White examined exhibit a very limited and peculiar sort of competition. If the principal mechanism for determining which products to sell and at what prices is constant surveillance of competitor firms in order to achieve parity in provision, then the idea that an orientation to efficiency generates 'competitive' pricing seems to be thoroughly mistaken. Other studies indicate that the motor of competitive rivalry is often comparatively subdued in comparison with other forces operating within particular markets. Baker *et al.* (1998), building upon the argument of Fligstein (1996) that markets can be analysed as a political process, provide a suggestive approach to evaluating the role of competition in the making and reproduction of particular markets. They examined the survival rates of relationships between advertising agencies and their clients in the USA. They distinguished between three sets of processes – competition, power and institutional forces – for each of which a number of empirical indicators could be furnished, in order to assess their relative importance in explaining the trajectory of the market for advertising services. They indicated that the rules which were adumbrated in the period during which advertising services were initially established – rules which included remuneration as a rate of commission at 15 per cent of the cost of a campaign, the exclusivity of the relationship between agency and client, and an associated presumption of long-term loyalty – continued to hold sway at the end of the twentieth century. These were precisely institutional conventions which stabilised markets and reduced direct competition between agencies as suppliers. Thus rates at which contracts between agencies and clients were dissolved, when new business might be put to open tender or when clients sought new or multiple suppliers of services, were comparatively few. The destabilising effects of competition were thus weak, mitigated both by institutional rules and by the operation of particular structures of power. For instance, organisational size, financial status and centrality within markets influenced rates of dissolution of contracts.

This schema seems fruitful in that it allows us to distinguish degrees of competitiveness and to chart their consequences. In this regard it is important to appreciate that it is not simply the rules governing directly competitive behaviour which constitute institutional forces. A full list would have to include legal regulations, informal rules or norms, tacit agreements among organisations about procedures and mutually acceptable forms of competition, inter-organisational collaborations and alliances, as well as interpersonal ties between employees of different firms. Moreover, this is not just a matter of interpersonal acquaintanceship and mutual accommodation among incumbents of positions in adjacent firms. Workers have identities, or there are claims and obligations upon them, other than as incumbents of a position in an organisation. Claims upon them also arise from their occupational and professional affiliations. The occupational associations of practitioners exert an influence over appropriate levels of competition, partly through policing of professional standards applied to particular operations. The extent of competition permitted and existing between medical practices is restricted in a way fundamentally different from that which obtains between small retailers. It is also the case that where the circulation of information is an essential element of a production process, levels of collaboration are required, such that over-competitive or over-zealous appropriation or exploitation of the knowledge shared among members of a 'college' may be punished by subsequent exclusion from the network of information exchange. As Lane (1991) reports, studies show that excessive competitiveness on the part of individuals frequently hampers their progress and success. The relatively high levels of collaboration among cultural producers in the east end of London, examined by Tonkiss (chapter 6) illustrate some of these points, and this contrasts strongly with the case of the software industry reported by Athreye (chapter 8).

Ultimately, then, we might argue that markets are institutions, with particular norms and rules, which are based not upon ruthless competition between autonomous and anonymous suppliers in pursuit of limited demand, but upon socially ordained and regulated processes. It is partly competitive, but importantly socially embedded, a product of co-operation, collaboration and collusion.

The agenda

Besides our general call for more open theoretical debate, the issues discussed above define an agenda for research in terms of the institutional foundations of a market system and an agenda for detailed research on the evolution of particular markets.

Concerning the first of these topics, we have suggested that the most important task is to understand the relationship between market systems and economic change. In this regard, it is impossible to separate the role of markets in generating new knowledge from the role of competition in translating new knowledge into economic change. The competitive process forms a bridge between the generation of new knowledge and its economic consequences. Thus it is not surprising that all serious scholars of capitalism have understood the central role that innovation plays in the long-term transformation of the system and have understood how the knowledge which underpins innovation arises from within the system. Hence, market institutions, in relation to other knowledge-creating institutions, have a fundamental role in facilitating different forms of response to innovation and in shaping the kinds of innovations which are generated and accepted.

A further dimension requires development. Not only has the analysis of innovation been dominated by an excessively technological perspective, but it has been driven almost exclusively by the idea that innovation relates exclusively to the problem of supply and production (Harvey *et al.*, 2001). Equally important is the role of consumer knowledge and the fact that innovation depends upon consumers changing their behaviour. There is very little concrete analysis of consumption in this domain and we need to understand more clearly the role of consumption in the emergence, growth, stabilisation and decline of particular markets. We know much more about strategies for targeting markets by suppliers than we do about the behaviour of customers. Certainly the latter do not compete like suppliers do, and the principles that might explain how different aggregates of individuals come to select the same products are highly contested and probably therefore poorly understood.

In relation to the second topic, there is a need for the detailed analysis of the full conditions for the emergence of particular markets and their subsequent development. The contributors to this volume have pointed to the enormous range of factors involved in the formation and operation of particular markets. The examples drawn from retailing (Harvey, chapter 4) and from the football-entertainment industry (Michie and Oughton, chapter 7) illustrate the specificity and variability of market arrangements. It is clear that the history of the development of these markets has been conditioned by very different kinds of influences, socially constructed in specific contexts of time and place. Theories of markets need to be sensitive to the full range of forms that particular markets can take and proper consideration of alternative taxonomies of market types should be an important part of future inquiry. We might, for instance, analyse the distinctive features of different types of market – product, labour, capital – and their interconnectedness with different types of intermediation and exchange process. This might usefully form a platform for the comparative empirical study of the variety of market types across different industrial sectors and nation states. One problem facing any taxonomy of markets will be the question of boundaries. Slater in chapter 5 uncovered some of the critical conditions under which a market can be constructed and deconstructed, drawing attention to the processes of social cognition and classification affecting the stability of markets. In addition, Best (chapter 9) identified the importance of spatial boundaries, implying a geographical dimension to the distributed innovation processes which characterise current arrangements.

A deeper issue in the working of market processes involves the social construction of economic categories which give shape to business practices and public understanding of economic activity. Here the role of formal economic thinking is of importance, but how that thinking is translated by individuals into knowledge and practice is not very clear. Therefore, it seems important to explore the understanding that economic agents have of their own practice. For instance, it would be interesting to explore the perceptions, understanding and practical operations of key and powerful actors in industry and government regarding the nature and limits of competitive processes in different national and sectoral contexts. In this regard, wider use of qualitative, even ethnographic, methods of investigation might elucidate a range of views prevailing at any one time and their change over time. We have already drawn attention to the relative neglect of the role of consumers in relation to innovation and the competitive process more generally. This is to emphasise the role of markets in generating and disseminating information which influences changes in consumption behaviour. For example, the complex of connections between the behaviours of firms and their customers, market research organisations and their clients, advertisers and their audiences provide a nexus through which economic knowledge impacts on everyday activities.

Finally, if defining characteristics of market systems are the rate and the manner in which they develop from within, then it follows that the incidence of the costs and benefits of change will be very unevenly distributed across the members of a particular society. At one level this requires a form of welfare analysis beyond the logic of Paretian economics. More fundamentally, however, it demands re-examination of the ethical dimensions of the social and political case for market systems. The normative presumption in favour of markets, noted by both Nelson and Sayer (chapters 1 and 2), should be challenged more widely and more frequently. We have suggested that this can be fruitfully explored in terms of the virtues of the market. Collective public concern about the general social consequences of competitive market relations should be re-established as a *raison d'être* for empirical studies of market behaviour.

References

Baker, W., Faulkner, R. and Fisher, G. (1998), 'Hazards of the market: the continuity and dissolution of interorganizational market relationships', *American Sociological Review*, 63(2), pp. 147–77.

Becker, G. (1975), *Human Capital: A Theoretical and Empirical Analysis*, 2nd edn, New York, National Bureau of Economic Research.

Bowles, S. (1998), 'Endogenous preferences: the cultural consequences of markets and other economic institutions', *Journal of Economic Literature*, 36, pp. 75–111.

Burgess, A. (2001), 'Flattering consumption: creating a Europe of the consumer', *Journal of Consumer Culture*, 1(1), pp. 93–118.

Burt, R. S. (1992), *Structural Holes: The Social Structure of Competition*, Cambridge; MA, Harvard University Press.

Callon, M. (1998), *The Laws of the Market*, Sociological Review monograph series, Oxford, Blackwell.

Casson, M. (1982), *The Entrepreneur: An Economic Theory*, London, Martin Robertson.

Fligstein, N. (1996), 'Markets as politics: a political cultural approach to market institutions', *American Sociological Review*, 61(4), pp. 656–73.

Harvey, M., McMeekin, A., Randles, S., Southerton, D., Tether, B. and Warde, A. (2001), *Between Demand and Consumption: A Framework for Research*, CRIC Discussion Paper, No. 40, Manchester, University of Manchester.

Harvey, M., Beynon, H. and Quilley, S. (2002), *The Human Tomato: Investigations Into Biological and Socio-economic Variety*, Cheltenham, Edward Elgar.

Heilbron, J. (2001), 'Economic sociology in France', *European Societies*, 3(1), pp. 41–68.

Knight, F. (1934), *The Ethics of Competition*, Chicago, IL; Chicago University Press.

Krier, D. (1999), 'Assessing the new synthesis of economics and sociology: promising themes for contemporary analysis of economic life', *The American Journal of Economics and Sociology*, 58, pp. 669–96.

Kuttner, R. (1999), *Everything For Sale: The Virtues and Limits of Markets*, Chicago, IL, Chicago University Press.

Lane, R. E. (1991), *The Market Experience*, Cambridge, Cambridge University Press.

Lie, J. (1997), 'Sociology of markets', *Annual Review of Sociology*, 23, pp. 241–60.

Loasby, B. (1999), *Knowledge, Institutions and Evolution in Economics*, London, Routledge.

Marshall, A. (1919), *Industry and Trade*, London, Macmillan.

Marshall, T. H. (1950), *Citizenship and Social Class: And Other Essays*, Cambridge, Cambridge University Press.

Miller, D. (2002), 'Some things are virtual (but not the internet)', in DuGay, P. and Pryke, M. (eds), *Cultural Economy: Cultural Analysis and Commercial Life*, London, Sage.

Nelson, R. and Winter, S. (1982), *An Evolutionary Theory of Economic Change*, Cambridge, MA, Belknap.

O'Neill, J. (1998), *The Market: Ethics, Knowledge and Politics*, London, Routledge.

Polanyi, K. (1944), *The Great Transformation: The Political and Economic Origins of Our Time*, Boston, MA, Beacon.

Ray, L. and Sayer, A. (eds) (1999), *Culture and Economy After the Cultural Turn*, London, Sage.

Schor, J. (1998), *The Overspent American: Upscaling, Downshifting and the Consumer*, New York, Basic Books.

Slater, D. (2002), 'From calculation to alienation: disentangling economic abstractions', *Economy and Society*, 31(2), pp. 234–49.

Slater, D. and Tonkiss, F. (2001), *Market Society: Markets and Modern Social Thought*, Cambridge, Polity.

Smelser, N. and Swedberg, R. (eds) (1994), *A Handbook of Economic Sociology*, Princeton, NJ, Princeton University Press.

Stigler, J. (1951), 'The division of labour is limited by the extent of the market', *The Organization of Industry*, Chicago, IL, Chicago University Press, chapter 12.

Swedberg R. (1987), 'Economic sociology: past and present', *Current Sociology*, 35(1), pp. 1–221.

Swedberg, R. (1990), *Economics and Sociology*, Princeton, NJ, Princeton University Press.

Swedberg, R. (1998), *Max Weber and the Idea of Economic Sociology*, Princeton, NJ, Princeton University Press.

Thompson, E. P. (1971), 'The moral economy of the English crowd in the eighteenth century', *Past and Present*, 50, pp. 78–98.

Weber, M., 1922, 'Sociological categories of economic action' in Swedberg, R. (1999), *Max Weber: Essays in Economic Sociology*, Princeton, NJ, Princeton University Press.

White, H. C. (1981), 'Where do markets come from?', *American Journal of Sociology*, 87(3), pp. 517–47.

Zelizer, V. (1988), 'Beyond the polemics on the market: establishing a theoretical and empirical agenda', *Sociological Forum*, 3(3), pp. 614–34.

Index